THE
unofficial GUIDE®
ᵀᴼWalt Disney World® with Kids

4TH EDITION

THE *unofficial* GUIDE®

TO Walt Disney World® with Kids

4TH EDITION

BOB SEHLINGER

WILEY

Please note that prices fluctuate in the course of time, and travel information changes under the impact of many factors that influence the travel industry. We therefore suggest that you write or call ahead for confirmation when making your travel plans. Every effort has been made to ensure the accuracy of information throughout this book, and the contents of this publication are believed correct at the time of printing. Nevertheless, the publishers cannot accept responsibility for errors or omissions or for changes in details given in this guide or for the consequences of any reliance on the information provided by the same. Assessments of attractions and so forth are based upon the author's own experience, and therefore, descriptions given in this guide necessarily contain an element of subjective opinion, which may not reflect the publisher's opinion or dictate a reader's own experience on another occasion. Readers are invited to write the publisher with ideas, comments, and suggestions for future editions.

Published by:
John Wiley & Sons, Inc.
111 River Street
Hoboken, NJ 07030

Produced by Menasha Ridge Press

Cover design by Michael J. Freeland

Interior design by Michele Laseau

For information on our other products and services or to obtain technical support please contact our Customer Care Department within the U.S. at ☎ 800-762-2974, outside the United States at ☎ 317-572-3993 or fax 317-572-4002.

John Wiley & Sons, Inc. also publishes its books in a variety of electronic formats. Some content that appears in print may not be available in electronic formats.

ISBN 0-7645-8824-9

Manufactured in the United States of America

5 4 3 2 1

CONTENTS

LIST *of* MAPS

ACKNOWLEDGMENTS

PSYCHOLOGISTS DR. KAREN TURNBOW, Dr. Gayle Janzen, and Dr. Joan Burns provided much insight concerning the experiences of young children at Walt Disney World.

Many thanks also to Megan Parks for production and editorial work on this book. Annie Long and Steve Jones earned our appreciation for their fine work and for keeping tight deadlines in providing the typography. Cartography was provided by Steve Jones, and the index was prepared by Donna Riggs.

THE
unofficial GUIDE®
ᵀᴼWalt Disney World® with Kids

4TH EDITION

INTRODUCTION

 ## HOW *come* "UNOFFICIAL"?

DECLARATION OF INDEPENDENCE

THE AUTHOR AND RESEARCHERS OF this guide specifically and categorically declare that they are and always have been totally independent of the Walt Disney Company, Inc.; of Disneyland, Inc.; of Walt Disney World, Inc.; and of any and all other members of the Disney corporate family not listed.

The authors believe in the wondrous variety, joy, and excitement of the Walt Disney World attractions. At the same time, we recognize that Walt Disney World is a business, with the same profit motivations as businesses the world over. In this guide we represent and serve you, the consumer. If a restaurant serves bad food, or a gift item is overpriced, or a certain ride isn't worth the wait, we can say so, and in the process we hope to make your visit more fun, efficient, and economical.

WHY SO MANY BOOKS?

WE'VE BEEN WRITING ABOUT WALT DISNEY World for 20 years. When we started, Walt Disney World more or less consisted of the Magic Kingdom theme park and a few hotels. Since then, Walt Disney World has grown to the size of a city and is equally if not more complex. Our comprehensive *Unofficial Guide to Walt Disney World,* tipping the scales at more than 800 pages, still provides the most in-depth and objective coverage of any Walt Disney World guide and is our basic reference work on the subject.

As thorough as we try to make *The Unofficial Guide to Walt Disney World,* there is not sufficient space to share all of the tips and information that may be important and useful to some of our readers. Thus, we have developed five additional Walt Disney World guides, all designed to work in conjunction with what we call "the big book." Each of the five, including this guide for families with children, provides specialized information tailored to very specific Walt Disney World visitors. Although some tips from the big book (like arriving at the theme parks early) are echoed or elaborated herein, most of the information is unique and was developed especially for *The Unofficial Guide to Walt Disney World with Kids.* Just as there's not space in the big book for the family-oriented material presented here, we likewise can't cram all of the detailed information from *The Unofficial Guide to Walt Disney World* into this guide. Rather, the two guides are designed to work together and complement each other.

Besides *The Unofficial Guide to Walt Disney World* and *The Unofficial Guide to Walt Disney World with Kids,* the following titles are available:

Beyond Disney: The Unofficial Guide to Universal, Sea-World, and the Best of Central Florida, by Bob Sehlinger and Katie Brandon

Inside Disney: The Incredible Story of Walt Disney World and the Man Behind the Mouse, by Eve Zibart

Mini-Mickey: The Pocket-Sized Unofficial Guide to Walt Disney World, by Bob Sehlinger

The Unofficial Guide to Walt Disney World for Grown-ups, by Eve Zibart

Mini-Mickey is a nice, portable, *Cliffs Notes* version of *The Unofficial Guide to Walt Disney World.* Updated annually, it distills information from this comprehensive guide to help short-stay or last-minute visitors quickly plan their limited hours at Walt Disney World. *Inside Disney* is a behind-the-scenes unauthorized history of Walt Disney World, and it is loaded with all the amazing facts and great stories that we can't squeeze into the big book. *The Unofficial Guide to Walt Disney World for Grown-Ups* helps adults traveling without children make the most of their Disney vacation, and *Beyond Disney* is a complete consumer guide to the non-Disney attractions, restaurants, and nightlife in Orlando and central Florida. All of the guides are available from Wiley, Inc. and at most bookstores.

THE MUSIC OF LIFE

ALTHOUGH IT IS COMMON IN OUR CULTURE to see life as a journey from cradle to grave, Alan Watts, a noted late–20th century philosopher, saw it somewhat differently. He viewed life not as a journey but as a dance. In a journey, he said, you are trying to get somewhere, and are consequently always looking ahead, anticipating the way stations, and thinking about the end. Though the journey metaphor is popular, particularly in the West, it is generally characterized by a driven, goal-oriented mentality: a way of living and being that often inhibits those who subscribe to the journey metaphor from savoring each moment of life.

When you dance, by contrast, you hear the music and move in harmony with the rhythm. Like life, a dance has a beginning and an end. But unlike a journey, your objective is not to get to the end, but to enjoy the dance while the music plays. You are totally in the moment and care nothing about where on the floor you stop when the dance is done.

As you begin to contemplate your Walt Disney World vacation, you may not have much patience for a philosophical discussion about journeys and dancing. But, you see, it is relevant. If you are like most travel guide readers, you are apt to plan and organize, to anticipate and control, and you like things to go smoothly. And, truth be told, this leads us to suspect that you are a person who looks ahead and is outcome-oriented. You may even feel a bit of pressure concerning your vacation. Vacations, after all, are special events and expensive ones as well. So you work hard to make the most of your vacation.

We also believe that work, planning, and organization are important, and at Walt Disney World they are essential. But if they become your focus, you won't be able to hear the music and enjoy the dance. Though a lot of dancing these days resembles highly individualized seizures, there was a time when each dance involved specific steps, which you committed to memory. At first you were tentative and awkward, but eventually the steps became second nature and you didn't think about them anymore.

Metaphorically, this is what we want for you and your children or grandchildren as you embark on your Walt Disney World vacation. We want you to learn the steps ahead of time, so that when you're on your vacation and the music plays, you will be able to hear it, and you and your children will dance with grace and ease.

YOUR PERSONAL TRAINERS

WE'RE YOUR WALT DISNEY WORLD PERSONAL trainers. We will help you plan and enjoy your Walt Disney World vacation. Together we will make sure that it really *is* a vacation, as opposed to say, an ordeal or an expensive way to experience heat stroke. Our objective, simply put, is to ensure that you and your children have fun.

Because this book is specifically for adults traveling with children, we'll concentrate on your special needs and challenges. We'll share our most useful tips as well as the travel secrets of more than 18,000 families interviewed over the years we've covered Walt Disney World. For a more detailed, comprehensive coverage of Walt Disney World itself, pick up a copy of *The Unofficial Guide to Walt Disney World*.

YES, YOU CAN DO IT

WE'LL START BY SAYING THAT BOTH ENJOYING and surviving a Walt Disney World vacation are possible. Millions of parents and grandparents have done it, and so can you. We do not, however, advise winging it. Your best shot at having a really great vacation comes from fully understanding the unique challenges of touring Walt Disney World with children.

▉ ABOUT *this* GUIDE

WALT DISNEY WORLD HAS BEEN OUR BEAT for two decades, and we know it inside out. During those years we have observed many thousands of parents and grandparents trying—some successfully, others less so—to have a good time at Walt Disney World. Some of these, owing to unfortunate dynamics within the family, were doomed right from the start. Others were simply overwhelmed by the size and complexity of Walt Disney World; whereas still others fell victim to a lack of foresight, planning, and organization.

Walt Disney World is a better destination for some families than for others. Likewise, some families are more compatible on vacation than others. The likelihood of experiencing a truly wonderful Walt Disney World vacation transcends the theme parks and attractions offered. In fact, the theme parks and attractions are the only constants in the equation. The variables that will define the experience and determine its success or failure are intrinsic to your family: things like attitude, sense of humor, cohesiveness, stamina, flexibility, and conflict resolution.

The simple truth is that Walt Disney World will test you as a family. It will overwhelm you with choices and force you to make decisions about how to spend your time and money. It will wear you down physically as you cover mile after mile on foot and wait in lines touring the theme parks. You will have to respond to surprises (both good and bad), deal with hyperstimulation as well as disappointment, and be able to reconcile your actual experience with sometimes unrealistic expectations.

This guide will forewarn and forearm you. It will help you decide whether a Walt Disney World vacation is a good idea for you and your family at this particular time. It will help you sort out and address the attitudes and family dynamics that can ruin your good time. Most important, it will provide the confidence that comes with thorough self-examination coupled with good planning and realistic expectations.

LETTERS AND COMMENTS FROM READERS

MANY OF THOSE WHO USE *The Unofficial Guide to Walt Disney World* write us to make comments or share their own strategies for visiting Walt Disney World. We appreciate all such input, both positive and critical, and encourage our readers to continue writing. Readers' comments and observations are frequently incorporated into revised editions of the *Unofficial Guide* and have contributed immeasurably to its improvement.

Privacy Policy

If you write us or return our reader-survey form, you can rest assured that we won't release your name and address to any mailing-list companies, direct-mail advertisers, or other third party. Unless you instruct us otherwise, we will assume that you do not object to being quoted in a future edition.

How to Write the Author

Bob Sehlinger
The Unofficial Guide to Walt Disney World with Kids
P.O. Box 43673
Birmingham, AL 35243

When you write, be sure to put a return address on your letter as well as the envelope; sometimes envelopes and letters get separated. It's also a good idea to include your phone number.

You can also send us e-mail at **UnofficialGuides@Menasha Ridge.com.** Remember, our work often requires that we be out of the office for long periods of time, and *Unofficial Guide* mail and e-mail are not forwarded to us when we're traveling. So forgive us if our response is a little slow; we will respond as soon as possible when we return.

A QUICK TOUR *of* *a* BIG WORLD

WALT DISNEY WORLD ENCOMPASSES 43 square miles, an area twice as large as Manhattan and roughly the same size as Boston. Situated strategically in this vast expanse are the Magic Kingdom, Epcot, Disney-MGM Studios, and the Animal Kingdom theme parks; two water parks; two night-time entertainment areas; a sports complex; several golf courses, hotels, and campgrounds; almost 100 restaurants; four large, interconnected lakes; a shopping complex; three convention venues; a nature preserve; and a complete transportation system consisting of four-lane highways, elevated monorails, and a system of canals.

THE MAJOR THEME PARKS

The Magic Kingdom

When people think of Walt Disney World, most think of the Magic Kingdom. It comprises Cinderella Castle and the collection of adventures, rides, and shows symbolizing the Disney cartoon characters. Although the Magic Kingdom is only one element of Disney World, it remains its heart. The Magic Kingdom is divided into seven areas or "lands," six of which are arranged around a central hub. First encountered is Main Street, U.S.A., which connects the Magic Kingdom entrance with the central hub. Clockwise around the hub are Adventureland, Frontierland, Liberty Square, Fantasyland, and Tomorrowland. Mickey's Toontown Fair, the first new land in the Magic Kingdom since the park opened, is situated along the Walt Disney Railroad on three acres between Fantasyland and Tomorrowland. Access is through Fantasyland or Tomorrowland or via the railroad. Three hotels (the Contemporary, Polynesian, and Grand Floridian Beach resorts) are close to the Magic Kingdom and are directly connected to it by monorail and boat. Two additional hotels, Shades of Green (operated by the Department of Defense) and Disney's Wilderness Lodge Resort, are nearby but aren't served by the monorail.

Epcot

Epcot opened in October 1982. Divided into two major areas, Future World and World Showcase, the park is twice as big as the Magic Kingdom and comparable in scope. Future World consists of futuristic pavilions relating to different themes concerning humankind's creativity and technological advancement. World Showcase, arranged around a 41-acre lagoon, presents the architectural, social, and cultural heritages of almost a dozen nations, with each country represented by replicas of famous landmarks and local settings familiar to world travelers. Epcot is more education-oriented than the Magic Kingdom and has been repeatedly characterized as a sort of permanent World's Fair.

The five Epcot resort hotels—Disney's Beach Club and Villas, Disney's Yacht Club, Disney's BoardWalk and Villas, the Walt Disney World Swan and the Walt Disney World Dolphin—are within a 5- to 15-minute walk of Epcot's "back door," the International Gateway entrance. The hotels are also linked to the park by boat. Epcot is connected to the Magic Kingdom and its resort hotels by monorail.

Disney-MGM Studios

This 100-acre theme park opened in 1989 and is divided into two areas. The first is a theme park focusing on the past, present, and future of the motion picture and television industries. This section contains movie-theme rides and shows and covers about half of the Disney-MGM complex. Highlights include a re-creation of Hollywood and Sunset boulevards from Hollywood's Golden Age; movie stunt demonstrations; a children's play area; and four high-tech rides: *The Twilight Zone* Tower of Terror, Star Tours, the Rock 'n' Roller Coaster, and The Great Movie Ride.

The second Disney-MGM area is a working motion picture and television production facility encompassing three soundstages, a backlot of streets and sets, and creative support services. Public access to this area is limited to studio tours, which take visitors behind the scenes for crash courses on Disney animation and moviemaking, including (on occasion) the opportunity to witness the actual shooting of a feature film, television show, or commercial.

Disney-MGM Studios is linked to other Walt Disney World areas by highway and canal but not by monorail. Guests can park in the Studios' pay parking lot or commute by bus. Patrons staying in Epcot resort hotels can reach the Studios by boat.

Disney's Animal Kingdom

More than five times the size of the Magic Kingdom, the Animal Kingdom combines zoological exhibits with rides, shows, and live entertainment. The park is arranged somewhat like the Magic Kingdom, in a hub-and-spoke configuration. A lush tropical rain forest called The Oasis serves as Main Street, funneling visitors to Discovery Island at the center of the park. Dominated by the park's central icon, the 14-story-tall, hand-carved Tree of Life, Discovery Island is the park's center, with services, shopping, and dining. From Discovery Island, guests can access the theme areas: Africa, Asia, DinoLand U.S.A., and Camp Minnie-Mickey. Africa, the largest of the theme areas at 100 acres, features free-roaming herds in a re-creation of the Serengeti Plain. Guests tour in open-air safari vehicles.

Disney's Animal Kingdom has its own pay parking lot and is connected to other Disney World destinations by the Disney bus system. Although there are no hotels at the Animal Kingdom, the Animal Kingdom Lodge, All-Star, and Coronado Springs resorts are nearby.

THE WATER THEME PARKS

THERE ARE TWO MAJOR SWIMMING THEME parks in Walt Disney World: Typhoon Lagoon and Blizzard Beach. Typhoon Lagoon is distinguished by a wave pool capable of making six-foot waves. Blizzard Beach is the newest Disney water park and features more slides than Typhoon Lagoon. Both parks are beautifully landscaped, with great attention to aesthetics and atmosphere. Typhoon Lagoon and Blizzard Beach have their own adjacent parking lots.

OTHER WALT DISNEY WORLD VENUES

Downtown Disney (Downtown Disney Marketplace, Pleasure Island, and Disney's West Side)

Downtown Disney is a large shopping, dining, and entertainment complex encompassing the Downtown Disney Marketplace on the east, the gated (i.e., admission required) Pleasure Island nighttime entertainment venue in the middle, and Disney's West Side on the west. Downtown Disney Marketplace is home to the largest Disney character merchandise store in the world, upscale resort-wear and specialty shops, and several restaurants, including the tacky but popular Rainforest Cafe.

Part of the Downtown Disney complex, Pleasure Island is a six-acre nighttime entertainment center where one cover charge gets a visitor into any of eight nightclubs. The clubs have different themes and feature a variety of shows and activities. Music ranges from pop/rock to hip-hop to Celtic. For the hungry, there are several restaurants, including a much-hyped Planet Hollywood.

Disney's West Side combines nightlife, shopping, dining, and entertainment. Dan Aykroyd's House of Blues serves Cajun/Creole dishes in its restaurant and electric blues in its music hall. Bongos, a Cuban nightclub and cafe created by Gloria and Emilio Estefan, offers Caribbean flavors and rhythms. Wolfgang Puck Cafe, sandwiched among pricey boutiques (including a three-level Virgin Records megastore) is the West Side's prestige eatery. In the entertainment department, you'll find a 24-screen cinema; a permanent showplace for the extraordinary, 70-person cast of Cirque du Soleil; and DisneyQuest, a high-tech, interactive virtual reality and electronic games venue. Downtown Disney can be accessed via Disney buses from most Walt Disney World locations.

Disney's BoardWalk

Located near Epcot, Disney's BoardWalk is an idealized replication of an East Coast turn-of-the-century waterfront resort. Open all day, the BoardWalk features upscale restaurants, shops and galleries, a brewpub, an ESPN sports bar, a nightclub with dueling pianos (New Orleans Pat O'Brien's–style), and a dance club. Although there is no admission fee for the BoardWalk per se, individual clubs levy a cover charge at night. Besides the public facilities, the BoardWalk fronts a 378-room deluxe hotel and a 532-unit time-share development. The BoardWalk is within walking distance of the Epcot resorts and the International Gateway of the Epcot theme park. Boat transportation is available from Disney-MGM Studios, with buses serving other Disney World locations.

Disney's Wide World of Sports

Covering 200 acres, Disney's Wide World of Sports is a state-of-the-art competition and training facility consisting of a 7,500-seat ballpark, a field house, and venues for baseball, softball, tennis, track and field, beach volleyball, and 27 other sports. In addition to being the spring-training home of the Atlanta Braves, the complex hosts a mind-boggling calendar of professional and amateur competitions. Although Walt

Disney World guests are welcome at the complex as paid spectators, none of the facilities are available for use by guests unless they are participants in a scheduled competition.

DISNEYSPEAK POCKET TRANSLATOR

ALTHOUGH IT MAY COME AS A SURPRISE to many, Walt Disney World has its own somewhat peculiar language. Here are some of terms you are likely to bump into:

DISNEYSPEAK	ENGLISH DEFINITION
Adventure	Ride
Attraction	Ride or theater show
Attraction Host	Ride operator
Audience	Crowd
Backstage	Behind the scenes, out of view of customers
Bull Pen	Queuing area
Cast Member	Employee
Character	Disney character impersonated by an employee
Costume	Work attire or uniform
Dark Ride	Indoor ride
Day Guest	Any customer not staying at a Disney resort
Face Character	A character that does not wear a head-covering costume (Snow White, Cinderella, Jasmine, etc.)
General Public	Same as day guest
Greeter	Employee positioned at an attraction entrance
Guest	Customer
Hidden Mickeys	Frontal silhouette of Mickey's head worked subtly into the design of buildings, railings, vehicles, golf greens, attractions, and just about anything else
In Rehearsal	Operating, though not officially open
Lead	Foreman or manager, the person in charge of an attraction
On Stage	In full view of customers
Preshow	Entertainment at an attraction prior to the feature presentation
Resort Guest	A customer staying at a Disney resort
Role	An employee's job
Security Host	Security guard
Soft Opening	Opening a park or attraction before its stated opening time
Transitional Experience	An element of the queuing area and/or preshow that provides a story line or information essential to understanding the attraction

PART ONE

BASIC CONSIDERATIONS

IS WALT DISNEY WORLD *for* YOU?

ALMOST ALL VISITORS ENJOY WALT DISNEY World on some level and find things to see and do that they like. In fact, for many, the theme park attractions are just the tip of the iceberg. The more salient question, then (since this is a family vacation), is whether the members of your family basically like the same things. If you do, fine. If not, how will you handle the differing agendas?

A mother from Toronto wrote a couple of years ago describing her husband's aversion to Disney's (in his terms) "phony, plastic, and idealized version of life." Touring the theme parks, he was a real cynic and managed to diminish the experience for the rest of the family. As it happened, however, dad's pejorative point of view didn't extend to the Disney golf courses. So mom packed him up and sent him golfing while the family enjoyed the theme parks.

If you have someone in your family who doesn't like theme parks or, for whatever reason, doesn't care for Disney's brand of entertainment, it helps to get the attitude out in the open. Our recommendation is to deal with the person up front. Glossing over or ignoring the contrary opinion and hoping that "Tom will like it once he gets there" is naive and unrealistic. Either leave Tom at home, or help him discover and plan activities that he will enjoy, resigning yourself in the process to the fact that the family won't be together at all times.

DIFFERENT FOLKS, DIFFERENT STROKES

IT'S NO SECRET THAT WE AT THE *Unofficial Guides* believe thorough planning is an essential key to a successful Walt Disney World vacation. It's also no secret that our emphasis on planning rubs some folks the wrong way. The author's sister and her husband, for example, are spontaneous people and do not appreciate the concept of detailed planning or, more particularly, following one of our touring plans when they visit the theme parks. To them the most important thing is to relax, take things as they come, and enjoy the moment. Sometimes they arrive at Epcot at 10:30 in the morning (impossibly late for us *Unofficial Guide* types), walk around enjoying the landscaping and architecture, and then sit with a cup of espresso watching *Unofficial Guide* readers race around the park like maniacs. They would be the first to admit that they don't see many attractions, but experiencing attractions is not what lights their sparklers.

Not coincidentally, most of our readers are big on planning. When they go to the theme park they want to experience the attractions, and the shorter the lines the better. In a word, they are willing to sacrifice some spontaneity for touring efficiency.

We want you to have the best possible time, whatever that means to you, so plan (or not) according to your preference. The point here is that most families (unlike my sister and her husband) are not entirely in agreement on this planning versus spontaneity issue. If you are a serious planner and your oldest daughter and husband are free spirits, you've got the makings of a problem. In practice, the way this and similar scenarios shake out is that the planner (usually the more assertive or type-A person) just takes over. Sometimes daughter and husband go along and everything works out, but just as often they feel resentful. There are as many ways of developing a win/win compromise as there are well-intentioned people on different sides of this situation. How you settle it is up to you. We're simply suggesting that you examine the problem and work out the solution *before* you go on vacation.

TYPES OF PARENTS AND
TYPES OF CHILDREN

MOST PARENTS TRY HARD TO DO THE BEST JOB they can with their children. However, ten minutes of observing parents and children in line for *Dumbo* will clearly reveal that some moms and dads have a greater aptitude for parenting than others.

Some parents are, for lack of a better word, naturals at the job. Every moment in the company of their children is treasured and enjoyed. These parents, who take everything in cheerful stride, view parenting as a happy, pleasant pastime. Their children are their best friends, the people whose company they enjoy most. Naturals understand that their children have altered their lives, but view the alteration as an enhancement as opposed to an imposition or sacrifice. For these parents, the parent-child relationship is the cornerstone of family life, and the day-to-day life of the family is its logical function.

At the opposite end of the spectrum are those parents for whom every act is an effort, who feel oppressed by their parental responsibility and obligation, and who must really work at being a parent. These are the parents who preface their opinions with statements like, "I wouldn't trade my kids for anything in the world, but . . . ." Usually parents who lack a real comfort level with children (their own as well as those of other families), they are fully cognizant of, but never totally adjusted to, the way their children have changed their lives. Generally speaking, they are effective as parents and take "the job" very seriously, but derive minimal joy from parenting. They prefer the company of adults and create opportunities to "recharge their batteries" away from the kids. For these parents, the parent-child relationship is somewhat tenuous, so family functionality is primarily achieved through the introduction of structure and rules. For the purpose of this discussion, we will call these parents "structuring parents."

In two-parent households, both parents might be cut from the same mold, be polar opposites, or (more likely) occupy a space on the parenting continuum somewhere in between. As a general rule, some fusion occurs that both incorporates and modifies the basic parenting type of the two individuals.

Kids, of course, also come in assorted personalities. In fact, I have always been amazed by the extent to which a child's basic personality manifests itself even as an infant. Even those who support the proposition that "there are no bad children, only bad parents" acknowledge that there is a genetic dimension to personality that, learned behaviors notwithstanding, makes some children more happy, easygoing, and mellow while others are more temperamental and difficult.

In the context of a Disney vacation, it is useful to locate your parenting type, that of your partner, your combined parenting type on the parenting continuum, and your child's basic personality type on the personality continuum.

PARENTING TYPE/CHILD PERSONALITY CONTINUUM	
Parenting Continuum	
Natural	Structuring
Child Personality Continuum	
Easygoing	Temperamental

If you and your partner are naturals and your child is easygoing, you could vacation on Mars and have a good time. At Walt Disney World, the most child-friendly of destinations, you'll coast right along. If your children are not altogether easygoing, a little advance planning and on-site attention to things like getting enough rest and not overloading the itinerary will keep things mellow.

Conversely, if you and your partner are structuring parents, your family will have to plan in greater detail and work harder to have a successful vacation. Because rules that apply at home are more difficult to administer while traveling, structuring parents often have a tough time rolling with the punches. If you have easygoing kids, Walt Disney World will be a nearly perfect vacation venue because the theme parks will provide much of the structure and organization that you work so hard to provide at home. You won't have to worry, for example, about what to do; filling the hours and days will be a snap. You'll also discover that Disney frames and structures the visits of all guests in subtle (and sometimes not so subtle) ways, ways that will remove much of the burden of initiating structure when adapting to the new environment.

If you are a structuring parent and your children are sometimes difficult, your best bet is to put Walt Disney World off for a few years. Older children, even somewhat temperamental ones, are better able to adjust to things not going their way than are younger children. Additionally, because older children are more independent and physically capable, they are able to function more completely in the adult-oriented world that structuring parents prefer.

Most parents, of course, are neither purely structuring nor natural, but fall somewhere in between. Analyzing your own parenting tendencies and style, however, provides some critical insight into how things are likely to work on vacation with different types of children.

In case you are wondering, the author is definitely *not* a natural. Even with really great kids, he struggled a lot, and he struggles still. Once, however, in a moment of monumental clarity, he articulated an insight that has subsequently become known as "Sehlinger's Law." Although you've probably never heard of it, we'll bet you a pound cake to a penny that you are familiar with the experience. Sehlinger's Law postulates that "the number of adults required to take care of an active toddler is equal to the number of adults present, plus one."

THE NATURE OF THE BEAST

THOUGH MANY PARENTS DON'T REALIZE IT, there is no law that says you must take your kids to Walt Disney World. Likewise, there's no law that says you will enjoy Walt Disney World. And although we will help you make the most of any visit, we can't change the basic nature of the beast . . . er, mouse. A Walt Disney World vacation is an active and physically demanding undertaking. Regimentation, getting up early, lots of walking, waiting in lines, fighting crowds, and (often) enduring heat and humidity are as intrinsic to a Walt Disney World vacation as stripes are to a zebra. Especially if you're traveling with children, you'll need a sense of humor, more than a modicum of patience, and the ability to roll with the punches.

unofficial **TIP**
You can enjoy a perfectly wonderful time in the World if you are realistic, organized, and prepared.

KNOW THYSELF AND NOTHING TO EXCESS

THIS GOOD ADVICE WAS MADE AVAILABLE to ancient Greeks courtesy of the oracle of Apollo at Delphi, who gave us permission to pass it along to you. First, concerning the "know thyself" part, we want you to do some serious thinking concerning what you want in a vacation. We also want you to entertain the notion that having fun and deriving pleasure from your vacation may be very different indeed from doing and seeing as much as possible.

Because Walt Disney World is expensive, many families confuse "seeing everything" in order to "get our money's worth" with having a great time. Sometimes the two are compatible, but more often they are not. So, if sleeping in, relaxing with the paper over coffee, sunbathing by the pool, or taking a nap rank high on your vacation hit parade, you need to accord them due emphasis on your Disney visit (are you listening?), even if it means you see less of the theme parks.

Which brings us to the "nothing to excess" part. At Walt Disney World, especially if you are touring with children, less is definitely more. Trust us, you cannot go full tilt dawn to dark in the theme parks day after day. First you'll get tired, then you'll get cranky, and then you'll adopt a production mentality ("we've got three more rides and then we can go back to the hotel"). Finally, you'll hit the wall because you just can't maintain the pace.

unofficial **TIP**
Get a grip on your needs and preferences before you leave home, and develop an itinerary that incorporates all the things that make you happiest.

Plan on seeing Walt Disney World in bite-size chunks with plenty of sleeping, swimming, napping, and relaxing in between. Ask yourself over and over in both the planning stage and while you are at Walt Disney World: what will contribute the greatest contentedness, satisfaction, and harmony? Trust your instincts. If stopping for ice cream or returning to the hotel for a dip feels like more fun than seeing another attraction, do it—even if it means wasting the remaining hours of an expensive admissions pass.

■ THE AGE THING

THERE IS A LOT OF SERIOUS COGITATION among parents and grandparents in regard to how old a child should be before embarking on a trip to Walt Disney World. The answer, not always obvious, stems from the personalities and maturity of the children, and the personalities and parenting style of the adults.

Walt Disney World for Infants and Toddlers

We believe that traveling with infants and toddlers is a great idea. Developmentally, travel is a stimulating learning experience for even the youngest of children. Infants, of course, will not know Mickey Mouse from a draft horse, but will respond to sun and shade, music, bright colors, and the extra attention they receive from you. From first steps to full mobility, toddlers respond to the excitement and spectacle of Walt Disney World, though of course in a much different way than do you. Your toddler will prefer splashing in fountains and clambering over curbs and benches to experiencing most attractions, but no matter: he or she will still have a great time.

Somewhere between 4 and 6 years of age, your child will experience the first vacation that he or she will remember as an adult. Though more likely to remember the comfortable coziness of the hotel room than the theme parks, the child will be able to experience and comprehend many attractions and will be a much fuller participant in your vacation. Even so, his or her favorite activity is likely to be swimming in the hotel pool.

As concerns infants and toddlers, there are good reasons and bad reasons for vacationing at Walt Disney World. A good reason for taking your little one to Walt Disney World is that you want to go and there's no one available to care for your child during your absence. Philosophically, we are very much against putting your life (including your vacation) on hold until your children are older.

Especially if you have children of varying ages (or plan to, for that matter) it's better to take the show on the road than to wait until the youngest reaches the perceived ideal age.

unofficial **TIP**
Traveling with infants and toddlers sharpens parenting skills and makes the entire family more mobile and flexible, resulting in a richer, fuller life for all.

If your family includes a toddler or infant, you will find everything from private facilities for breast-feeding to changing tables in both men's and women's restrooms to facilitate baby's care. Your whole family will be able to tour together with fewer hassles than on a day's picnic outing at home.

A bad reason, however, for taking an infant or toddler to Walt Disney World is that, through some misguided logic, you think Walt Disney World is the perfect vacation destination for babies. Believe us, it's not, so think again if you are contemplating Walt Disney World primarily for your child's enjoyment. For starters, attractions are geared more toward older children and adults. Even designer play areas like Tom Sawyer Island in the Magic Kingdom are developed with older children in mind.

By way of example, the author has a friend who bought a video camcorder when his first child was born. He delighted in documenting his son's reaction to various new experiences on video. One memorable night when the baby was about 18 months old, he taped the baby eating a variety of foods (from whipped cream to dill pickles) that he had never tried before. While some of the taste sensations elicited wild expressions and animated responses from the baby, the exercise was clearly intended for the amusement of Dad, not junior. Likewise with Walt Disney World, you might score a few memorable photos for the scrapbook as your child reacts to the noise, crowds, and attractions, but don't fool yourself into thinking that the infant or toddler is getting much out of it.

Along similar lines, remember when you were little and you got that nifty electric train for Christmas, the one Dad wouldn't let you play with? Did you ever wonder who that train was really for? Ask yourself the same question about your vacation to Walt Disney World. Whose dream are you trying to make come true: yours or your child's?

If you elect to take your infant or toddler to Walt Disney World, rest assured that their needs have been anticipated. The major theme parks have centralized facilities for infant and toddler care. Everything necessary for changing diapers, preparing formula, and warming bottles and food is available. At the Magic Kingdom, the Baby Center is next to the Crystal Palace at the end of Main Street. At Epcot, Baby Services is near the Odyssey Center, right of Test Track in Future World. At Disney-MGM Studios, Baby Care is in the Guest Relations Building left of the entrance. At the Animal Kingdom, Baby Changing/Nursing is in Discovery Island in the center of the park. Dads in charge of little ones are welcome at the centers and can use most services offered. In addition, men's rooms in the major theme parks have changing tables.

> *unofficial* **TIP**
> Baby supplies, including disposable diapers, formula, and baby food are for sale, and there are rockers and special chairs for nursing mothers.

Infants and toddlers are allowed to experience any attraction that doesn't have minimum height or age restrictions. But as a Minneapolis mother reports, some attractions are better for babies than others:

Theater and boat rides are easier for babies (ours was almost 1 year old, not yet walking). Rides where there's a bar that comes down are doable, but harder. Peter Pan was our first encounter with this type, and we had barely gotten situated when I realized he might fall out of my grasp. The standing auditorium films are too intense; the noise level is deafening, and the images inescapable. You don't have a rating system for babies, and I don't expect to see one, but I thought you might want to know what a baby thought (based on his reactions).

At the Magic Kingdom: Jungle Cruise—Didn't get into it. Pirates—Slept through it. Riverboat—While at Aunt Polly's, the horn made him cry. Aunt Polly's—Ate while watching the birds in relative quiet. Small World—Wide-eyed, took it all in. Peter Pan—Couldn't really sit on the seat. A bit dangerous. He didn't get into it. Carousel of Progress—Long talks; hard to keep him quiet; danced during song. The Timekeeper—Too loud. Dinosaur at

*beginning scared him. Walt Disney World Railroad—
Liked the motion and scenery.* Tiki Birds—*Loved it.
Danced, clapped, sang along.*

At Epcot: Honey, I Shrunk the Audience—*We skipped
due to recommendation of Disney worker that it got too
loud and adults screamed throughout. Journey into Imagination—Loved it. Tried to catch things with his hands.
Bounced up and down, chortled. The Land—Watchful,
quiet during presentation.* Food Rocks—*Loved it, danced.
El Río del Tiempo—Loved it.*

The same mom also advises:

*We used a baby sling on our trip and thought it was great
when standing in the lines—much better than a stroller,
which you have to park before getting in line (and navigate
through crowds). My baby was still nursing when we went
to Walt Disney World. The only really great place I found
to nurse in the Magic Kingdom was a hidden bench in the
shade in Adventureland in between the freezee stand (next
to Tiki Birds) and the small shops. It is impractical to go to
the baby station every time, so a nursing mom better be
comfortable about nursing in very public situations.*

Two points in our reader's comment warrant elaboration.
First, the rental strollers at all of the major theme parks are
designed for toddlers and children up to 3
and 4 years old, but are definitely not for
infants. Still, if you bring a supply of pillows and padding, the rental strollers can
be made to work. You can alternatively
bring your own stroller, but unless it's collapsible, you will not be able to take it on
Disney trams, buses, or boats.

Even if you opt for a stroller (your own or
a rental), we nevertheless recommend that
you also bring a baby sling or baby/child
backpack. Simply put, there will be many
times in the theme parks when you will have to park the
stroller and carry your child. As an aside, if you haven't
checked out baby slings and packs lately, you'll be amazed by
some of the technological advances made in these products.

The second point that needs addressing is our reader's per-
ception that there are not many good places in the theme parks
for breast-feeding unless you are accustomed to nursing in public. Many nursing moms recommend breast-feeding during a
dark Disney theater presentation. This only works, however, if
the presentation is long enough for the baby to finish nursing.

unofficial **TIP**
In addition to pro-
viding an alternative
to carrying your
child, a stroller
serves as a handy
cart for diaper bags,
water bottles, and
other items you
deem necessary.

The Hall of Presidents at the Magic Kingdom and *The American Adventure* at Epcot will afford you about 23 and 29 minutes, respectively. In addition, neither production includes noise or special effects that will frighten your infant, although you can expect fairly loud volume levels for narration and music. *Impressions de France* in the French pavilion at Epcot's World Showcase is only 18 minutes long, but is very quiet and relaxing. For the time being, unfortunately, there are no theater presentations at the Animal Kingdom that offer sufficient quiet and adequate time to nurse. At the Disney-MGM Studios, *Voyage of the Little Mermaid* will work if your child can get filled up in 15 minutes.

Many Disney shows run back to back with only a minute or two in between to change the audience. If you want to breast-feed and require more time than the length of the show, tell the cast member on entering that you want to breast-feed and ask if you can remain in the theater and watch a second showing while your baby finishes.

If you can adjust to nursing in more public places with your breast and the baby's head covered with a shawl or some such, nursing will not be a problem at all. Even on the most crowded days, you can always find a back corner of a restaurant or a comparatively secluded park bench or garden spot to nurse. Finally, the baby centers, with their private nursing rooms, are centrally located in all of the parks except the Disney-MGM Studios.

Walt Disney World for 4-, 5-, and 6-Year-Olds

Four-, five-, and six-year-olds vary immensely in their capacity to comprehend and enjoy Walt Disney World. With this age group the go/no-go decision is a judgment call. If your child is sturdy, easygoing, fairly adventuresome, and demonstrates a high degree of independence, the trip will probably work. On the other hand, if your child tires easily, is temperamental, or is a bit timid or reticent in embracing new experiences, you're much better off waiting a few years. Whereas the travel and sensory-overload problems of infants and toddlers can be addressed and (usually) remedied on the go, discontented 4- to 6-year-olds have the ability to stop a family dead in its tracks, as this mother of three from Cape May, New Jersey, attests:

> My 5-year-old was scared pretty bad on Snow White our first day at Disney World. From then on for the rest of the trip we had to coax and reassure her before each and every ride before she would go. It was like pulling teeth.

If you have a retiring, clinging, and/or difficult 4- to 6-year-old who, for whatever circumstances, will be part of your group, you can sidestep or diminish potential problems with a bit of pretrip preparation. Even if your preschooler is plucky and game, the same prep measures (described later in this section) will enhance his or her experience and make life easier for the rest of the family.

The Ideal Age

Although our readers report both successful trips as well as disasters with children of all ages, the consensus ideal children's ages for family compatibility and togetherness at Walt Disney World are 8 to 12 years. This age group is old enough, tall enough, and sufficiently stalwart to experience, understand, and appreciate practically all Disney attractions. Moreover, they are developed to the extent that they can get around the parks on their own steam without being carried or collapsing. Best of all, they are still young enough to enjoy being with mom and dad. From our experience, ages 10 to 12 are better than 8 and 9, though what you gain in maturity is at the cost of that irrepressible, wide-eyed wonder so prevalent in the 8- and 9-year-olds.

Walt Disney World for Teens

Teens love Walt Disney World, and for parents of teens the "World" is a nearly perfect, albeit expensive vacation choice. Although your teens might not be as wide-eyed and impressionable as their younger sibs, they are at an age where they can sample, understand, and enjoy practically everything Walt Disney World has to offer—and we do mean *everything*. Teens for example, delight in playing adult at Pleasure Island, Walt Disney World's nighttime entertainment complex, hopping from club to club (teens and even younger children are eligible for admission to some Disney nightclubs, but are not allowed to purchase alcohol).

For parents, Walt Disney World is a vacation destination where you can permit your teens an extraordinary amount of freedom. The entertainment is wholesome, the venues are safe, and the entire complex of hotels, theme parks, restaurants, and shopping centers is accessible via the Walt Disney World transportation system. The transportation system allows you, for example, to enjoy a romantic dinner and an early bedtime while your teens take in the late-night fireworks at the theme parks. After the fireworks, a Disney bus, boat, or monorail will deposit them safely back at the hotel.

Because most adolescents relish freedom, you may have difficulty keeping your teens with the rest of the family. Thus, if one of your objectives is to spend time with your teenage children during your Disney World vacation, you will need to establish some clear-cut guidelines regarding togetherness and separateness before you leave home. Make your teens part of the discussion and try to meet them halfway in crafting a decision everyone can live with. For your teens, touring on their own at Walt Disney World is tantamount to being independent in a large city. It's intoxicating, to say the least, and can be an excellent learning experience, if not a rite of passage. In any event, we're not suggesting that you just turn them loose. Rather, we are just attempting to sensitize you to the fact that for your teens, there are some transcendent issues involved.

Most teens crave the company of other teens. If you have a solitary teen in your family, do not be surprised if he or she wants to invite a friend on your vacation. If you are invested in sharing intimate, quality time with your solitary teen, the presence of a friend will make this difficult, if not impossible. However, if you turn down the request to bring a friend, be prepared to go the extra mile to be a companion to your teen at Walt Disney World. Expressed differently, if you're a teen, it's not much fun to ride Space Mountain by yourself.

One specific issue that absolutely should be addressed before you leave home is what assistance (if any) you expect from your teen in regard to helping with younger children in the family. Once again, try to carve out a win/win compromise. Consider the case of the mother from Indiana who had a teenage daughter from an earlier marriage and two children under age 10 from a second marriage. After a couple of vacations where she thrust the unwilling teen into the position of being a surrogate parent to her stepsisters, the teen declined henceforth to participate in family vacations.

Many parents have written the *Unofficial Guide* asking if there are unsafe places at Walt Disney World or places where teens simply should not be allowed to go. Although the answer depends more on your family values and the relative maturity of your teens than on Walt Disney World, the basic answer is no. Though it's true that teens (or adults, for that matter) who are looking for trouble can find it anywhere, there is absolutely nothing at Walt Disney World that could be construed as a precipitant or a catalyst. Be advised, however, that adults consume alcohol at most Walt Disney World restaurants and that drinking is a very visible part of the Pleasure Island club scene. Also, be aware that some of the movies available at the cinemas at the West Side of Downtown Disney demand the same discretion you exercise when allowing your kids to see movies at home.

As a final aside, if you allow your teens some independence and they are getting around on the Walt Disney World transportation system, expect some schedule slippage. There are no posted transportation schedules other than when service begins in the morning and when service terminates at night. Thus, to catch a bus, for example, you just go to a bus station and wait for the next bus to your Disney World destination. If you happen to just miss the bus, you might have to wait 15 to 45 minutes (more often 15 to 20 minutes) for the next one. If punctuality is essential, advise your independent teens to arrive at a transportation station an hour before they are expected somewhere in order to allow sufficient time for the commute.

ABOUT INVITING *your* CHILDREN'S FRIENDS

IF YOUR CHILDREN WANT TO INVITE friends on your Walt Disney World vacation, give your decision careful thought. There's more involved here than might be apparent. First, consider the logistics of numbers. Is there room in the car? Will you have to leave something at home that you had planned on taking to make room in the trunk for the friend's luggage? Will additional hotel rooms or a larger condo be required? Will the increased number of people in your group make it hard to get a table at a restaurant?

If you determine that you can logistically accommodate one or more friends, the next step is to consider how the inclusion of the friend will affect your group's dynamics. Generally speaking, the presence of a friend will make it harder to really connect with your own children. So if one of your vacation goals is an intimate bonding experience with your children, the addition of friends will probably frustrate your attempts to realize that objective.

If family relationship building is not necessarily a primary objective of your vacation, it's quite possible that the inclusion of a friend will make life easier for you. This is especially true in the case of only children, who may otherwise depend exclusively on you to keep them happy and occupied. Having a friend along can take the pressure off and give you some much-needed breathing room.

If you decide to allow a friend to accompany you, limit the selection to children you know really well and whose parents you also know. Your Walt Disney World vacation is not the time to include "my friend Eddie from school" whom you've never met. Your children's friends who have spent time in your home will have a sense of your parenting style, and you will have a sense of their personality, behavior, and compatibility with your family. Assess the prospective child's potential to fit in well on a long trip. Is he or she polite, personable, fun to be with, and reasonably mature? Does he or she relate well to you and to the other members of your family?

Because a Walt Disney World vacation is not, for most of us, a spur-of-the-moment thing, you should have adequate time to evaluate potential candidate friends. A trip to the mall including a meal in a sit-down restaurant will tell you volumes about the friend. Likewise, inviting the friend to share dinner with the family and then spend the night will provide a lot of relevant information. Ideally this type of evaluation should take place early on in the normal course of family events, before you discuss the possibility of a friend joining you on your vacation. This will allow you to size things up without your child (or the friend) realizing that an evaluation is taking place.

By seizing the initiative, you can guide the outcome. Ann, a Springfield, Ohio, mom, for example, anticipated that her 12-year-old son would ask to take a friend on their vacation. As she pondered the various friends her son might propose, she came up with four names. One, an otherwise sweet child, had a medical condition that Ann felt unqualified to monitor or treat. A second friend was overly aggressive with younger children and was often socially inappropriate for his age. Two other friends, Chuck and Marty, with whom she had had a generally positive experience, were good candidates for the trip. After orchestrating some opportunities to spend time with each of the boys, she made her decision and asked her son, "Would you like to take Marty with us to Disney World?" Her son was delighted, and Ann had diplomatically preempted having to turn down friends her son might have proposed.

We recommend that *you* do the inviting, instead of your child, and that the invitation be extended parent to parent. Observing this recommendation will allow you to query the friend's parents concerning food preferences, any medical conditions, how discipline is administered in the friend's family, how the friend's parents feel about the way you administer discipline, and the parents' expectation regarding religious observations while their child is in your care.

Before you extend the invitation, give some serious thought to who pays for what. Make a specific proposal for financing the trip a part of your invitation, for example, "There's room for Marty in the hotel room, and transportation's no problem because we're driving. So we'll just need you to pick up Marty's meals, theme park admissions, and spending money."

unofficial **TIP**
We suggest that you arrange for the friend's parents to reimburse you after the trip for things like restaurant meals and admissions. This is much easier than trying to balance the books after every expenditure.

A FEW WORDS *for* SINGLE PARENTS

BECAUSE SINGLE PARENTS GENERALLY are also working parents, planning a special getaway with your children can be the best way to spend some quality time together. But remember, the vacation is not just for your child—it's for you, too. You might invite a grandparent or a favorite aunt or uncle along; the other adult provides nice company for you, and your child will benefit from the time with family members.

Don't try to spend every moment with your children on vacation. Instead, plan some activities for your children with other children. Disney educational programs for children, for example, are worth considering. Then take advantage of your free time to do what you want to do: read a book, have a massage, take a long walk, or enjoy a catnap.

"HE *who* HESITATES *is* LAUNCHED!"
Tips and Warnings for Grandparents

SENIORS OFTEN GET INTO PREDICAMENTS caused by touring with grandchildren. Run ragged and pressured to endure a blistering pace, many seniors just concentrate on surviving Walt Disney World rather than enjoying it. The theme parks have as much to offer older visitors as they do children, and seniors must either set the pace or dispatch the young folks to tour on their own.

An older reader from Alabaster, Alabama, writes:

The main thing I want to say is that being a senior is not for wussies. At Disney World particularly, it requires courage and pluck. Things that used to be easy take a lot of effort, and sometimes your brain has to wait for your body to catch up. Half the time, your grandchildren treat you like a crumbling ruin and then turn around and trick you into getting on a roller coaster in the dark. What you need to tell seniors is that they have to be alert and not trust anyone. Not their children or even the Disney people, and especially not their grandchildren. When your grandchildren want you to go on a ride, don't follow along blindly like a lamb to the slaughter. Make sure you know what the ride is all about. Stand your ground and do not waffle. He who hesitates is launched!

If you don't get to see much of your grandchildren, you might think that Walt Disney World is the perfect place for a little bonding and togetherness. Wrong! Walt Disney World sends children into system overload and precipitates behaviors that pose a challenge even to adoring parents, never mind grandparents. You don't take your grandchildren straight to Disney World for the same reason you don't buy your 16-year-old son a Ferrari: handling it safely and well requires a lot of experience.

Begin by spending time with your grandchildren in an environment that you can control. Have them over one at a time for dinner and to spend the night. Check out how they respond to your oversight and discipline. Most of all, zero in on whether you are compatible, enjoy each other's company, and have fun together. Determine that you can set limits and that they will accept those limits. When you reach this stage, you can contemplate some outings to the zoo, the movies, the mall, or the state fair. Gauge how demanding your grandchildren are when you are out of the house. Eat a meal or two in a full-service restaurant to get a sense of their social skills and their ability to behave appropriately. Don't expect perfection, and be prepared to modify your behavior a little, too. As a senior friend of mine told her husband (none too decorously), "You can't see Walt Disney World sitting on a stick."

If you have a good relationship with your grandchildren and have had a positive one-on-one experience taking care of them, you might consider a trip to Walt Disney World. If you do, we have two recommendations. First, visit Walt Disney World without them to get an idea of what you're getting into. A scouting trip will also provide you an opportunity to enjoy some of the attractions that won't be on the itinerary when you return with the grandkids. Second, if you are considering a trip of a week's duration, you might think about buying a Disney package that combines four days at Walt Disney World with a three-day cruise on the *Disney Magic* or the *Disney Wonder*. In addition to being a memorable experience for your grandchildren, the cruise provides plenty of structure for children of almost every age, thus allowing you to be with them but also to have some time off. Call the Disney Cruise Line at ☎ 800-951-3532 or visit **www.disneycruise.com.**

A Dozen Tips for Grandparents

1. It's best to take one grandchild at a time, two at the most. Cousins can be better than siblings because they don't fight as much.

2. Let your grandchildren help plan the vacation, and keep the first one short. Be flexible, and don't overplan.

3. Discuss mealtimes and bedtime. Fortunately, many grandparents are on an early dinner schedule, which works nicely with younger children. Also, if you want to plan a special evening out, be sure to make the reservation ahead of time.

4. Gear plans to your grandchildren's age levels, because if they're not happy, you won't be happy.

5. Create an itinerary that offers some supervised activities for children in case you need a rest.

6. If you're traveling by car, this is the one time we highly recommend headphones. Kids' musical tastes are vastly different from most grandparents. It's simply more enjoyable when everyone can listen to his or her own preferred style of music, at least for some portion of the trip.

7. Take along a nightlight.

8. Carry a notarized statement from parents for permission for medical care in case of an emergency. Also be sure you have insurance information and copies of any prescriptions for medicines the kids may be on. Ditto for eyeglass prescriptions.

9. Tell your grandchildren about any medical problems you may have so they can be prepared if there's an emergency.

10. Many attractions and hotels offer discounts for seniors, so be sure you check ahead of time for bargains.

11. Plan your evening meal early to avoid long waits. And make advance reservations if you're dining in a popular spot, even if it's early. Take some crayons and paper to keep kids occupied.

12. If planning a family-friendly trip seems overwhelming, try Grandtravel, a tour operator/travel agent aimed at kids and

their grandparents (call ☎ 800-47-7651 or visit **www.grandtrvl.com**).

Ten Additional Tips from Molly Staub

Travel writer Molly Arost Staub is everybody's go-to-person for information on traveling with grandchildren. Here are her tips on doing Walt Disney World with the grandkids:

A WORD OF CAUTION Times have changed since your children were young. These days, keep a lookout (and hold hands with little ones) at all times. It's not the innocent world we (or our children) grew up in. Carry a cell phone in case of problems, and make sure you know how to use it.

THE PERFECT SOUNDTRACK If you're driving, borrow some age-appropriate tapes or CDs from your children so your grandkids won't keep asking, "Are we there yet?"

EXPECT SUNSHINE Don't forget sun hats, sunglasses, and sunscreen. And bring bottles of water.

SLEEP TIGHT Leave the tents and backpacks to your kids' generation; you've earned a bit of comfort by now. Choose a Disney hotel so you can hop on a bus or monorail. You will also be eligible for admission to the park prior to opening time through the Extra Magic Hours morning early entry program. There's the added bonus of easily returning to your room for two-generation naps or refreshing dips in the pool. Choose a hotel on the monorail (if it fits your budget) so you can watch the Magic Kingdom fireworks across the lake (instead of traipsing back to the park after a tiring day). A good budget choice is Disney's Port Orleans Resort Riverside. The more upscale Polynesian Resort hosts a luau in which little ones are invited onstage to join in a hula. At the Animal Kingdom Lodge, children will gladly gaze out the windows at the giraffes and zebras roaming just beyond, instead of staring endlessly at the TV screen.

STAY "SEASIDE" A particularly nostalgic lodging option with multigenerational appeal is Disney's BoardWalk Inn. Recall the boardwalk of your youth—whether it was Atlantic City, Coney Island, or Wildwood—by staying at the elaborately themed property. You can "walk the boards" again, smell the cotton candy, ride on a bicycle built for two, and swear you hear the seagulls.

GLOBETROTTING Epcot's World Showcase has become more youngster-friendly thanks to newer hands-on activities. The varied foods and live shows provide good introductions to other cultures and may stimulate a desire to travel—maybe even taking an exotic trip with the grands.

MEALTIME WITH MICKEY Splurge on one character breakfast. Even the most sophisticated little ones will forget about their Game Boys for a hug from Snow White or Goofy, and will thank you for being the best grandparents in the world.

PERSONALIZE YOUR TRIP Use your time at the theme parks to share bits of family history. Kids relish hearing stories of when their parents were little, as well as when grandparents were young in the "olden days." At Disney-MGM Studios, grands wax nostalgic for the 1940s and 1950s on Disney's Hollywood Boulevard, while a meal at the Prime Time Cafe is a howl, and a good way to help young ones understand you didn't grow up in the horse-and-buggy days. Watching the tiny black-and-white TVs and eating at a chrome-and-formica table, share the story of going to see *Mary Poppins* when it was first released—and see if you can still sing "Supercalifragilisticexpialidocious." Perhaps your house was the first on the block to get color TV, or maybe you were really deprived and only got three TV stations.

ROLL ON If one of your party—grandparent or grand-child—tires easily, bring or rent a wheelchair. Not only will it save aching feet and legs, but cast members often offer those guests preferential treatment in the lines.

RELIVE A LITTLE It's fun revisiting some attractions that appealed to your own children—and perhaps taught valu-able lessons—to find they've been updated with newer music or sets appealing to today's youngsters.

ORDER *and* DISCIPLINE *on the* ROAD

OK, OK, WIPE THAT SMIRK OFF YOUR FACE. Order and discipline on the road may seem like an oxymoron to you, but you won't be hooting when your 5-year-old launches a screaming stem-winder in the middle of Fantasyland. Your willingness to give this subject serious consideration before you leave home may well be the most important element of your pre-trip preparation.

Discipline and maintaining order are more difficult when traveling than at home because everyone is, as a Boston mom put it, "in and out" (in strange surroundings and out of the normal routine). For children, it's hard to contain excitement and anticipation that pop to the surface in the form of fidgety hyperactivity, nervous energy, and sometimes, acting out. Confinement in a car, plane, or hotel room only exacerbates the situation, and kids are often louder than normal, more aggressive with siblings, and much more inclined to push the envelope of parental patience and control. Once in the theme parks, it doesn't get much better. There's more elbowroom, but there's also overstimulation, crowds, heat, miles of walking. All this coupled with marginal or inadequate rest, can lead to meltdown in the most harmonious of families.

Sound parenting and standards of discipline practiced at home, applied consistently, will suffice to handle most situations on vacation. Still, it's instructive to study the hand you are dealt when traveling. For starters, aside from being jazzed and ablaze with adrenaline, your kids may believe that rules followed at home are somehow suspended when traveling. Parents reinforce this misguided intuition by being inordinately lenient in the interest of maintaining peace in the family. While some of your home protocols (cleaning your plate, going to bed at a set time, etc.) might be relaxed to good effect on vacation, differing from your normal approach to discipline can precipitate major misunderstanding and possibly disaster.

unofficial **TIP**
Discuss your vacation needs with your children and explore their wants and expectations as well, before you depart on your trip.

Children, not unexpectedly, are likely to believe that a vacation (especially a vacation to Walt Disney World) is expressly for them. This reinforces their focus on their own needs and largely erases any consideration of yours. Such a mindset dramatically increases their sense of hurt and disappointment when you correct them or deny them something they want. An incident that would hardly elicit a pouty lip at home could well escalate to tears or defiance when traveling.

The stakes are high for everyone on a vacation; for you because of the cost in time and dollars, but also because your vacation represents a rare opportunity for rejuvenation and renewal. The stakes are high for your children too. Children tend to romanticize travel, building anticipation to an almost unbearable level. Discussing the trip in advance can ground expectations to a certain extent, but a child's imagination will, in the end, trump reality every time. The good news is that you can take advantage of your children's emotional state to establish pre-agreed rules and conditions for their conduct while on vacation. Because your children want what's being offered sooooo badly, they will be unusually accepting and conscientious regarding whatever rules are agreed upon.

According to child psychologist Dr. Karen Turnbow, successful response to (or avoidance of) behavioral problems on the road begins with a clear-cut disciplinary policy at home. Both at home and on vacation the approach should be the same, and should be based on the following key concepts:

1. LET EXPECTATIONS BE KNOWN. Discuss what you expect from your children but don't try to cover every imaginable situation. Cover expectations in regard to compliance with parental directives, treatment of siblings, resolution of disputes, schedule (including wake-up and bedtimes), courtesy and manners, staying together, and who pays for what.

2. EXPLAIN THE CONSEQUENCES OF NONCOMPLIANCE. Detail very clearly and firmly the consequence of not meeting expectations. This should be very straightforward and unambiguous. If you do X (or don't do X) this is what will happen.

3. WARN YOUR KIDS. You're dealing with excited, expectant children, not machines, so it's important to issue a warning before meting out discipline. It's critical to understand that we're talking about one unequivocal warning rather than multiple warnings or nagging. These last undermine your credibility and make your expectations appear relative or less than serious. Multiple warnings or nagging also effectively passes control of the situation from you to your child (who may continue to act out as an attention-getting strategy).

4. FOLLOW THROUGH. If you say you're going to do something, do it. Period. Children must understand that you are absolutely serious and committed.

5. BE CONSISTENT. Inconsistency makes discipline a random event in the eyes of your children. Random discipline encourages random behavior, which translates to a nearly total loss of parental control. Long-term, both at home and on the road, your response to a given situation or transgression must be perfectly predictable. Structure and repetition, essential for a child to learn, cannot be achieved in the absence of consistency.

Although the above are the five biggies, there are several corollary concepts and techniques that are worthy of consideration.

First, understand that whining, tantrums, defiance, sibling friction, and even holding the group up are ways in which children communicate with parents. Frequently the object or precipitant of a situation has little or no relation to the unacceptable behavior. A fit may on the surface appear to be about the ice cream you refused to buy little Robby, but there's almost always something deeper, a subtext that is closer to the truth (this is the reason why ill behavior often persists after you give in to a child's demands). As often as not the real cause is a need for attention. This need is so powerful in some children that they will subject themselves to certain punishment and parental displeasure to garner the attention they crave.

To get at the root cause of the behavior in question requires both active listening and empowering your child with a "feeling vocabulary." Active listening is a concept that's been around a long time. It involves being alert not only to what a child says, but also to the context in which it is said, to the language used and possible subtext, to the child's emotional state and body language, and even to what's not said. Sounds complicated, but it's basically being attentive to the larger picture, and more to the point, being aware that there is a larger picture.

Helping your child to develop a feeling vocabulary consists of teaching your child to use words to describe what's going on. The idea is to teach the child to articulate what's really troubling him, to be able to identify and express emotions and mood states in language. Of course learning to express feelings is a lifelong experience, but it's much less dependent on innate sensitivity than being provided the tools for expression and being encouraged to use them.

It all begins with convincing your child that you're willing to listen attentively and take what he's saying seriously. Listening to your child, you help him transcend the topical by reframing the conversation to address the underlying emotional state(s). That his brother hit him may have precipitated the mood, but the act is topical and of secondary importance. What you want is for your child to be able to communicate how that makes him feel, and to get in touch with those emotions. When you reduce an incident (hitting) to the emotions triggered (anger, hurt, rejection, etc.) you have the foundation for helping him to develop constructive coping strategies. Not only are being in touch with one's feelings and developing constructive coping strategies essential to emotional well-being, they also beneficially affect behavior. A child who can tell his mother why he is distressed is a child who has discovered a coping strategy far more effective (not to mention easier for all concerned) than a tantrum.

Children are almost never too young to begin learning a feeling vocabulary. And helping your child to be in touch with, and try to communicate, his emotions, will stimulate you to focus on your feelings and mood states in a similar way.

SIX MORE TIPS

UNTIL YOU GET THE ACTIVE LISTENING and feeling vocabulary going, be careful not to become part of the problem. There's a whole laundry list of adult responses to bad behavior that only make things worse. Hitting, swatting, yelling, name calling, insulting, belittling, using sarcasm, pleading, nagging, and inducing guilt (as in: "We've spent thousands of dollars to bring you to Disney World and now you're spoiling the trip for everyone") figure prominently on the list.

Responding to a child appropriately in a disciplinary situation requires thought and preparation. Following are key things to keep in mind and techniques to try when your world blows up while waiting in line for Dumbo.

1. BE THE ADULT. It's well understood that children can punch their parents' buttons faster and more lethally than just about anyone or anything else. They've got your number, know precisely how to elicit a response, and are not reluctant to go for the jugular. Fortunately (or unfortunately) you're the adult, and to deal with a situation effectively, you must act like one. If your kids get you ranting and caterwauling, you effectively abdicate your adult status. Worse, you suggest by way of example that being out of control is an acceptable expression of hurt or anger. No matter what happens, repeat the mantra, "I am the adult in this relationship."

2. FREEZE THE ACTION. Being the adult and maintaining control almost always translates to freezing the action, to borrow a sports term. Instead of a knee-jerk response (at a maturity level closer to your child's than yours), freeze the action by disengaging. Wherever you are or whatever the family is doing, stop in place and concentrate on one thing, and one thing only: getting all involved calmed down. Practically speaking, this usually means initiating a time-out. It's essential that you take this action immediately. Grabbing your child by the arm or collar and dragging him toward the car or hotel room only escalates the turmoil by prolonging the confrontation and by adding a coercive physical dimension to an already volatile emotional event. If for the sake of people around you (as when a toddler throws a tantrum in church), it's essential to retreat to a more private place, chose the first place available. Firmly sit the child down and refrain from talking to him until you've both cooled off. This might take a little time, but the investment is worthwhile. Truncating the process is like trying to get on your feet too soon after surgery.

3. ISOLATE THE CHILD. You'll be able to deal with the situation more effectively and expeditiously if the child is isolated with one parent. Dispatch the uninvolved members of your party for a Coke break or have them go on with the activity or itinerary without you (if possible) and arrange to rendezvous later at an agreed time and place. In addition to letting the others get on with their day, isolating the offending child with one parent relieves him of the pressure of being the group's focus of attention and object of anger. Equally important, isolation frees you from the scrutiny and expectations of the others in regard to how to handle the situation.

4. REVIEW THE SITUATION WITH THE CHILD. If, as discussed above, you've made your expectations clear, stated the consequences of failing those expectations, and have administered a warning, review the situation with the child and follow through with the discipline warranted. If, as often occurs, things are not so black and white, encourage the child to communicate his feelings. Try to uncover what occasioned the acting out. Lecturing and accusatory language don't work well here, nor do threats. Dr. Turnbow suggests a better approach (after the child is calm) is to ask, "What can we do to make this a better day for you?"

5. FREQUENT TANTRUMS OR ACTING OUT. The preceding four points relate to dealing with an incident as opposed to a chronic condition. If a child frequently acts out or throws tantrums, you'll need to employ a somewhat different strategy.

Tantrums are cyclical events evolved from learned behavior. A child learns that he can get your undivided attention by acting out. When you respond, whether by scolding, admonishing, threatening, or negotiating, your response further draws you into the cycle and prolongs the behavior. When you accede to the child's demands you reinforce the effectiveness of the tantrum and raise the cost of capitulation next time around. When a child thus succeeds in monopolizing your attention, he effectively becomes the person in charge.

To break this cycle, you must disengage from the child. The object is to demonstrate that the cause and effect relationship (i.e., tantrum elicits parental attention) is no longer operative. This can be accomplished by refusing to interact with the child as long as the untoward behavior continues. Tell the child that you're unwilling to discuss his problem until he calms down. You can ignore the behavior, remove yourself from the child's presence (or visa versa), or isolate the child with a time-out. The important thing is to disengage quickly and decisively with no discussion or negotiation.

Most children don't pick the family vacation as the time to start throwing tantrums. The behavior will be evident before you leave home and home is the best place to deal with it. Be forewarned, however, that bad habits die hard, and that a child accustomed to getting attention by throwing tantrums will not simply give up after a single instance of disengagement. More likely, the child will at first escalate the intensity and length of his tantrums. By your consistent refusal over several weeks (or even months) to respond to his behavior, however, he will finally adjust to the new paradigm.

Children are cunning as well as observant. Many understand that a tantrum in public is embarrassing to you and that you're more likely to cave in than you would at home. Once again, consistency is the key, along with a bit of anticipation. When traveling, it's not necessary to retreat to the privacy of a hotel room to isolate your child. You can carve out space for time-out almost anywhere: on a theme park bench, in a park, in your car, in a restroom, even on a sidewalk. You can often spot the warning signs of an impending tantrum and head it off by talking to the child before he reaches an explosive emotional pitch.

> *unofficial* **TIP**
> Tantrums are about getting attention. Giving your child attention when things are on an even keel often pre-empts acting out.

6. SALVAGE OPERATIONS. Who knows what evil lurks in the hearts of children? What's for sure is that they are full of surprises, and sometimes the surprises are not good. If your sweet child manages to pull a boner of mammoth proportions, what do you do? This happened to an Ohio couple, resulting in the offending kid pretty much being grounded for life. Fortunately there were no injuries or lives lost, but the parents had to determine what to do for the remainder of the vacation. For starters, they split the group. One parent escorted the offending child back to the hotel where he was effectively confined to his guest room for the duration. That evening, the parents arranged for in-room sitters for the rest of the stay. Expensive? You bet, but better than watching your whole vacation go down the tubes.

A family at Walt Disney World's Magic Kingdom theme park had a similar experience, although the offense was of a more modest order of magnitude. Because it was their last day of vacation, they elected to place the child in time-out, in the theme park, for the rest of the day. One parent monitored the culprit while the other parent and the siblings enjoyed the attractions. At agreed times the parents would switch places. Once again, not ideal, but preferable to stopping the vacation.

Visiting Walt Disney World is a bit like childbirth—you never really believe what people tell you, but once you have been through it yourself, you know exactly what they were saying!

—Hilary Wolfe, a mother and *Unofficial Guide*
reader from Swansea, United Kingdom

GATHERING INFORMATION

IN ADDITION TO THIS GUIDE, we recommend that you obtain:

1. **THE WALT DISNEY TRAVEL COMPANY FLORIDA VACATIONS BROCHURE AND VIDEO/DVD** This video/DVD and brochure describe Walt Disney World in its entirety, list rates for all Disney resort hotels and campgrounds, and describe Disney World package vacations. They're available from most travel agents or by calling the Walt Disney Travel Company at ☎ 407-828-8101 or 407-934-7639. Be prepared to hold. When you get a representative, tell them you want the video or DVD vacation planner that lists the benefits and costs of the various packages.

2. **THE DISNEY CRUISE LINE BROCHURE AND DVD** This brochure provides details on vacation packages that combine a cruise on the Disney Cruise Line with a stay at Disney World. Disney Cruise Line also offers a free DVD that tells all you need to know about Disney cruises and then some. To obtain a copy, call ☎ 800-951-3532 or order at **www.disney cruise.disney.go.com/disneycruiseline**.

3. **THE UNOFFICIAL GUIDE TO WALT DISNEY WORLD WEB SITE** Our Web site, **www.touringplans.com,** offers a free online trip organizer, 50 different touring plans, and updates on changes at Walt Disney World, among other features. The site is described more fully later in this chapter.

4. **ORLANDO MAGICARD** If you're considering lodging outside Disney World or if you think you might patronize out-of-the-World attractions and restaurants, obtain an Orlando Magicard, a Vacation Planner, and the *Orlando Official Accommodations Guide* (all free) from the Orlando Visitors Center. The Magicard entitles you to discounts for hotels, restaurants, ground transportation, shopping malls, dinner theaters, and non-Disney theme parks and attractions. The Orlando Magicard can be conveniently downloaded from a new Web site, **www.orlandoinfo. com/magicard.** To order the accommodations guide, call ☎ 800-643-9492. For additional information and materials, call ☎ 407-363-5872 weekdays during business hours. Allow four weeks for delivery by mail.

> *un*official **TIP**
> Request information as far in advance as possible and allow four weeks for delivery. Make a checklist of information you request, and follow up if you haven't received your materials within six weeks.

5. **FLORIDA TRAVELER DISCOUNT GUIDE** Another good source of discounts on lodging, restaurants, and attractions statewide is the *Florida Traveler Discount Guide,* published by Exit Information Guide. The guide is free, but you pay $3 for handling ($5 if shipped to Canada). Call ☎ 352-371-3948, Monday–Friday, 8 a.m.–5 p.m. EST, or go to **www.travelerdiscountguide.com** and order online. To order by mail, write to 4205 N.W. Sixth Street, Gainesville, FL 32609. Similar guides to other states are available at the same number. Also, print hotel coupons free from their **www.roomsaver.com** Web site.

6. **KISSIMMEE–ST. CLOUD TOUR AND TRAVEL SALES GUIDE** This full-color directory of hotels and attractions is one of the most complete available and is of particular interest to those who intend to lodge outside Disney World. It also lists rental houses, time-shares, and condominiums. For a copy, call the Kissimmee–St. Cloud Convention and Visitors Bureau at ☎ 800-327-9159 or 407-944-2400; or access **www.florida kiss.com.**

7. **GUIDEBOOK FOR GUESTS WITH DISABILITIES** Each park's *Guidebook for Guests with Disabilities* is available online at **www.disneyworld.com.**

Recommended Web Sites

The *Unofficial Guide* data-collection director, Len Testa, has combed the Web, looking for the best Disney sites. Here are Len's picks:

BEST OFFICIAL THEME-PARK SITE The official Walt Disney World Web site (**www.disneyworld.com**) contains information on ticket options, park hours, attraction height requirements, disabled guest access, and the like.

BEST GENERAL UNOFFICIAL SITES *The Walt Disney World Information Guide* (**www.allearsnet.com**) is the first Web site we recommend to friends interested in going to Disney World. It contains information on virtually every hotel, restaurant, and activity in the World. Want to know what the rooms look like at Disney resorts before you book one? This site has photos—sometimes for each floor of a resort. The Web site is updated several times per week and includes menus from Disney restaurants, ticketing information, maps, driving directions, and more.

We also read **www.mouseplanet.com** on a weekly basis. Besides timely information, MousePlanet delivers detailed, multipart stories on a wide range of Disney theme-park subjects, including restaurants, resorts, and transportation. The site hosts a lively set of discussion boards featuring a wide range of theme-park topics, and their "updates" section is the most comprehensive available.

UNOFFICIAL GUIDE WEB SITES *The Unofficial Guide to Walt Disney World* Web site can be found at **www.touringplans.com.** The official Web site of the *Unofficial Guide* Travel and Lifestyle Series, providing in-depth information on all the *Unofficial Guides* in print, is at **www.theunofficialguides.com.**

The official Web site for this guide, **www.touringplans.com,** has quite a few useful features: the most recent additions include more than 50 touring plans for the Disney theme parks.

Our Web site also features a comprehensive, free online trip planner that allows you to keep track of all your trip details, including packing checklists, flight information, ground transportation, lodging, budgets, and daily activities in each of the parks. Best of all, you can optionally share trip details with family, friends, and others. So, for example, your travel agent can update your organizer, and you'll be able to see the new information immediately.

BEST MONEY-SAVING SITE Mary Waring's **www.mousesavers. com** is the kind of Web site for which the Internet was invented. It keeps an updated list of discounts and reservation codes for use at Disney resorts. The codes are separated into categories such as "For anyone" and "For residents of certain states." Anyone calling the Disney central reservations office (☎ 407-w-DISNEY) can use a current code and get the discounted rate. Savings can be considerable. Two often-overlooked features are the discount codes for rental cars and non-Disney hotels in the area.

BEST DISNEY DISCUSSION BOARDS The best online discussions of all things Disney can be found at **www.disboards. com.** With almost 70,000 members and 7 million posts, the discussion boards are the most active and popular on the Web. Posting a question on any aspect of an upcoming trip is likely to get you helpful responses from lots of folks who've been in the same situation.

BEST SITE FOR WDW LIVE ENTERTAINMENT SCHEDULES Orlando resident Steve Soares posts the daily performance schedule a week in advance for every live show in Walt Disney World. This information is invaluable if you're trying to integrate these shows into our touring plans. Visit **http:// pages.prodigy.net/stevesoares** for details.

BEST ORLANDO WEATHER INFORMATION Printable 15-day forecasts for the Orlando area are available from **www. accuweather.com.** The site is especially useful in winter and spring, when temperatures can vary dramatically. During summer, the ultraviolet-index forecasts will help you choose between a tube and a keg of sunscreen.

BEST SAFETY SITE All children younger than 6 must be properly restrained when traveling by car. Check **www.buckleup florida.com** to learn about Florida child-restraint requirements.

BEST WEB SITE FOR ORLANDO TRAFFIC, ROADWORK, AND CON- STRUCTION INFORMATION Visit **www.expresswayauthority. com** for the latest information on road work in the Orlando and Orange County areas. The site also contains detailed maps, directions, and toll-rate information for the most popular tourist destinations.

Important Walt Disney World Telephone Numbers

When you call the main information number, you'll be offered a menu of options for recorded information on operating hours, recreation areas, shopping, entertainment, tickets, reservations, and driving directions. If you're using a rotary telephone, your call will be forwarded to a representative. If you're using a touch-tone phone and have a question not covered by recorded information, press 8 at any time to speak to a representative.

General Information	☎ 407-824-4321
General Information for the Hearing Impaired	☎ 407-939-8255
Accommodations/Reservations	☎ 407- W-DISNEY or 407-824-8000
Blizzard Beach Information	☎ 407-560-3400
Centracare	☎ 407-238-3000
The Crossroads	☎ 407-239-7777
Disney Main Gate	☎ 407-397-7032
Kissimmee	☎ 407-390-1888
Lake Buena Vista	☎ 407-934-2273
Dining Advance Reservations	☎ 407-WDW-DINE
Disabled Guests Special Requests	☎ 407-939-7807
DisneyQuest	☎ 407-828-4600
Disney's Wide World of Sports	☎ 407-939-2139
Golf Reservations and Information	☎ 407-WDW-GOLF or 407-939-4653
Guided Tour Information	☎ 407-WDW-TOUR or 407-939-8687
Outdoor Recreation Reservations and Information	☎ 407-WDW-PLAY or 407-939-7529
Pleasure Island Information	☎ 407-939-2648
Resort Dining and Recreational Information	☎ 407-WDW-DINE or 407-939-3463
Tennis Reservations/Lessons	☎ 407-939-7529
Typhoon Lagoon Information	☎ 407-560-4141
Walt Disney Travel Company	☎ 407-828-3232
Weather Information	☎ 407-827-4545
Wrecker Service	☎ 407-824-0976

▮ ALLOCATING TIME

DURING WALT DISNEY WORLD'S FIRST DECADE, a family with a week's vacation could enjoy the Magic Kingdom and now-defunct River Country and still have several days for the beach or other local attractions. Since Epcot opened in 1982, however, Disney World has steadily been enlarging to monopolize the family's entire week. Today, with the addition of Blizzard Beach, Typhoon Lagoon, Disney-MGM Studios, the Animal Kingdom, and Downtown Disney, you should allocate six days for a whirlwind tour (seven to ten days if you're old-fashioned and insist on a little relaxation during your vacation). If you don't have six or more days, or think you might want to venture beyond the edge of "the World," be prepared to make some hard choices.

A seemingly obvious point lost on many families is that Walt Disney World is not going anywhere. There's no danger that it will be packed up and shipped to Iceland anytime soon. This means that you can come back if you don't see everything this year. Disney has planned it this way, of course, but that doesn't matter. It's infinitely more sane to resign yourself to the reality that seeing everything during one visit is impossible. We recommend, therefore, that you approach Walt Disney World the same way you would an eight-course Italian dinner: leisurely, with plenty of time between courses. The best way not to have fun is to cram too much into too little time.

WHEN TO GO TO WALT DISNEY WORLD

LET'S CUT TO THE ESSENCE: WALT DISNEY World between June 12 and August 18 is rough. You can count on large summer crowds as well as Florida's trademark heat and humidity. Avoid these dates if you can. Ditto for Memorial Day weekend at the beginning of the summer and Labor Day weekend at the end. Other holiday periods (Thanksgiving, Christmas, Easter, spring break, and so on) are extremely crowded, but the heat is not as bad.

The best time of year to visit Walt Disney World is in the fall, especially November before Thanksgiving and December before Christmas. Excluding New Year's and other national holidays, January and February are also good, although the weather is generally not as nice as it is in the fall. March and April bring spring break and Easter crowds, though it is sometimes possible (depending on the school and liturgical calendars) to find certain weeks in this period that are not too busy. Late April and May as well as the beginning of June are pretty good crowd-wise, but are hot and often rainy. Crowds in late August are more tolerable than the heat.

So, parents, what to do? If your children are of preschool age, definitely go during a cooler, less-crowded time. If you have school-age children, look first for an anomaly in your school-year schedule: in other words, a time when your kids will be out of school when most other schools are in session. Anomalies are most often found at the beginning or end of the school year (for example, school starts late or lets out early), at Christmas, or at spring break. In the event that no such anomalies exist, and providing that your kids are good students, our recommendation is to ask permission to take your children out of school either just before or after the Thanksgiving holiday. Teachers can assign lessons that can be made up at home over the Thanksgiving holiday, either before or after your Walt Disney World vacation.

If none of the foregoing is workable for your family, consider visiting Walt Disney World the week immediately before school starts (excluding Labor Day weekend) or the week immediately after school lets out (excluding Memorial Day weekend). This strategy should remove you from the really big mob scenes by about a week.

Incidently, taking your kids out of school for more than a few days is problematic. We have received well-considered letters from parents and teachers who don't think taking kids out of school is such a hot idea. A Fairfax, Virginia, dad put it thus:

> My wife and I do not encourage families to take their children out of school in order to avoid the crowds at Walt Disney World during the summer months. My wife is an eighth-grade science teacher of chemistry and physics. She has parents pull their children, some honor-roll students, out of school for vacations only to discover when they return that the students are unable to comprehend the material. Several students have been so thoroughly lost in their assignments that they ask if they can be excused from the tests. Parental suspicions [about] the quality of their children's education should be raised when children go to school for six hours a day yet supposedly can complete this same instruction with "less than an hour of homework" each night.

Likewise, a high-school teacher from Louisville, Kentucky, didn't mince words on this subject:

> Teachers absolutely hate it when a kid misses school for a week because: (a) parents expect a neat little educational packet to take with them as if every minute can be planned—not practicable; (b) when the kid returns he is going to be behind, and it is difficult to make up classroom instruction [at the time] when the kid needs it.
>
> If a parent bothers to ask my opinion, I tell them bluntly it's their choice. If the student's grades go down, then they have to accept that as part of their family decision. I have a student out this entire week, skiing in Colorado. There's no way she can make up some of the class activities (and that's exactly what I told her mom).

If you are left with the choice of going during the hot, busy summer or not going at all, take heart. You can still have a great time, but you will probably see less. If you elect to go this route, visit as early in June or as late in August as possible, avoiding July. Set up your touring itinerary to visit the parks early in the morning and late in the evening with swimming and napping in between.

Though we strongly recommend going to Walt Disney World at less busy times of year, you should know that there are trade-offs. The parks often open late and close early on fall, winter, and spring days. When they open as late as 10 a.m., everyone arrives about the same time, making it hard to beat the crowd. A late opening coupled with an early closing drastically reduces the hours available for touring. Even when crowds are small, it's difficult to see a big park like the Magic Kingdom or Epcot between 10 a.m. and 6 p.m. Early closing (before 8 p.m.) also usually means that evening parades or fireworks are eliminated. And, because these are slow times at Disney World, some rides and attractions may be closed for maintenance or renovation. Finally, central Florida temperatures fluctuate wildly during the late fall, winter, and early spring; daytime lows in the 40s are not uncommon.

unofficial **TIP**
If you must visit during the busy summer season, cut your visit short by one or two days so that you will have the weekend or a couple of vacation days remaining when you get home to recuperate.

Selecting the Day of the Week for Your Visit

We receive thousands of emails and letters from readers each year asking which park is the best bet on a particular day. Because there are now so many variables (about 26) to consider when recommending a specific best park for a given date, we've created a computer program that weighs all the variables and provides the answer. The results are posted in a Crowd Condition Calendar posted on our Web site **www. touringplans.com.** Once you've decided the dates of your visit to Walt Disney World, access the Web site and check out your dates on the Crowd Condition Calendar (no charge). The calendar will tell you the park to visit (and to avoid) for each day of your visit. If you don't have regular Internet access, the information is worth a trip to an Internet café or to a your local library to obtain.

Extra Magic Hours

"Extra Magic Hours" is a perk for families staying at a Walt Disney World resort, including the Swan, Dolphin, and Shades of

unofficial **TIP**
You'll need to have a Park-Hopping option on your theme-park admission to take advantage of the Extra Magic Hours at both the Disney-MGM Studios and Animal Kingdom on Tuesdays (see chart below).

Green, and the Hilton in the Downtown Disney resort area. On selected days of the week, Disney resort guests will be able to enter a Disney theme park one hour earlier, or stay in a selected theme park up to three hours later than the official park-operating hours. Theme park visitors not staying at a Disney resort may stay in the park for Extra Magic Hour evenings, but cannot experience any rides, attractions, or shows. In other words, they can shop and eat.

WHAT'S REQUIRED? A valid admission ticket is required to enter the park, and you must show your Disney Resort I.D. when entering. For evening Extra Magic Hours, you must pick up a wristband inside the park at least two hours before park closing if you want to experience any of the rides or attractions.

WHEN ARE EXTRA MAGIC HOURS OFFERED? The regular Extra Magic Hours schedule is shown below. Note that the schedule is subject to change, especially during holidays and other periods of peak attendance.

EXTRA MAGIC HOURS SCHEDULE *(subject to change)*		
	MORNING	**EVENING**
Monday	Epcot	–
Tuesday	Disney-MGM Studios	Animal Kingdom
Wednesday	–	Magic Kingdom
Thursday	–	Epcot
Friday	Magic Kingdom	–
Saturday	Animal Kingdom	–
Sunday	Disney-MGM Studios	–

WHAT DO EXTRA MAGIC HOURS MEAN TO YOU? Crowds are likely to be larger when the theme parks host an Extra Magic Hours session. If you're not staying at a Disney resort, we suggest avoiding the park hosting Extra Magic Hours, if at all possible.

unofficial **TIP**
Extra Magic Hours draw more Disney resort guests to the host park, which results in longer lines than you'd otherwise experience.

If you're staying at a Disney resort, there are a couple of strategies you can employ to cut down on your wait in lines. One strategy is to avoid the park hosting Extra

Magic Hours entirely, if possible. If you can be at the park when it opens, a second strategy would be to visit the park offering a morning Extra Magic Hours session until lunchtime, then visit another, less-crowded park in the afternoon.

PLANNING *your* WALT DISNEY WORLD VACATION BUDGET

HOW MUCH YOU SPEND DEPENDS on how long you stay at Walt Disney World. But even if you only stop by for an afternoon, be prepared to drop a bundle. Later we'll show you how to save money on lodging. This section will give you some sense of what you can expect to pay for admissions and food. And we'll help you decide which admission option will best meet your needs.

> *unofficial* **TIP**
> Try **www.touring plans.com** before your trip to Walt Disney World—it's free and considers almost all of the different ticket options.

Walt Disney World Admission Options

In an effort to accommodate vacations of various durations and activities, Disney offers a number of different admission options to its theme parks. These options range from the basic "One Day, One Park" ticket, good for a single entry into any one of Disney's theme parks, to the top of the line Premium Annual Pass, good for 365 days of admission into every theme and water park Disney operates, plus DisneyQuest and Pleasure Island.

We wrote a computer program to help you figure out which of the many Disney admission options is best for you. You can use the program by visiting our Web site at **www. touringplans.com.** All you have to do is answer a few simple questions relating to the theme parks you intend to visit, whether you intend to stay at a Disney or non-Disney hotel, etc. (nothing personal). The program will then identify the four least-expensive ticket options for your vacation.

Magic Your Way

In January 2005, Walt Disney World pretty much chunked its entire panoply of admission options and introduced a completely new array of theme-park tickets in a program called "Magic Your Way." The new scheme applies to both one-day and multiday passports and begins with a "Base Ticket" (also referred to in some Disney literature as a "Starter Pass").

Features that were previously bundled with certain tickets, such as the ability to visit more than one park per day ("park hopping"), or the inclusion of admission to Disney's minor venues (Typhoon Lagoon, Blizzard Beach, Pleasure Island, DisneyQuest, etc.) are now available as individual add-ons to the Base Ticket.

As before, there is a volume discount. The more days of admission you purchase, the lower the cost per day. For example, if you buy an adult Five-Day Base Ticket for $205.54 (taxes included), each day will cost $41.11, as compared to $63.63 a day for a one-day pass. Base Tickets can be purchased from one to up to ten days. The Base Ticket admits you to exactly one Disney theme park per day. Unlike Disney's previous multiday tickets, you cannot use a Base Ticket to visit more than one park per day.

Under the old system, unused days on multiday passports were good indefinitely. Now passes expire 14 days from the first day of use.

Base Ticket Add-On Options

Navigating the Magic Your Way program is much like ordering dinner in an upscale restaurant where all menu selections are à la carte: lots of choices, mostly expensive, virtually all of which require some thought.

Three add-on options are offered with the Base Ticket, each at an additional cost:

PARK HOPPING Adding this feature to your Base Ticket allows you to visit more than one theme park per day. The cost is a flat $37.28 (tax included) on top of the Base Ticket price and covers the total number of days' admission you buy. It's an exorbitant price for one or two days but becomes more affordable the longer your stay.

NO EXPIRATION DATE Adding this option to your ticket means that unused admissions to the major theme parks and the swimming parks, as well as other minor venues, never expire. The No Expiration option ranges from $10.65 with tax for a two-day ticket, to $58.57 for tickets with seven or more days. This option is not available on one-day tickets.

"PLUS PACK" A "plus" is a single admission to one of Disney's water parks (Blizzard Beach and Typhoon Lagoon), DisneyQuest, or Pleasure Island. The cost is a flat $47.93, and the number of pluses per ticket is tied to the number of days' admission you buy. One-, two-, and three-day tickets come with two pluses; four- and five-day tickets get three

MAGIC YOUR WAY ADMISSION CHART						
TICKET TYPE						
7-Day	6-Day	5-Day	4-Day	3-Day	2-Day	1-Day
BASE TICKET ADULTS						
$212	$209	$206	$197	$182	$127	$64
$30/day	$35/day	$41/day	$49/day	$60/day	$63/day	$64/day
BASE TICKET CHILDREN (ages 9 and under)						
$170	$167	$165	$158	$146	$102	$51
$24/day	$28/day	$33/day	$39/day	$49/day	$51/day	$51/day
PARK HOPPER ADD-ON						
$37	$37	$37	$37	$37	$37	$37
$5/day	$6/day	$7/day	$9/day	$12/day	$19/day	$37/day
PLUS PACK ADD-ON						
$48 for 5 visits	$48 for 4 visits	$48 for 3 visits	$48 for 3 visits	$48 for 2 visits	$48 for 2 visits	$48 for 2 visits
$10/visit	$12/visit	$16/visit	$16/visit	$24/visit	$24/visit	$24/visit
PREMIUM TICKET ADULTS						
$297	$294	$291	$282	$267	$212	$149
$42/day	$49/day	$58/day	$71/day	$89/day	$106/day	$149/day
PREMIUM TICKET CHILDREN (ages 9 and under)						
$256	$252	$250	$243	$231	$187	$136
$37/day	$42/day	$50/day	$61/day	$77/day	$94/day	$136/day
NO EXPIRATION ADD-ON						
$59	$48	$37	$16	$11	$11	N/A

All prices include tax and are rounded to the nearest dollar.

pluses; six-day tickets merit four pluses; and five pluses are accorded to seven- through ten-day tickets.

PREMIUM PASSES A Premium Pass is simply a Base Ticket bundled with the Park Hopping and Plus Pack features. The No Expiration add-on can also be purchased for Premium Passes.

If you visit Walt Disney World every year, here's how to save big bucks. Let's say you usually take your vacation during summer. This year, plan your Disney vacation for July and buy an Annual Passport. Next year, go in June. Because Annual Passports start on the date of purchase, those you buy this year will still be good for next year's vacation if you go a month earlier! If you spend four days each year at Disney World (eight days in the two consecutive years), you'll cut your daily admission to about $40 per adult. The longer your Disney vacation, of course, the more you save with the Annual Passport. If you visit the theme parks seven days each year, your admission will be less than $30 per day. As a bonus, Annual Passports qualify you for big discounts at Disney resorts.

FOOD

EVERY TIME YOU BUY A SODA AT THE theme parks it's going to set you back about $2.50, and everything else from hot dogs to salad is comparably high. You can say, "Oh well, we're on vacation," and pay the exorbitant prices, or you can plan ahead and save big bucks. For comparison purposes, let's say that a family of two adults and two young teens arrives at Walt Disney World on Sunday afternoon and departs for home the following Saturday after breakfast. During that period the family eats six breakfasts, five lunches, and six dinners. What those meals cost, of course, depends on where and what they eat. It is possible for them to rent a condo and prepare all of their own meals, but they didn't travel all the way to Walt Disney World to cook. So, let's be realistic and assume that they will eat their evening meals out (this is what most families do, because, among other reasons, they're too tired to think about cooking). It may be just burgers or pizza, but they eat dinner in a restaurant.

That leaves breakfast and lunch to contend with. Here, basically, are the options. Needless to say, there are dozens of other various combinations. They could eat all of their meals in full-service restaurants, for example, but the bottom line is that most people don't, so we'll just keep this relatively simple.

1. Eat breakfast in their room out of their cooler or fridge and prepare sandwiches and snacks to take to the theme parks in their hip packs. Carry water bottles or rely on drinking fountains for water. Cost: $121 for family of four for six days (does not include dinners or food purchased on travel days)

2. Eat breakfast in their room out of their cooler or fridge, carry snacks in their hip packs, and buy lunch at Disney counter-service restaurants. Cost: $288 for family of four for six days (does not include dinners or food purchased on travel days)

3. Eat breakfast at their hotel restaurant, buy snacks from vendors, and eat lunch at Disney counter-service restaurants. Cost: $532 for family of four for six days (does not include dinners or food purchased on travel days)

In case you're wondering, these are the foods on which

we've based our grocery costs for those options where break-fast, lunch, and/or snacks are prepared from the cooler:

BREAKFAST Cold cereal (choice of two), breakfast pastries, bananas, orange juice, milk, and coffee.

LUNCH Cold cuts or peanut butter and jelly sandwiches, condiments (mayo, mustard, etc.), boxed juice, apples.

SNACKS Packaged cheese or peanut butter crackers, boxed juice, and trail mix (combination of M&Ms, nuts, raisins, and so on).

If you opt to buy groceries, you can stock up on food for your cooler at the Publix Supermarket on the corner of FL 535 and Vineland Road. A second, more upscale (and pricier) store is the Goodings Supermarket in the Disney-owned Crossroads Shopping Center on FL 535 opposite the entrance to the Disney Hotel Plaza and Downtown Disney. Finally, there's a Winn Dixie about a mile north of the Crossroads Center on FL 535.

Projected costs for snacks purchased at the theme parks are based on drinks (coffee or sodas) twice a day and pop-corn once each day. Counter-service meal costs assume basic meals (hot dogs, burgers, fries, and soda or coffee). Hotel breakfast expense assumes eggs, bacon, and toast, or pan-cakes with bacon, and juice, milk, or coffee to drink.

HOW MUCH DOES IT COST PER DAY AT WALT DISNEY WORLD?

A TYPICAL DAY WOULD COST $443.70, excluding lodging and transportation, for a family of four—Mom, Dad, 12-year-old Tim, and 8-year-old Sandy—driving their own car and staying outside the World. They plan to be in the area for a week, so they buy Five-Day Base Tickets with Park-Hopping Option. Here's a breakdown:

HOW MUCH DOES A DAY COST?	
Breakfast for four at Denny's with tax and tip	$26.00
Epcot parking fee	8.00
One day's admission on a 5-Day Base Ticket with Park-Hopping Option	
Dad: Adult 5-Day with tax = $243 divided by five (days)	48.60
Mom: Adult 5-Day with tax = $243 divided by five (days)	48.60
Tim: Adult 5-Day with tax = $243 divided by five (days)	48.60
Sandy: Child 5-Day with tax = $202 divided by five (days)	40.40

HOW MUCH DOES A DAY COST? (CONTINUED)	
Morning break (soda or coffee)	13.50
Fast-food lunch (sandwich or burger, fries, soda), no tip	35.00
Afternoon break (soda and popcorn)	18.00
Dinner at Italy (no alcoholic beverages) with tax & tip	118.00
Souvenirs (Mickey T-shirts for Tim and Sandy) with tax*	39.00
One-Day total (without lodging or transportation)	$443.70
Cheer up; you won't have to buy souvenirs every day.	

■ BABYSITTING

CHILDCARE CENTERS Childcare isn't available inside the theme parks, but each Magic Kingdom resort connected by monorail or boat, two Epcot resorts (Yacht and Beach Club resorts), and Animal Kingdom Lodge have a childcare center for potty-trained children older than 3 years. Services vary, but children generally can be left between 4:30 p.m. and midnight. Milk and cookies, and blankets and pillows are provided at all centers, and dinner is provided at most. Play is supervised but not organized, and toys, videos, and games are plentiful. Guests at any Disney resort or campground may use the services.

The most elaborate of the childcare centers (variously called "clubs" or "camps") is Neverland Club at the Polynesian Resort. The rate for ages 4 to 12 is $10 per hour per child.

All clubs accept reservations (some six months in advance!) with a credit-card guarantee. Call the club directly or reserve through Disney central reservations at ☎ 407-WDW-DINE. Most clubs require a 24-hour cancellation notice and levy a hefty penalty of $15 per child for no-shows. A limited number of walk-ins are usually accepted on a first-come, first-served basis.

If you're staying in a Disney resort that doesn't offer a childcare club and you don't have a car, you're better off using in-room babysitting. Trying to take your child to a club in another hotel via Disney bus requires a 50- to 90-minute trip each way. By the time you have deposited your little one, it will almost be time to pick him up again.

Childcare clubs close at or before midnight. If you intend to stay out late, in-room babysitting is your best bet.

Kinder-Care Learning Centers also operate childcare facilities at Disney World. Developed for use by Disney employees, the centers now also take guests' children on a space-available basis. Kinder-Care provides services much like a hotel club's, except that the daytime "Learning While Playing Development Program" is more structured and educational. Employees are certified in CPR and first aid. Kinder-Care is open Monday through Friday, 6 a.m. to 9 p.m., and Saturday and Sunday, 6 a.m. to 6 p.m. Accepted are ages 1 (provided they're walking and can eat table food) through 12; $10 per hour, per child. For reservations, call ☎ 407-827-5437 or 407-824-3290.

CHILDCARE CLUBS*		
HOTEL/PHONE	NAME OF PROGRAM	AGES
Animal Kingdom Lodge ☎ 407-938-4785	Simba's Cubhouse	4–12
Dolphin ☎ 407-934-4241	Camp Dolphin	4–12
Grand Floridian Beach Resort ☎ 407-824-1666	Mouseketeer Club	4–12
The Hilton ☎ 407-812-9300	All About Kids	4–12
Polynesian Resort ☎ 407-824-2000	Neverland Club	4–12
Swan ☎ 407-934-1621	Camp Dolphin	4–12
Wilderness Lodge & Villas ☎ 407-824-1083	Cub's Den	4–12
Wyndham Palace ☎ 407-812-9300	All About Kids	All
Yacht and Beach Club resorts ☎ 407-934-7000	Sandcastle Club	4–12

IN-ROOM BABYSITTING Three companies provide in-room sitting in Walt Disney World and surrounding tourist areas, including the International Drive/Orange County Convention Center area, the Universal Orlando area, and the Lake Buena Vista area. They are **Kid's Nite Out** (a Kinder-Care company), **All About Kids,** and the **Fairy Godmothers** (no kidding). Kid's Nite Out also serves hotels in the greater Orlando area, including downtown. All three provide sitters older than age 18 who are insured, bonded, and trained in CPR. Some sitters have advanced medical/first-aid training and/or education credentials. All sitters are screened, reference-checked, and

Babysitting Services

KID'S NITE OUT ☎ 407-828-0920 or 800-696-8105 kidsniteout.com	**ALL ABOUT KIDS** ☎ 407-812-9300 or 800-728-6506 www.all-about-kids.com	**FAIRY GODMOTHERS** ☎ 407-277-5724
HOTELS SERVED All Orlando, WDW hotels, and WDW area hotels	**HOTELS SERVED** All WDW hotels and some outside WDW area	**HOTELS SERVED** All WDW hotels and all hotels in the general WDW area
SITTERS Male and female	**SITTERS** Male and female	**SITTERS** Mothers and grandmothers
MINIMUM CHARGES 4 hours	**MINIMUM CHARGES** 4 hours	**MINIMUM CHARGES** 4 hours
BASE HOURLY RATES 1 child $14 2 children $16.50 3 children $19 4 children $21.50	**BASE HOURLY RATES** 1 child $11 2 children $12 3 children $13 4 children $14	**BASE HOURLY RATES** 1 child $12 2 children $12 3 children $12 4 children $14
EXTRA CHARGES Transportation fee $8; starting after 9 p.m. +$2 per hour	**EXTRA CHARGES** Transportation fee $8; starting after 9 p.m. +$2 per hour	**EXTRA CHARGES** Transportation fee $12; starting after 10 p.m. +$2 per hour
CANCELLATION DEADLINE 24 hours prior to service when reservation is made	**CANCELLATION DEADLINE** 3 hours prior to service	**CANCELLATION DEADLINE** 3 hours prior to service
FORM OF PAYMENT AE, D, MC, V; gratuity in cash	**FORM OF PAYMENT** Cash or travelers checks for actual payment; gratuity in cash. Credit card to hold reservation	**FORM OF PAYMENT** Cash or travelers checks for actual payment; gratuity in cash
THINGS SITTERS WON'T DO Transport children in private vehicle; take children swimming; give baths	**THINGS SITTERS WON'T DO** Transport children; give baths	**THINGS SITTERS WON'T DO** Transport children; give baths. Swimming is at sitter's discretion.

police-checked. In addition to caring for your children in your guest room, the sitters will, if you direct (and pay), take your children to the theme parks or other venues. Many sitters arrive loaded with reading books, coloring books, and games. All three services offer bilingual sitters.

SPECIAL PROGRAMS FOR CHILDREN

SEVERAL PROGRAMS FOR CHILDREN ARE available, but they are somewhat lacking the educational focus of the old curriculum.

GRAND ADVENTURES IN COOKING This experience originates at the Grand Floridian at Walt Disney World, where children cook treats and decorate a chef hat and apron. Tuesday–Friday, 10–11:45 a.m., $30 per child (ages 4–10). Limited space; reservations can be made up to 120 days in advance, ☎ 407-WDW-DINE.

LET THE KIDS PLAY PIRATE This program originates at the Grand Floridian and is open to all Walt Disney World resort guests ages 4–10. Children don bandannas and cruise to other resorts situated on Bay Lake and the Seven Seas Lagoon, following a treasure map and discovering clues along the way. At the final port of call the kids gobble down a snack and locate the buried treasure (doubloons, beads, and rubber bugs!). The two-hour cruise operates Monday, Wednesday, Thursday, and Saturday; 9:30–11:30 a.m. and costs $30 per child. Reservations can be made up to 120 days in advance by calling ☎ 407-WDW-DINE.

WONDERLAND TEA PARTY Although the name of this enchanting soiree is enough to make most boys break out in hives, it is nevertheless available at the Grand Floridian on Monday through Friday afternoons at 1:30 p.m. for $30 per child (ages 4–10). The program consists of making cupcakes, arranging flower bouquets, and having lunch and tea with characters from Alice in Wonderland. Reservations can be made by calling ☎ 407-WDW-DINE up to 120 days in advance.

JR. FISHING EXCURSIONS One-hour fishing excursions on Bay Lake and Lake Buena Vista are available for children ages 6–12; the cost is $30 per child. A similar outing is available at Disney's BoardWalk and Disney's Yacht Club and Beach Club resorts for ages 6–12 at a tariff of $30 per child. Soft drinks and all fishing equipment are provided. No parents are allowed along. Dockside Outing offers cane-pole fishing daily 9 a.m.–5 p.m. at Fort Wilderness Resort and Campground, Port Orleans, and Coronado Springs; $3.75 per half hour, advance reservations not required. For reservations or additional information, call ☎ 407-WDW-PLAY.

In our opinion, the excursions are far too short for the hefty price tags. By the time the kids are loaded on the boat, travel to the fishing spot, get baited up and receive instruction, there's not much time left for fishing. If you wish to take a child fishing yourself, canoes and poles are available for rent at Disney's Fort Wilderness Campground at the Bike Barn, open daily.

MAGIC KINGDOM FAMILY MAGIC TOUR This is a two-hour guided tour of the Magic Kingdom for the entire family. Even children in strollers are welcome. The tour combines information about the Magic Kingdom with the gathering of clues that ultimately lead the group to a character greeting at the tour's end. Definitely not for the self-conscious, the tour involves skipping, hopping, and walking sideways as you progress from land to land. There's usually a marginal plot such as saving Wendy from Captain Hook, in which case the character at the end of tour is Wendy. You get the idea. The tour departs daily at 10 a.m. The cost is $25 per person plus a valid Magic Kingdom admission. The maximum group size is 18 persons. Reservations can be made up to one year in advance by calling ☎ 407-WDW-TOUR.

DISNEY'S THE MAGIC BEHIND OUR STEAM TRAINS You must be age 10 or older for this three-hour tour, presented every Monday, Thursday, and Saturday. Kicking off at 7:30 a.m., you join the crew of the Walt Disney World Railroad as they prepare their steam locomotives for the day. Cost is $40, all tours attached, per person plus a valid Magic Kingdom admission. Call ☎ 407-WDW-TOUR for additional information and reservations.

BIRTHDAYS AND SPECIAL OCCASIONS

IF SOMEONE IN YOUR FAMILY CELEBRATES a birthday while you're at Disney World, don't keep it a secret. A Lombard, Illinois, mom put the word out and was glad she did:

> My daughter was turning five while we were there and I asked about special things that could be done. Our hotel asked me who her favorite character was and did the rest. We came back to our room on her birthday and there were helium balloons, a card, and a Cinderella 5x7 photo autographed in ink!! When we entered the Magic Kingdom, we received an "It's My Birthday Today" pin (FREE!), and at the restaurant she got a huge cupcake with whipped cream, sprinkles, and a candle. IT PAYS TO ASK!!

An Ohio mom celebrated her child's first haircut at the Magic Kingdom barber shop:

> The barber shop at the entrance of MK makes a big deal with baby's first haircut—pixie dust, photos, a certificate, and "free" mouse ears hat! ($12 total).

PART THREE

WHERE *to* STAY

WHEN TRAVELING WITH CHILDREN, your hotel is your home away from home, your safe harbor, and your sanctuary. Staying in a hotel, an activity usually reserved for adults, is in itself a great adventure for children. They take in every detail and delight in such things as having a pool at their disposal and obtaining ice from a noisy machine. Of course, it is critical that your children feel safe and secure, but it adds immeasurably to the success of the vacation if they really like the hotel.

In truth, because of their youth and limited experience, kids are far less particular about hotels than adults tend to be. A spartan room and a small pool at a budget motel will make most kids happier than a beagle with a lamb chop. But kids' memories are like little steel traps, so once you establish a lodging standard, that's pretty much what they'll expect every time. A couple from Gary, Indiana, stayed at the pricey Yacht Club Resort at Walt Disney World because they heard that it offered a knockout swimming area (true). When they returned two years later and stayed at Disney's All-Star Resorts for about a third the price, their 10-year-old carped all week. If you're on a budget, it's better to begin with more modest accommodations and move up to better digs on subsequent trips as finances permit.

"You Can't Roller Skate in a Buffalo Herd"

FOR YOUR SANITY AND ENJOYMENT, and for the protection of your vacation investment, you absolutely must get your family some midday rest.

This was a song title from the 1960s. If we wrote that song today we'd call it, "You Can't Have Fun at Disney World if You're Drop-Dead Tired." Believe us, Walt Disney World is an easy place to be penny-wise and pound-foolish. Many families who cut lodging expenses by booking a budget hotel end up so far away from Walt Disney World that it is a major hassle to return to the hotel in the middle of the day for swimming and a nap. By trying to spend the whole day at the theme parks, however, they wear themselves out quickly, and the dream vacation suddenly disintegrates into short tempers and exhaustion. And don't confuse this advice as a sales pitch for Disney hotels. There are, you will find, dozens of hotels outside Walt Disney World that are as close or closer to certain Disney theme parks than some of the resorts inside the World. Our main point—in fact, our only point—is to make it easy on yourself to return to your hotel when the need arises.

unofficial **TIP**
In our opinion, if you are traveling with a child age 12 or younger, one of your top priorities should be to book a hotel within easy striking distance of the parks.

SOME BASIC CONSIDERATIONS

COST

A NIGHT IN A HOTEL AT DISNEY WORLD or the surrounding area can run anywhere from $40 to $900. Clearly, if you are willing to sacrifice some luxury and don't mind a 10- to 25-minute commute, you can really cut your lodging costs by staying outside Walt Disney World. Hotels in Walt Disney World tend to be the most expensive, but they also offer some of the highest quality as well as a number of perks not enjoyed by guests who stay outside of Walt Disney World.

COSTS PER NIGHT OF DISNEY RESORT HOTEL ROOMS	
Grand Floridian	$349–$870
Polynesian Resort	$304–$720
Swan (Westin)	$259–$409
Dolphin (Sheraton)	$259–$409
Beach Club Resort	$294–$675

Beach Club Villas	$294–$449
Yacht Club Resort	$294–$680
BoardWalk Inn	$294–$625
BoardWalk Villas	$294–$459
Wilderness Lodge	$199–$490
Wilderness Lodge Villas	$284–$449
Saratoga Springs	$259–$379
Old Key West Resort	$259–$379
Contemporary Resort	$244–$560
Fort Wilderness Resort	$234–$339
Animal Kingdom Lodge	$199–$620
Coronado Springs Resort	$134–$209
Caribbean Beach Resort	$134–$209
Port Orleans Resort	$134–$209
All-Star Resorts	$77–$119
Pop Century Resorts	$77–$119

WHAT IT COSTS TO STAY IN THE DOWNTOWN DISNEY RESORT AREA	
DoubleTree Guest Suites Resort	$118–$328
Hilton	$134–$345
Wyndham Palace	$149–$299
Hotel Royal Plaza	$82–$220
Holiday Inn at Walt Disney World	$99–$180
Grosvenor Resort	$79–$220
Lake Buena Vista Resort	$89–$259

LOCATION AND TRANSPORTATION OPTIONS

ONCE YOU HAVE DETERMINED YOUR BUDGET, think about what you want to do at Walt Disney World. Will you go to all four theme parks, or will you concentrate on one or two? If you intend to use your own car, the location of your Disney hotel isn't especially important unless you plan to spend most of your time at the Magic Kingdom. (Disney transportation is always more efficient than your car in this case because it bypasses the Transportation and Ticket Center and deposits you at the theme park entrance.)

Most convenient to the Magic Kingdom are the monorail hotels, the Grand Floridian, the Contemporary, and the Polynesian resorts. Linked by direct boat to the Magic Kingdom is the Wilderness Lodge.

Most convenient to Epcot and Disney-MGM Studios are the BoardWalk Inn and Villas, Yacht and Beach Club Resorts, and Swan and Dolphin. Though all are within easy walking distance of Epcot's International Gateway, boat service is also available. Vessels also connect Epcot hotels to Disney-MGM Studios. Epcot hotels are best for guests planning to spend most of their time at Epcot and/or Disney-MGM Studios.

unofficial **TIP**
For the record, the resorts within walking distance of the International Gateway (the back door, so to speak) of Epcot are expensive and are a long, long walk from Future World, the section of Epcot where families tend to spend most of their time.

If you plan to use Disney transportation and intend to visit all four major parks and one or more of the swimming theme parks, book a centrally located resort with good transportation connections. The Epcot resorts and the Polynesian, Caribbean Beach, and Port Orleans resorts fill the bill.

Though not centrally located, the All-Star, Animal Kingdom Lodge, and Coronado Springs resorts have very good bus service to all Walt Disney World destinations and are closest to the Animal Kingdom. Independent hotels on US 192 near the entrance to Walt Disney World are also just a few minutes from the Animal Kingdom. Wilderness Lodge and Fort Wilderness Campground have the most convoluted and inconvenient transportation service of the Disney hotels. The Old Key West Resort is also transportationally challenged, that is, buses run less frequently than at other Disney resorts.

COMMUTING TO AND FROM THE THEME PARKS

FOR VISITORS LODGING INSIDE WALT DISNEY WORLD With three important exceptions, the fastest way to commute from your hotel to the theme parks and back is in your own car. And although many Walt Disney World guests use the Disney Transportation System and appreciate not having to drive, in the final analysis, based on timed comparisons, it is almost always less time-consuming to drive. The exceptions are these: (1) commuting to the Magic Kingdom from the hotels on the monorail (Grand Floridian, Polynesian, and Contemporary Resorts); (2) commuting to the Magic Kingdom from any Disney hotel by bus or boat; and (3) commuting to Epcot on the monorail from the Polynesian Resort via the Transportation and Ticket Center.

If you stay at the Polynesian Resort, you can catch a direct monorail to the Magic Kingdom, and by walking 100 yards or so to the Transportation and Ticket Center, you can catch a direct monorail to Epcot. Located at the nexus of the monorail system, the Polynesian is indisputably the most convenient of all hotels. From either the Magic Kingdom or Epcot, you can return to your hotel quickly and easily whenever you desire. Sound good? It is, but it costs between $300 and $700 per night.

Second to the Polynesian in terms of convenience are the Grand Floridian and Contemporary resorts, also on the Magic Kingdom monorail, but they cost as much or more as the Polynesian. Less expensive Disney hotels transport you to the Magic Kingdom by bus or boat. For reasons described below, this is more efficient than driving your own car.

DRIVING TIME TO THE THEME PARKS FOR VISITORS LODGING OUTSIDE WALT DISNEY WORLD For vacationers staying outside Walt Disney World, we've calculated the approximate commuting time to the major theme parks' parking lots from several off-World lodging areas. Add a few minutes to our times to pay your parking fee and park. Once parked at the Transportation and Ticket Center (Magic Kingdom parking lot), it takes an average of 20 to 30 more minutes to reach the Magic Kingdom. To reach Epcot from its parking

DRIVING TIME TO THE THEME PARKS				
MINUTES TO: FROM	MAGIC KINGDOM PARKING LOT	EPCOT PARKING LOT	DISNEY-MGM STUDIOS PARKING LOT	ANIMAL KINGDOM PARKING LOT
Downtown Orlando	35	31	33	37
North International Drive and Universal Studios	24	21	22	26
Central International Drive–Sand Lake Road	26	23	24	27
South International Drive and Sea World	18	15	16	20
FL 535	12	9	10	13
US 192, north of I-4	10–15	7–12	5–10	5–10
US 192, south of I-4	10–18	7–15	5–13	5–12

lot, add 7 to 10 minutes. At Disney-MGM Studios and the Animal Kingdom, the lot-to-gate transit time is 5 to 10 minutes. If you haven't purchased your theme park admission in advance, tack on another 10 to 20 minutes.

SHUTTLE SERVICE FROM HOTELS OUTSIDE WALT DISNEY WORLD Many hotels in the Walt Disney World area provide shuttle service to the theme parks. They represent a fairly carefree alternative for getting to and from the parks, letting you off near the entrance (except for the Magic Kingdom), and saving you the cost of parking. The rub is that they might not get you there as early as you desire (a critical point if you take our touring advice) or be available at the time you wish to return to your lodging. Also, be forewarned that most shuttle services do not add vehicles at park opening or closing times. In the morning, your biggest problem is that you might not get a seat. At closing time, however, and sometimes following a hard rain, you can expect a lot of competition for standing space on the bus. If there's not room for everyone, you might have to wait 30 minutes to an hour for the next shuttle.

CONVENIENCE CONVENIENTLY DEFINED Conceptually, it's easy to grasp that a hotel that is closer is more convenient than one that is far away. But nothing is that simple at Walt Disney World, so we'd better tell you exactly what you're in for. If you stay at a Walt Disney World resort and use the Disney transportation system, you'll have a five- to ten-minute walk to the bus stop, monorail station, or dock (whichever applies). Once there, buses, trains, or boats generally run about every 15 to 25 minutes, so you might have to wait a short time for your transportation to arrive. Once on board, most conveyances make additional stops en route to your destination, and many take a less-than-direct route. Upon arrival, however, they deposit you fairly close to the entrance of the theme park. Returning to your hotel is the same process in reverse and takes about the same amount of time.

Regardless of whether you stay in Walt Disney World or not, if you use your own car, here's how your commute shakes out. After a one- to five-minute walk from your room to your car, you drive to the theme park, stopping to pay a parking fee or showing your Disney ID for free parking (if you are a Disney resort guest). Disney cast members then direct you to a parking space. If you arrive early, your space may be close enough to the park entrance (Magic Kingdom excepted) to walk. If you park farther afield, a Disney tram will come along every five minutes to collect you and transport you to the entrance.

At the Magic Kingdom, the entrance to the theme park is away-and-gone, separated from the parking lot by the Transportation and Ticket Center (TTC) and the Seven Seas Lagoon. After parking at the Magic Kingdom lot, you take a tram to the TTC and there board a ferry or monorail (your choice) for the trip across the lagoon to the theme park. All this is fairly time consuming and is to be avoided if possible. The only way to avoid it, however, is to lodge in a Disney hotel and commute directly to the Magic Kingdom entrance via Disney bus, boat, or monorail. Happily, all of the other theme parks are situated adjacent to their parking lots.

Because families with children tend to spend more time on average at the Magic Kingdom than at the other parks, and because it's so important to return to your hotel for rest, the business of getting around the lagoon can be a major consideration when choosing a place to stay; the extra hassle of crossing the lagoon (to get back to your car) makes coming and going much more difficult. The half hour it takes to commute to your hotel via car from the Animal Kingdom, Disney-MGM Studios, or Epcot takes an hour or longer from the Magic Kingdom. If you stay in a Disney hotel and use the Disney transportation system, you may have to wait five to ten minutes for your bus, boat, or monorail, but it will take you directly from the Magic Kingdom entrance to your hotel, bypassing the lagoon and the TTC.

DINING

DINING FIGURES INTO THE DISCUSSION OF where to stay only if you don't plan to have a car at your disposal. If you have a car, you can go eat wherever you want. Alternatively, if you plan on using the Disney Transportation System (for Disney hotel guests) or the courtesy shuttle of your non-Disney hotel, you will either have to dine at the theme park or at or near your hotel. If your hotel offers a lot of choice or if there are other restaurants within walking distance, then there's no problem. If your hotel is somewhat isolated and offers limited selection, you'll feel like the people on a canoe trip the author once took who ate northern pike at every meal for a week because that's all they could catch.

At Walt Disney World, although it's relatively quick and efficient to commute from your Disney hotel or campground to the theme parks, it's a long, arduous process requiring transfers to travel from hotel to hotel. Disney hotels that are somewhat isolated and that offer limited dining choices include the Old Key West, Caribbean Beach, All-Star, Pop Century, Animal Kingdom Lodge, Coronado Springs, and

Wilderness Lodge resorts as well as the Fort Wilderness Campground and most of the Saratoga Springs Resort.

If you want a condo-type accommodation so that you have more flexibility for meal preparation than eating out of a cooler, the best deals in Walt Disney World are the Wilderness Homes and Cabins (prefab log cabins) at the Fort Wilderness Campground. Other Disney lodgings with kitchens are available at the BoardWalk Villas, Old Key West, Saratoga Springs, Wilderness Lodge Villas, and the Beach Club Villas, but all are much more expensive than the cabins at the campground. Outside Walt Disney World, there are an ever-increasing number of condos available, and some are very good deals. See our discussion of lodging outside of Walt Disney World later in this chapter.

THE SIZE OF YOUR GROUP

LARGER FAMILIES AND GROUPS MAY BE interested in how many people can stay in a Disney resort room, but only Lilliputians would be comfortable in a room filled to capacity. Groups requiring two or more rooms should consider condo/suite/villa accommodations, either in or out of Walt Disney World. If there are more than six in your party, you will need either two hotel rooms, a suite (see Wilderness Lodge below), or a condo.

unofficial **TIP**
The most cost-efficient lodging in Walt Disney World for groups of five or six people are the cabins at Fort Wilderness Campground. Both sleep six adults plus a child or toddler in a crib.

HOTEL	MAXIMUM OCCUPANCY PER ROOM
All-Star Resorts	4 people plus child in crib
Animal Kingdom Lodge	2 to 5 people plus child in crib
Beach Club Resort	5 people plus child in crib
Beach Club Villas	Studio: 4 people; 2-bedroom, 8 people Grand Villa: 12 people; all plus child in crib
BoardWalk Inn	4 people plus child in crib
BoardWalk Villas	Studio: 4 people; 2-bedroom, 8 people Grand Villa: 12 people; all plus child in crib
Caribbean Beach Resort	4 people plus child in crib
Contemporary Resort	5 people plus child in crib
Coronado Springs Resort	4 people plus child in crib
Dolphin (Sheraton)	4 people

Fort Wilderness Homes	6 people plus child in crib
Grand Floridian Beach Resort	4 or 5 people plus child in crib
Old Key West Resort	Studio: 4 people; 2-bedroom, 8 people Grand Villa: 12 people; all plus child in crib
Polynesian Resort	5 people plus child in crib
Pop Century Resort	4 people plus child in crib
Port Orleans French Quarter	4 people plus child in crib
Port Orleans Riverside	4 people plus child in crib or trundle bed
Saratoga Springs	Studio: 4 people; 2-bedroom, 8 people Grand Villa: 12 people; all plus child in crib
Swan (Westin)	4 people
Wilderness Lodge	4 people plus child in crib; junior suites with bunk beds accommodate 6 people
Wilderness Lodge Villas	Studio: 4 people; 2-bedroom, 8 people Grand Villa: 12 people; all plus child in crib
Yacht Club Resort	5 people plus child in crib

STAYING IN OR OUT OF THE WORLD: WEIGHING THE PROS AND CONS

1. COST If cost is your primary consideration, you'll lodge much less expensively outside Walt Disney World.

2. EASE OF ACCESS Even if you stay in Walt Disney World, you're dependent on some mode of transportation. It may be less stressful to use Disney transportation, but with the single exception of commuting to the Magic Kingdom, the fastest, most efficient, and most flexible way to get around usually is a car. If you're at Epcot, for example, and want to take the kids back to Disney's Grand Floridian Beach Resort for a nap, forget the monorail. You'll get back much faster in your own car.

A reader from Raynham, Massachusetts, who stayed at the Caribbean Beach Resort (and liked it very much) writes:

> Even though the resort is on the Disney bus line, I recommend renting a car if it [fits] one's budget. The buses do not go directly to many destinations and often you have to switch at the Transportation and Ticket Center. Getting a

unofficial TIP
If you share a room with your children, you all need to hit the sack at the same time. Establish a single compromise bedtime, probably a little early for you and a bit later than the child's usual weekend bedtime. Observe any nightly rituals you practice at home, such as reading a book before lights out.

> [bus] seat in the morning is no problem [because] they
> allow standees. Getting a bus back to the hotel after a hard
> day can mean a long wait in line."

It must be said that the Disney Transportation System is
about as efficient as is humanly possible. No matter where
you're going, you rarely wait more than 15 to 20 minutes for
a bus, monorail, or boat. It is only for the use and benefit of
Disney guests, nevertheless it is public transportation, and
users must expect the inconveniences inherent in any transportation system: conveyances that arrive and depart on their
schedule, not yours; the occasional need to transfer; multiple
stops; time lost loading and unloading large numbers of pas-
sengers; and, generally, the challenge of understanding and
using a complex transportation network.

3. SPLITTING UP If your party will likely split up to tour (as
frequently happens in families with children of widely varying ages), staying in the World offers more transportation
options, thus more independence. Mom and Dad can take
the car and return to the hotel for a relaxed dinner and early
bedtime, while the teens remain in the park for evening
parades and fireworks.

4. SLOPPING THE PIGS If you have a large crew that chows
down like pigs at the trough, you may do better staying outside the World, where food is far less expensive.

5. VISITING OTHER ORLANDO-AREA ATTRACTIONS If you plan
to visit Sea World, Kennedy Space Center, the Universal theme
parks, or other area attractions, it may be more convenient to
stay outside the World. Don't, however, book a hotel halfway
to Orlando because you think you might run over to Universal
or Sea World for a day. Remember the Number One Rule:
"Stay close enough to Walt Disney World to return to your hotel for rest in the middle of the day."

WALT DISNEY WORLD LODGING

BENEFITS OF STAYING IN WALT DISNEY WORLD

IN ADDITION TO PROXIMITY—ESPECIALLY easy access to
the Magic Kingdom—Walt Disney World resort hotel and
campground guests are accorded other privileges and
amenities unavailable to those staying outside the World.

Though some of these perks are only advertising gimmicks, others are potentially quite valuable. Here are the benefits and what they mean:

1. EXTRA MAGIC HOURS AT THE THEME PARKS Disney World lodging guests (excluding guests at the independent hotels of Downtown Disney Resort Area, except for the Hilton) are invited to enter a designated park one hour earlier than the general public each day or to enjoy a designated theme park for three hours after it closes to the general public in the evening. Disney guests are also offered specials on admission, including discount tickets to the water parks. These benefits are subject to change without notice.

Early entry can be quite valuable if you know how to use it. It can also land you in gridlock.

2. THEME All of the Disney hotels are themed, in pointed contrast to non-Disney hotels, which are, well, mostly just hotels. Each Disney hotel is designed to make you feel you're in a special place or period of history. See page 67 for a chart depicting the various hotels and their respective themes.

Theming is a huge attraction for children, firing their imaginations and really making the hotel an adventure and a memorable place. Some resorts carry off their themes better than others, and some themes are more exciting. The Wilderness Lodge, for example, is extraordinary. The lobby opens eight stories to a timbered ceiling supported by giant columns of bundled logs. One look eases you into the Northwest wilderness theme. Romantic and isolated, the lodge is heaven for children.

The Animal Kingdom lodge replicates the grand safari lodges of Kenya and Tanzania and overlooks its own private African game preserve. By far the most exotic of the Disney resorts, it's made to order for families with children.

The Polynesian, also dramatic, conveys the feeling of the Pacific islands. It's great for families. Waterfront rooms in the Moorea building offer a perfect view of the Cinderella Castle and the Magic Kingdom fireworks across Seven Seas Lagoon. Kids don't know Polynesia from amnesia, but they like those cool "lodge" buildings and all the torches at night.

Grandeur, nostalgia, and privilege are central to the Grand Floridian, Yacht and Beach Club Resorts, Beach Club Villas, Saratoga Springs Resort, and the BoardWalk Inn and Villas. Although modeled after eastern seaboard hotels of different eras, the resorts are amazingly similar. Thematic distinctions are subtle and are lost on many guests. Children appreciate the creative swimming facilities of these resorts, but are relatively neutral toward the themes.

The Port Orleans Resort lacks the real mystery and sultriness of the New Orleans French Quarter, but it's hard to replicate the Big Easy in a sanitized Disney version. The Riverside section of Port Orleans, however, hits the mark with its antebellum Mississippi River theme, as does Old Key West Resort with its Florida Keys theme. The Caribbean Beach Resort's theme is much more effective at night, thanks to creative lighting. By day, the resort looks like a Miami condo development. Children like each of these resorts, even though the themes are a bit removed from their frame of reference. All four resorts are more spread out and the buildings built to a more human (two- or three-story) scale.

Coronado Springs Resort offers several styles of Mexican and Southwestern American architecture. Though the lake setting is lovely and the resort is attractive and inviting, the theme (with the exception of the main swimming area) isn't particularly stimulating. Coronado Springs feels more like a Scottsdale, Arizona, country club than a Disney resort.

The All-Star Resorts encompass 30 three-story, T-shaped hotels with almost 6,000 guest rooms. There are 15 themed areas: five celebrate sports (surfing, basketball, tennis, football, and baseball), five recall Hollywood movie themes, and five have musical motifs. The resorts' design, with entrances shaped like musical notes, Coke cups, and footballs, is somewhat adolescent, sacrificing grace and beauty for energy and novelty. Guest rooms are small, with décor reminiscent of a teenage boy's bedroom. Despite the themes, the All-Star Resorts lack sports, movies, and music. For children, staying at the All-Star Resorts is like being a permanent resident at a miniature golf course. They can't get enough of the giant footballs, Dalmatians, and guitars. On a more subjective level, kids intuit that the All-Star Resorts are pretty close to what you'd get all the time if Disney had 12-year-olds designing their hotels. They're cool, and the kids feel right at home.

The Pop Century Resort is almost a perfect clone of the All-Star Resorts, i.e., three-story, motel-style buildings built around a central pool, food court, and registration area. Aside from location, the only differences between the All-Star and Pop Century resorts are the decorative touches. Where the All-Star Resorts are distinguished (if you can call it that) by larger-than-life icons from sports, music, and movies, Pop Century draws its icons from various decades of the 20th century. Look for such oddities as building-size Big Wheel tricycles, hula hoops, and the like.

Pretense aside, the Contemporary, Swan, and Dolphin are essentially themeless, but architecturally interesting. The Contemporary is a 15-story, A-frame building with monorails running through the middle. Views from guest rooms in the Contemporary Tower are among the best at Walt Disney World. The Swan and Dolphin resorts are massive, yet whimsical. Designed by Michael Graves, they're excellent examples of "entertainment architecture." Children are blown away by the giant sea creature and swans atop the Dolphin and Swan and love the idea of the monorail running through the middle of the Contemporary.

WALT DISNEY WORLD RESORT HOTEL THEMES

HOTEL	THEME
All-Star Resorts	Sports, movies, and music
Animal Kingdom Lodge	East African game preserve lodge
Beach Club Resort and Villas	New England beach club of the 1870s
BoardWalk Inn	East Coast boardwalk hotel of the early 1900s
BoardWalk Villas	East Coast beach cottage of the early 1900s
Caribbean Beach Resort	Caribbean islands
Contemporary Resort	The future as perceived by past and present generations
Coronado Springs Resort	Northern Mexico and the American Southwest
Dolphin (Sheraton)	Modern Florida resort
Grand Floridian Beach Resort	Turn-of-the-20th-century luxury hotel
Old Key West Resort	Key West
Polynesian Resort	Hawaii/South Sea islands
Pop Century	Icons from various decades of the last century
Port Orleans French Quarter	Turn-of-the-20th-century New Orleans and Mardi Gras
Port Orleans Riverside	Old South plantation and bayou theme
Saratoga Springs	Upstate NY lakeside resort
Swan (Westin)	Modern Florida resort
Wilderness Lodge	National park grand lodge of the early 1900s in the American Northwest
Yacht Club Resort	New England seashore hotel of the 1880s

3. GREAT SWIMMING AREAS Walt Disney World resorts offer some of the most imaginative swimming facilities that you are likely to encounter anywhere. Exotically themed, beautifully landscaped, and equipped with slides, fountains, and smaller pools for toddlers, Disney resort swimming complexes are a quantum leap removed from the typical, rectangular, hotel swimming pool. Some resorts, like the Grand Floridian and the Polynesian, even offer a sand beach on the Seven Seas Lagoon in addition to swimming pools. Others, like the Caribbean Beach and Port Orleans resorts, have provided elaborate themed playgrounds near their swimming areas. Incidentally, lest there be any confusion, we are talking about Disney hotel swimming areas and not the Disney paid-admission water theme parks (Typhoon Lagoon and Blizzard Beach).

WALT DISNEY WORLD RESORT SWIMMING POOLS RATED AND RANKED	
Hotel	**Pool Rating**
1. Yacht and Beach Club Resorts (shared complex)	★★★★★
2. Port Orleans	★★★★½
3. Saratoga Springs	★★★★½
4. Wilderness Lodge and Villas	★★★★½
5. Animal Kingdom Lodge	★★★★
6. Coronado Springs Resort	★★★★
7. Dolphin and Swan	★★★★
8. Polynesian Resort	★★★★
9. Contemporary Resort	★★★½
10. BoardWalk Inn and Villas	★★★½
11. Grand Floridian Resort	★★★½
12. All-Star Resorts	★★★
13. Caribbean Beach Resort	★★★
14. Fort Wilderness Resort and Campground	★★★
15. Old Key West Resort	★★★
16. Pop Century Resort	★★★
17. Shades of Green	★★★

4. BABYSITTING AND CHILDCARE OPTIONS A number of options for babysitting, childcare, and children's programs are offered to Disney hotel and campground guests. All the resort hotels connected by the monorail, as well as several other Disney hotels, offer "clubs," or themed childcare centers, where potty-trained children ages 4 to 12 can stay while their adults go out.

Though somewhat expensive, the clubs do a great job and are highly regarded by children and parents. On the negative side, they're open only in the evening and not all Disney hotels have them. If you're staying at a Disney hotel that doesn't have a childcare club, you're better off using one of the private in-room babysitting services such as Fairy Godmothers or Kid's Nite Out (see page 50). In-room babysitting is also available at hotels outside Walt Disney World.

5. GUARANTEED THEME PARK ADMISSIONS On days of unusually heavy attendance, Disney resort guests are guaranteed admission to the theme parks. In practice, no guest is ever turned away until a theme park's parking lot is full. When this happens, that park most certainly will be packed to the point of absolute gridlock. Under such conditions, you would have to possess the common sense of an amoeba to exercise your guaranteed-admission privilege. The privilege, by the way, doesn't extend to the swimming parks: Blizzard Beach and Typhoon Lagoon.

6. CHILDREN SHARING A ROOM WITH THEIR PARENTS There is no extra charge per night for children younger than age 18 sharing a room with their parents. Many hotels outside Walt Disney World also observe this practice.

7. FREE PARKING Disney resort guests with cars don't have to pay for parking in the theme park lots, which saves about $8 per day.

HOW TO GET DISCOUNTS ON LODGING AT WALT DISNEY WORLD

THERE ARE SO MANY GUEST ROOMS in and around Walt Disney World that competition is brisk, and everyone, including Disney, wheels and deals to keep them filled. This has led to a more flexible discount policy for Walt Disney World hotels. Here are tips for getting price breaks:

unofficial **TIP**
If all you need is a room, booking through Central Reservations is better than booking online or through the Walt Disney Travel Company because Central Reservations offers better terms for cancellation and payment dates.

1. SEASONAL SAVINGS You can save $15–$50 per night on a Walt Disney World hotel room by scheduling your visit during the slower times of the year.

2. ASK ABOUT SPECIALS When you talk to Disney reservationists, inquire specifically about special deals. Ask, for example, "What special rates or discounts are available at Disney hotels during the time of our visit?"

3. KNOW THE SECRET CODE The folks at **www.mouse savers.com** keep an updated list of discounts and reservation codes for use at the Disney resorts. The codes are separated into categories such as "For anyone," "For residents of certain states," "Annual pass-holders" and so on. Special offers that Disney makes to specific individuals (typically via postcard mailings) are not listed on the site, since not everyone qualifies. The site, for example, might list code "CVZ," published in an ad in some Spanish-language newspapers and magazines, offering a rate of $65 per night for the All Star Resorts from April 22 through August 8 and $49 per night from August 9 until October 3. There are usually dozens of discounts listed on the site, covering almost all of the Disney resort hotels. Anyone calling the Disney Central Reservations Office, ☎ 407-W-DISNEY, using a current code can get the discounted rate.

4. TRAVEL AGENTS Travel agents are particularly good sources of information on time-limited special programs and discounts.

5. ORGANIZATIONS AND AUTO CLUBS Eager to sell rooms, Disney has developed time-limited programs with some auto clubs and other organizations. Recently, for example, AAA members were offered a 10–20% savings on Disney hotels, preferred parking at the theme parks, and discounts on package vacations. Such deals come and go, but the market suggests there will be more in the next year. If you're a member of AARP, AAA, or any travel club, ask if the group has a program before shopping elsewhere.

A WORD ABOUT CAMPING AT WALT DISNEY WORLD

FORT WILDERNESS CAMPGROUND IS A spacious resort campground for tent and RV camping. Fully equipped, air-conditioned log cabins also are available for rent. Campsites, "preferred" or "regular," are arranged on loops branching from three thoroughfares. The only difference between a preferred and regular campsite is that preferred sites are closer to the campground amenities (swimming pools, restaurants, and shopping). Each site has a 110- and 220-volt outlet, picnic table, and grill. Most RV sites have sanitary hook-ups. RV sites are roomy by eastern U.S. standards, but tent

unofficial **TIP**
When booking, tent campers should request a site on Loop 1,500, Cottontail Curl, or on Loop 2,000, Spanish Moss Lane. The better loops for RVers are Loops 200, 400, 500, and 1,400. All loops have a comfort station with showers, toilets, phones, an ice machine, and a coin laundry.

campers will probably feel a little cramped. On any day, about 90% of campers will be RVers.

Cabins offer a double bed and two bunk beds in the only bedroom, augmented by a Murphy bed (pulls down from the wall) in the living room. There is one rather small bathroom with shower and tub.

Aside from offering economy accommodations, Fort Wilderness Campground has a group camping area, evening entertainment, horseback riding, bike trails, jogging trails, swimming, and a petting farm. Access to the Magic Kingdom and Discovery Island is by boat from the Fort Wilderness landing on Bay Lake. Access to other destinations is by private car or shuttle bus.

If you rent a cabin, particularly in the fall or spring, keep abreast of local weather conditions. These accommodations are essentially mobile homes, definitely not the place you want to be if the area is under a tornado warning.

FORT WILDERNESS CAMPGROUND		
784 campsites	$38–$89 per night	boat/bus service
408 wilderness homes and cabins (sleeps 4–6)	$234–$339 per night	boat/bus service

LODGING *outside* WALT DISNEY WORLD

AT THIS POINT YOU'RE PROBABLY WONDERING how, as mentioned above, a hotel outside Walt Disney World could be as convenient as one inside Walt Disney World? Well, Mabel, Walt Disney World is a *muy largo* place, but like any city or state, it has borders. By way of analogy, let's say you want to stay in a hotel in Cincinnati, Ohio, but can't find one you can afford. Would you rather book a hotel in Toledo or Cleveland, which are both still in Ohio but pretty darn far away, or would you be willing to leave Ohio and stay just across the state line in Covington, Kentucky?

Just west of Walt Disney World on US 192 are a bunch of hotels and condos, some great bargains, that are closer to the Animal Kingdom and the Disney-MGM Studios than are many hotels in Walt Disney World. Similarly, there are hotels along Disney's east border, FL 535, that are exceptionally convenient if you plan to use your own car.

Lodging costs outside Walt Disney World vary incredibly. If you shop around, you can find a clean motel with a pool within 20 minutes of "the World" for as low as $35 a night. You also can find luxurious, expensive hotels. Because of hot competition, discounts abound.

SELECTING AND BOOKING A HOTEL OUTSIDE WALT DISNEY WORLD

THERE ARE THREE PRIMARY OUT-OF-THE-WORLD areas to consider:

1. INTERNATIONAL DRIVE AREA This area, about 15–20 minutes east of Walt Disney World, parallels I-4 on its southern side and offers a wide selection of both hotels and restaurants. Accommodations range from $40 to $320 per night. The chief drawbacks of the International Drive area are its terribly congested roads, countless traffic signals, and inadequate access to westbound I-4. While the biggest bottleneck is the intersection with Sand Lake Road, the mile of International Drive between Kirkman Road and Sand Lake Road stays in near-continuous gridlock. It's common to lose 25–35 minutes trying to navigate this stretch.

Hotels in the International Drive area are listed in the *Orlando Official Accommodations Guide* published by the Orlando/Orange County Convention and Visitors Bureau. For a copy, call ☎ 800-255-5786 or 407-363-5872.

2. LAKE BUENA VISTA AND THE I-4 CORRIDOR A number of hotels are situated along FL 535 and north of I-4 between Walt Disney World and I-4's intersection with the Florida Turnpike. These properties are easily reached from the interstate and are near a large number of restaurants, including those on International Drive. Most hotels in this area are listed in the *Orlando Official Accommodations Guide*.

3. US 192 This is the highway to Kissimmee, southeast of Walt Disney World. In addition to a number of large, full-service hotels are many small, privately owned motels that are often a good value. Several dozen properties on US 192 are closer to the Disney theme parks than are the more expensive hotels in Walt Disney World Village and the Disney Village Hotel Plaza. The number and variety of restaurants on US 192 has increased markedly in the past several years, easing the area's primary shortcoming.

Hotels on US 192 and in Kissimmee can be found in the *Kissimmee–St. Cloud Visitor's Guide;* call ☎ 800-327-9159 or check **www.floridakiss.com.**

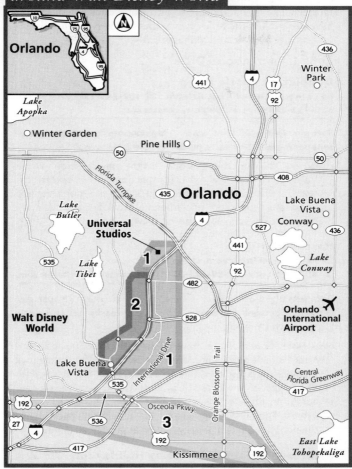

Hotel Concentrations around Walt Disney World

Orlando

Lake Apopka

○ Winter Garden

Pine Hills ○

Winter Park ○

Florida Turnpike

Orlando

Lake Butler

Universal Studios

Lake Tibet

Lake Buena Vista ○

Conway ○

Lake Conway

1

2

Walt Disney World

Lake Buena Vista

Orlando International Airport

1

International Drive

Orange Blossom Trail

Central Florida Greenway

Osceola Pkwy.

3

Kissimmee ○

East Lake Tohopekaliga

THE BEST HOTELS FOR FAMILIES OUTSIDE WALT DISNEY WORLD

WHAT MAKES A SUPER FAMILY HOTEL? Roomy accommodations, in-room fridge, great pool, free breakfast, child-care options, and programs for kids are but a few of the things the *Unofficial* hotel team checked out to select the top hotels for families from among hundreds of properties in the Walt Disney World area. You can be assured that these hotels understand the needs of a family. Though all the hotels listed below offer some type of shuttle service to the theme parks, some offer very limited service. Call the hotel before you book to find out what the shuttle schedule will be during your visit. Since families, like individuals, have different wants and needs, we have not ranked the following properties; they are listed geographically by zone and alphabetically.

Zone 1: International Drive

Doubletree Castle Hotel
8629 International Drive, Orlando; ☎ 407-345-1511 or 800-952-2785; www.doubletreecastle.com

---

Rate per night $100. **Pool** ★★★. **Fridge in room** Yes. **Maximum persons per room** 4. **Shuttle to parks** Yes (Disney, Universal, SeaWorld).

COMMENTS You can't miss this one—it's the only castle on I-Drive. Inside you'll find royal colors (purple dominates), opulent fixtures, and Renaissance music. Add $10 to the room rate and up to four people receive continental breakfast; two signature chocolate chip cookies come with every room.

Hard Rock Hotel
5800 Universal Boulevard, Orlando
☎ 407-503-ROCK or 888-322-5541; www.universalorlando.com

Rate per night $185. **Pool** ★★★★. **Fridge in room** $10 per day. **Maximum persons per room** 4. **Shuttle to parks** Yes (Universal, SeaWorld, Wet 'n Wild).

COMMENTS Located on the Universal property, the 650-room Hard Rock Hotel is nirvana for any kid interested in music, as rock memorabilia is displayed throughout the hotel. Guests are entitled to special privileges at Universal such as early theme-park admission on select days and all-day access to the Universal Express line-breaking program, plus delivery of packages to their hotel room and priority seating at select restaurants.

Nickelodeon Family Suites by Holiday Inn
14500 Continental Gateway Orlando
☎ 407-387-5437 or 866-GO2-NICK

Rate per night $137–$250. **Pools** ★★★★★. **Fridge in room** Yes. **Shuttle to parks** Yes (Disney only). **Maximum persons per room** 7. **Special comments** Complimentary hot breakfast buffet.

COMMENTS This resort is as kid-friendly as they come. Decked out in all themes Nickelodeon, the hotel is sure to please any fan of TV shows the likes of "Rugrats." Nickelodeon characters from the channel's many shows hang out in the resort's lobby and mall area. Guests can choose from one-, two-, and three-bedroom Kid Suites executed in a number of different themes—all very brightly and creatively decorated. The resort's two pools, Oasis and Lagoon, feature a water park complete with water cannons, rope ladders, geysers, and dump buckets, as well as two hot tubs for adults and a smaller play area for younger kids.

Portofino Bay Hotel
5601 Universal Boulevard, Orlando; ☎ 407-503-1000 or 888-322-5541; www.universalorlando.com

Rate per night $284. **Pools** ★★★★. **Fridge in room** Minibar; fridge available for $10 per day. **Maximum persons per room** 4. **Shuttle to parks** Yes (Universal, SeaWorld, Wet 'n Wild).

COMMENTS Also located in Universal, the 750-room Portofino Bay Hotel is themed like a seaside village on the Italian Riviera. Like at the Hard Rock Hotel, Portofino guests receive special theme-park privileges. Campo Portofino offers supervised activities from 5 p.m. to midnight for children ages 4–14 on Fridays and Saturdays. Cost is $12 per child.

Renaissance Orlando Resort
6677 Sea Harbor Drive, Orlando; ☎ 407-351-5555 or 800-327-6677; www.marriott.com.

Rate per night $200. **Pool** ★★★★. **Fridge in room** Yes. **Maximum persons per room** 4. **Shuttle to parks** Yes (Disney, Universal, and SeaWorld).

COMMENTS The Renaissance Orlando Resort does a lot of convention business. However, its large size and convenience to SeaWorld and Universal make it an acceptable alternative for families. Babysitting and child-care services available, and pets are permitted.

Sheraton Studio City
5905 International Drive, Orlando; ☎ 407-351-2100 or 800-327-1366; www.sheratonstudiocity.com

Rate per night $130. **Pool** ★★★. **Fridge in room** No. **Maximum persons per room** 4. **Shuttle to parks** Yes (Universal, SeaWorld, Wet 'n Wild).

COMMENTS It's not for little ones, but preteens and teens will love the hip atmosphere at Sheraton Studio City. And movie buffs will appreciate the theme—a tribute to feature films of the 1940s and 1950s. The hotel is across from Wet 'n Wild.

Sheraton World Resort
10100 International Drive, Orlando; ☎ **407-352-1100 or 800-327-0363; www.sheratonworld.com**

Rate per night $130–$150. **Pools** ★★★★. **Fridge in room** Yes. **Maximum persons per room** 4. **Shuttle to parks** Yes (Disney only).

COMMENTS A good option if you're visiting nearby SeaWorld, the 28-acre Sheraton World Resort offers plenty of room for kids to roam. And with three heated pools, two kiddie pools, a small playground, an arcade, and a complimentary mini golf course (very mini, indeed), this resort offers more than enough kid-friendly diversions.

ZONE 2: LAKE BUENA VISTA AND I-4 CORRIDOR

Hilton Walt Disney World
1751 Hotel Plaza Boulevard, Lake Buena Vista; ☎ **407-827-4000 or 800-782-4414; www.hilton-wdwv.com**

Rate per night $209. **Pools** ★★★★. **Fridge in room** Minibar. **Maximum persons per room** 4. **Shuttle to parks** Yes (Disney theme and water parks only)

COMMENTS Located in the Disney Village, the Hilton is an official Walt Disney World hotel and participates in the Extra Magic Hours program. One big family amenity offered by the Hilton is its character breakfast, on Sundays only from 8:30 to 11 a.m. Other important family amenities include babysitting services, an arcade, and a kiddie pool.

Holiday Inn SunSpree Resort
13351 FL 535, Lake Buena Vista; ☎ **407-239-4500 or 800-366-6299; www.sunspreeresorts.com**

Rate per night $120. **Pool** ★★★. **Fridge in room** Yes. **Maximum persons per room** 4–6. **Shuttle to parks** Yes (Disney only)

COMMENTS Put on your sunglasses—you'll know you're there when the multicolored exterior comes into view. Once inside, kids get into the action at their own check-in counter, where they'll receive a free goody bag. Max and Maxine, the character mascots here, come out to play with the kids at scheduled times during the day. But the big lures are the Kidsuites, which are 405-square-foot rooms with a separate themed play area for kids.

Hyatt Regency Grand Cypress
One Grand Cypress Boulevard, Lake Buena Vista;
☎ **407-239-1234; www.grandcypress.hyatt.com**

Rate per night $219. **Pool** ★★★★★. **Fridge in room** Minibar; fridge available on request. **Maximum persons per room** 4. **Shuttle to parks** Yes (Disney only).

COMMENTS There are myriad reasons to stay at this 1,500-acre resort, but the pool ranks number one. It's a sprawling, 800,000-gallon tropical paradise with a 125-foot water slide, ubiquitous waterfalls, caves and grottoes, and a suspension bridge. The Hyatt is also a golfer's paradise, with a 45-hole championship Jack Nicklaus–designed course, an 18-hole course, a 9-hole pitch-and-putt course, and a golf academy.

Marriott Village
8623 Vineland Avenue, Lake Buena Vista; ☎ **407-938-9001 or 877-682-8552; www.marriott.com**

Rate per night $119–$139. **Pools** ★★★. **Fridge in room** Yes. **Maximum persons per room** 4. **Shuttle to parks** Yes (Disney, Universal, SeaWorld, Wet 'n Wild).

COMMENTS This fully gated community includes a 388-room Fairfield Inn, a 400-suite Spring Hill Suites, and 312-room Courtyard. Whatever your budget, you'll find a room to fit it here. Each hotel features its own Kids Club. For kids ages 4–8, the themed clubs (backyard, tree house, and library) feature big-screen TVs, computer stations, and educational centers (for math and science, reading, and creative activities). Open approximately six hours per day, they have a staff member on duty at all times.

Sheraton Safari Hotel
12205 Apopka-Vineland Road, Lake Buena Vista
☎ **407-239-0444 or 800-423-3297; www.sheraton.com**

Rate per night $150. **Pool** ★★★. **Fridge in room** Safari suites only. **Maximum persons per room** 4–6. **Shuttle to parks** Yes (Disney complimentary; other parks for a fee).

COMMENTS A safari theme is nicely executed throughout this property—from the lobby dotted with African artifacts and native décor to the 79-foot python water slide dominating the pool. On-site amenities include a restaurant (children's menu available), deli, lounge, arcade, and fitness center. Should you want to escape for a night of strictly adult fun, babysitting services are available.

Sheraton Vistana Resort
8800 Vistana Center Drive, Lake Buena Vista; ☎ **407-239-3100;**
www.starwoodvo.com

Rate per night $184. **Pool** ★★★★. **Fridge in room** Minibar.
Maximum persons per room 4. **Shuttle to parks** Yes (Disney
complimentary; other parks for a fee).

COMMENTS The Sheraton Vistana is deceptively large, stretching
as it does across either side of Vistana Center Drive. Though
actually timeshares, the villas are rented nightly as well. If you
want to have a very serene retreat from your days in the
theme parks, this is an excellent home base.

Wyndham Palace
1900 Buena Vista Drive, Lake Buena Vista; ☎ **407-827-2727 or**
800-WYNDHAM; www.wyndham.com

Rate per night $150. **Pools** ★★★★. **Fridge in room** Minibar.
Maximum persons per room 4. **Shuttle to parks** Yes (Disney only).

COMMENTS Located in the Disney Village, the Wyndham Palace is
an upscale and convenient lodging choice. On Sunday, the
Wyndham offers a character breakfast at the Watercress Cafe.
Cost is $23 for adults and $13 for children. In-room babysitting is available.

ZONE 3: US 192

Comfort Suites Maingate Resort
7888 West US 192, Kissimmee; ☎ **407-390-9888**
www.comfortsuiteskissimmee.com

Rate per night $100. **Pool** ★★★. **Fridge in room** Yes. **Maximum
persons per room** 6. **Shuttle to parks** Yes (Disney, Universal,
SeaWorld, Wet 'n Wild).

COMMENTS This property has 150 spacious one-room suites with
double sofa bed, microwave, fridge, coffeemaker, TV, hair
dryer, and safe. The big plus for this place is its location—right
next door to a shopping center with just about everything a
traveling family could possibly need, including a walk-in medical clinic.

Gaylord Palms Resort
6000 West Osceola Parkway, Kissimmee; ☎ **407-586-0000**
www.gaylordpalms.com

Rate per night $200. **Pool** ★★★★★ **Fridge in room** Yes. **Maximum
persons per room** 4. **Shuttle to parks** Yes (Disney).

COMMENTS Though it strongly caters to a business clientele, the Gaylord Palms is still a nice (if pricey) family resort. The hotel wings are defined by the three themed, glass-roofed atriums: Key West, the Everglades, and St. Augustine. Children will enjoy wandering the themed areas, playing in the family pool (complete with giant water-squirting octopus), or participating in the La Petite Academy Kids Station, which organizes a range of games and activities for wee ones.

Holiday Inn Nikki Bird Resort
7300 West US 192, Kissimmee; ☎ 407-396-7300 or 800-20-OASIS; www.ichotelsgroup.com

Rate per night $110. **Pools** ★★★★ **Fridge in room** Yes. **Maximum persons per room** 5 (2 adults). **Shuttle to parks** Yes (Disney only).

COMMENTS In the Orlando hotel world, you're nobody unless you have a mascot. Here it's the Nikki Bird and Wacky the Wizard, who stroll the resort interacting with kids and posing for photos. This Holiday Inn offers standard guest rooms as well as Kidsuites. Kids 12 and under eat free from special menus with a paying adult; room service includes Pizza Hut pizza. Babysitting can be arranged through Kidsnite Out in-room services or at Camp Nikki, Wednesday–Sunday.

Howard Johnson EnchantedLand
4985 West US 192, Kissimmee; ☎ 407-396-4343 or 888-753-4343

Rate per night $125–$150. **Pool** ★★. **Fridge in room** Yes. **Maximum persons per room** 4. **Shuttle to parks** Yes (Disney, Universal, SeaWorld).

COMMENTS Fairies, dragons, and superheroes have invaded the HoJo. If you stay here, be sure you book what they call a Family Value Room: a standard room that has been transformed into a kids' suite. TV and VCR, microwave, fridge, coffeemaker, and safe. There's also a complimentary ice cream party nightly 7–7:30 pm.; Kids Theater each Friday and Saturday 7:30–9 p.m. with free popcorn; and arts, crafts, children's activities in Granny's playroom.

Radisson Resort Parkway
2900 Parkway Boulevard, Kissimmee; ☎ 407-396-7000 or 800-634-4774; www.radisson.com

Rate per night $149. **Pool** ★★★★★. **Fridge in room** Minibar. **Maximum persons per room** 4. **Shuttle to parks** Yes (Disney, Universal, SeaWorld).

COMMENTS The pool alone is worth a stay here, with a waterfall and water slide surrounded by lush palms and flowering plants, plus an additional smaller heated pool, two whirlpools, and a kiddie pool. But the Radisson Resort gets high marks in all areas, save the absence of an organized children's program. Dining options include Parkway Deli & Diner, with breakfast, lunch, and dinner buffets; a 1950s-style diner serving burgers, sandwiches, and shakes; and Pizza Hut pizza.

CONDOMINIUMS AND SUITE HOTELS

A LARGE NUMBER OF SUITE HOTELS AND condo resorts rent to vacationers in the Orlando/Kissimmee area for a week or less. Look for bargains, especially during off-peak periods. Reservations and information can be obtained from:

Condolink	☎ 800-733-4445
Holiday Villas	☎ 800-344-3959
Kissimmee–St. Cloud Reservations	☎ 800-333-5477
Vistana Resort	☎ 800-877-8787
Nickelodeon Family Suites by Holiday Inn	☎ 877-387-KIDS
Disney Home Vacations	☎ 407-396-9509

We frequently receive letters from readers extolling the virtues of renting a suite, condo, or vacation home. The following endorsement by a family from Glenmont, New York, is typical:

> I would recommend that you include the Vistana Resort in your hotel section. Such luxury for so little. On two past visits we stayed in Disney's Lake Buena Vista Hotel Village. To have two bedrooms, two baths, kitchen, dining room, living room, deck, and Jacuzzi for less money was heaven. The children could go to bed at 8:30, and we could stay up and have some privacy. The full kitchen saved $, too— especially at breakfast time. I highly recommend this for families. So close (five minutes to Epcot, ten to the Magic Kingdom, seven to SeaWorld) and convenient.

On the Internet check Vacation Rentals By Owner at **www.VRBO.com**. Other worthwhile sites include **www.Cyber Rentals.com** and **www.ResortQuest.com**.

GETTING A GOOD DEAL ON A ROOM OUTSIDE WALT DISNEY WORLD

HOTEL DEVELOPMENT AT WALT DISNEY WORLD has sharpened the competition among lodgings throughout the

Orlando/Kissimmee area. Hotels outside Walt Disney World, in particular, struggle to fill their guest rooms. Unable to compete with Disney resorts for convenience or perks, off-World hotels lure patrons in with bargain rates. The extent of the bargain depends on the season, day of the week, and local events. Here are tips and strategies for getting a good deal on a room outside Walt Disney World.

1. ORLANDO MAGICARD Orlando MagiCard is a discount program sponsored by the Orlando/Orange County Convention and Visitors Bureau. Cardholders are eligible for discounts of 20–50% at approximately 50 participating hotels. The MagiCard is also good for discounts at area attractions, including SeaWorld, the Universal parks, several dinner theaters, and Disney's Pleasure Island. Valid for up to six persons, the card isn't available for groups or conventions.

To obtain an Orlando MagiCard and a list of participating hotels and attractions, call ☎ 800-255-5786 or 407-363-5874. Anyone older than 18 is eligible, and the card is free. If you miss getting a card before you leave home, you can get one at the Convention and Visitors Bureau at 8723 International Drive in Orlando. When you call for a Magi-Card, also request the *Orlando Official Accommodations Guide* and the Orlando Vacation Planner.

2. EXIT INFORMATION GUIDE Exit Information Guide publishes a book of discount coupons for bargain rates at hotels statewide. The book is free in many restaurants and motels on main highways leading to Florida. Because most travelers make reservations before leaving home, picking up the coupon book en route doesn't help much. If you call and use a credit card, EIG will send the guide first class for $3 ($5 U.S. for Canadian delivery). Contact:

Exit Information Guide
4205 N.W. Sixth Street
Gainesville, FL 32609
☎ **352-371-3948**

3. HOTEL SHOPPING ON THE INTERNET Web sites we've found most dependable for Walt Disney Area hotel discounts are:

www.mousesavers.com	Best site for hotels in Disney World.
www.dreamsunlimitedtravel.com	Excellent for both Disney and non-Disney hotels
www.2000orlando-florida.com	Comprehensive hotel site
www.valuetrips.com	Specializes in budget accommodations

www.travelocity.com	Multidestination travel superstore
www.roomsaver.com	Provides discount coupons for hotels
www.floridakiss.com	Primarily US 192/Kissimmee area hotels
www.orlandoinfo.com	Good for hotel info; not user friendly for booking
www.orlandovacation.com	Great rates for a small number of properties including condos and home rentals
www.expedia.com	Largest of the multi-destination travel sites
www.hotels.com	Largest Internet hotel-booking service; many other sites link to hotels.com and their subsidiary, **hoteldiscounts.com**

Another tool in the hotel-hunting arsenal is **travel axe.com.** Travelaxe offers free software you can download on your PC (won't run on Macs) that will scan an assortment of the better hotel discount sites and find the cheapest rate (from among the sites scanned) for each of more than 200 Disney-area hotels. The site offers various filters such as price, quality rating, and proximity to a specific location (Walt Disney World, SeaWorld, the convention center, airport, etc.) to allow you to more narrowly define your search. As you'll see when you visit the Travelaxe site, the same software scans for best rates in cities throughout the United States and around the world.

unofficial **TIP**
Always call the hotel in question, not the hotel chain's national 800 number.

4. IF YOU MAKE YOUR OWN RESERVATION Reservationists at the toll-free number are often unaware of local specials. Always ask about specials before you inquire about corporate rates. Don't hesititate to bargain, but do it before you check in. If you're buying a hotel's weekend package, for example, and want to extend your stay, you can often obtain at least the corporate rate for the extra days.

OUT-OF-THE-WORLD CHILDREN'S PROGRAMS

MANY LARGE NON-DISNEY HOTELS OFFER supervised programs for children, some complimentary, some with fees. If you decide to take advantage of the kids' programs, call ahead to find out about specific children's events that are scheduled during your vacation. Ask about cost and the ages that can participate; the best programs divide children into age groups. Make reservations for activities your child might want to participate in. You can always cancel after arrival.

After checking in, visit with the kids' program staff. Ask about counselor-child ratio and whether the counselors are trained in first aid and CPR. Briefly introduce your children to the staff and setting, which typically will leave them wanting more, thereby easing the separation anxiety when they return to stay.

HOW *to* CHILDPROOF *a* HOTEL ROOM

TODDLERS AND SMALL CHILDREN UP TO 3 years of age (and sometimes older) can wreak mayhem if not outright disaster in a hotel room. They're mobile, curious, and amazingly fast, and they have a penchant for turning the most seemingly innocuous furnishing or decoration into a lethal weapon. Chances are you're pretty experienced when it comes to spotting potential dangers, but just in case you need a refresher course, here's what to look for.

Always begin by checking the room for hazards that you cannot neutralize, like balconies, chipping paint, cracked walls, sharp surfaces, shag carpeting, and windows that can't be secured shut. If you encounter anything that you don't like or is too much of a hassle to fix, ask for another room.

If you use a crib supplied by the hotel, make sure that the mattress is firm and covers the entire bottom of the crib. If there is a mattress cover, it should fit tightly. Slats should be 2⅜ inch (about the width of a soda can) or less apart. Test the drop sides to ensure that they work properly and that your child cannot release them accidentally. Examine the crib from all angles (including from underneath) to make sure it has been assembled correctly and that there are no sharp edges. Check for chipping paint and other potentially toxic substances that your child might ingest. Wipe down surfaces your child might touch or mouth to diminish the potential of infection transmitted from a previous occupant. Finally, position the crib away from drape cords, heaters, wall sockets, and air conditioners.

If your infant can turn over, we recommend changing him or her on a pad on the floor. Likewise, if you have a child seat of any sort, place it where it cannot be knocked over, and always strap your child in.

If your child can roll, crawl, or walk, you should bring about eight electrical outlet covers and some cord to tie cabinets shut and to bind drape cords and the like out of reach. Check for appliances, lamps, ashtrays, ice buckets, and anything else that your child might pull down on him- or herself. Have the hotel remove coffee tables with sharp edges, and both real and artificial plants that are within your child's reach. Round up items from table and counter tops such as matchbooks, courtesy toiletries, and drinking glasses and store them out of reach.

If the bathroom door can be accidentally locked, cover the locking mechanism with duct tape or a doorknob cover. Use the security chain or upper latch on the room's entrance door to ensure that your child doesn't open it without your knowledge.

Inspect the floor and remove pins, coins, and other foreign objects that your child might find. Don't forget to check under beds and furniture. One of the best tips we've heard came from a Fort Lauderdale, Florida, mother who crawls around the room on her hands and knees in order to see possible hazards from her child's perspective.

If you rent a suite or a condo, you'll have more territory to childproof and will have to deal with the possible presence of cleaning supplies, a stove, a refrigerator, cooking utensils, and low cabinet doors, among other things. Sometimes the best option is to seal off the kitchen with a folding safety gate.

DISNEY BOOT CAMP:
Basic Training for World-Bound Families

THE BRUTAL TRUTH *about* FAMILY VACATIONS

IT HAS BEEN SUGGESTED THAT THE PHRASE *family vacation* is a bit of an oxymoron. This is because you can never take a vacation from the responsibilities of parenting if your children are traveling with you. Though you leave work and normal routine far behind, your children require as much attention, if not more, when traveling as they do at home.

Parenting on the road is an art. It requires imagination and organization. Think about it: you have to do all the usual stuff (feed, dress, bathe, supervise, teach, comfort, discipline, put to bed, and so on) in an atmosphere where your children are hyperstimulated, without the familiarity of place and the resources you take for granted at home. Although it's not impossible—and can even be fun—parenting on the road is not something you want to learn on the fly, particularly at Walt Disney World.

The point we want to drive home is that preparation, or the lack thereof, will make or break your Walt Disney World vacation. Believe us, you do *not* want to leave the success of your expensive Disney vacation to chance. But don't confuse chance with good luck. Chance is what happens when you fail to prepare. Good luck is when preparation meets opportunity.

Your preparation can be organized into several categories, all of which we will help you undertake. Broadly speaking, you need to prepare yourself and your children mentally, emotionally, physically, organizationally, and logistically. You also need a basic understanding of Walt Disney World and a well-considered plan for how to go about seeing it.

MENTAL *and* EMOTIONAL PREPARATION

THIS IS A SUBJECT THAT WE WILL TOUCH ON here and return to many times in this book. Mental preparation begins with realistic expectations about your Disney vacation and consideration of what each adult and child in your party most wants and needs from their Walt Disney World experience. Getting in touch with this aspect of planning requires a lot of introspection and good, open family communication.

DIVISION OF LABOR

TALK ABOUT WHAT YOU AND YOUR PARTNER need and what you expect to happen on the vacation. This discussion alone can preempt some unpleasant surprises midtrip. If you are a two-parent (or two-adult) family, do you have a clear understanding of how the parenting workload is to be distributed? We have seen some distinctly disruptive misunderstandings in two-parent households where one parent is (pardon the legalese) the primary caregiver. Often, the other parent expects the primary caregiver to function on vacation as she (or he) does at home. The primary caregiver, on the other hand, is ready for a break. She expects her partner to either shoulder the load equally or perhaps even assume the lion's share so she can have a *real* vacation. However you divide the responsibility, of course, is up to you. Just make sure you negotiate a clear understanding *before* you leave home.

TOGETHERNESS

ANOTHER DIMENSION TO CONSIDER IS how much "togetherness" seems appropriate to you. For some parents, a vacation represents a rare opportunity to really connect with their children, to talk, exchange ideas, and get reacquainted. For others, a vacation affords the time to get a little distance, to enjoy a round of golf while the kids are participating in a program organized by the resort.

At Walt Disney World you can orchestrate your vacation to spend as much or as little time with your children as you desire, but more about that later. The point here is to think about your and your children's preferences and needs concerning your time together. A typical day at a Disney theme park provides the structure of experiencing attractions together, punctuated by periods of waiting in line, eating, and so on, which facilitate conversation and sharing. Most attractions can be enjoyed together by the whole family, regardless of age ranges.

This allows for more consensus and less dissent when it comes to deciding what to see and do. For many parents and children, however, the rhythms of a Walt Disney World day seem to consist of passive entertainment experiences alternated with endless discussions of where to go and what to do next. As a mother from Winston-Salem, North Carolina, reported, "Our family mostly talked about what to do next with very little sharing or discussion about what we had seen. [The conversation] was pretty task-oriented."

Two observations: First, fighting the crowds and keeping the family moving along can easily escalate into a pressure-driven outing. Having an advance plan or itinerary eliminates moment-to-moment guesswork and decision making, thus creating more time for savoring and connecting. Second, external variables such as crowd size, noise, and heat, among others, can be so distracting as to preclude any meaningful togetherness. These negative impacts can be moderated, as previously discussed (pages 41–43), by your being selective concerning the time of year, day of the week, and time of day you visit the theme parks. The bottom line is that you can achieve the degree of connection and togetherness you desire with a little advance planning and a realistic awareness of the distractions you will encounter.

LIGHTEN UP

PREPARE YOURSELF MENTALLY TO BE A little less compulsive on vacation about correcting small behavioral deviations and pounding home the lessons of life. Certainly, little Mildred will have to learn eventually that it's very un-Disney-like to take off her top at the pool. But there's plenty of time for that later. So what if Matt eats hamburgers for breakfast, lunch, and dinner every day? You can make him eat peas and broccoli when you get home and are in charge of meal preparation again. Roll with the little stuff, and remember when your children act out that they are wired to the max. At least some of that adrenaline is bound to spill out in undesirable ways. Coming down hard will send an already frayed little nervous system into orbit.

SOMETHING FOR EVERYONE

IF YOU TRAVEL WITH AN INFANT, toddler, or any child that requires a lot of special attention, make sure that you have some energy and time remaining for your

unofficial **TIP**
Try to schedule some time alone with each of your children, if not each day, then at least a couple of times during the trip.

other children. In the course of your planning, invite each child to name something special to do or see at Walt Disney World with mom or dad alone. Work these special activities into your trip itinerary. Whatever else, if you commit, write it down so that you don't forget. Remember, a casually expressed willingness to do this or that may be perceived as a promise by your children.

WHOSE IDEA WAS THIS ANYWAY?

THE DISCORD THAT MANY VACATIONING families experience arises from the kids being on a completely different wavelength from mom and dad. Parents and grandparents are often worse than children are when it comes to conjuring up fantasy scenarios of what a Walt Disney World vacation will be like. A Disney vacation can be many things, but believe us when we tell you that there's a lot more to it than just riding Dumbo and seeing Mickey.

In our experience, most parents and nearly all grandparents expect children to enter a state of rapture at Walt Disney World, bouncing from attraction to attraction in wide-eyed wonder, appreciative beyond words to their adult benefactors. What they get, more often than not, is not even in the same ballpark. Preschoolers will, without a doubt, be wide-eyed,

unofficial **TIP**
Short forays to the parks interspersed with naps, swimming, and quiet activities such as reading to your children will go a long way toward keeping things on an even keel.

but less with delight than a general sense of being overwhelmed by noise, crowds, and Disney characters as big as tool sheds. We have substantiated through thousands of interviews and surveys that the best part of a Disney vacation for a preschooler is the hotel swimming pool. With grade-schoolers and pre-driving-age teens you get near-manic hyperactivity coupled with periods of studied nonchalance. This last, which relates to the importance of being "cool," translates into a maddening display of boredom and a "been there, done that" attitude. Older teens are the exponential version of the younger teens and grade-schoolers, except without the manic behavior.

As a function of probability, you may escape some—but most likely not all—of the above behaviors. Even in the event that they are all visited on you, however, take heart, there are antidotes.

For preschoolers you can keep things light and happy by limiting the time you spend in the theme parks. The most critical point is that the overstimulation of the parks must be balanced by adequate rest and more mellow activities. For grade-schoolers and early teens, you can moderate the hyperactivity and false apathy by enlisting their help in planning the vacation, especially by allowing them to take a leading role in determining the itinerary for

unofficial **TIP**
The more information your children have before arriving at Walt Disney World, the less likely they will be to act out.

days at the theme parks. Being in charge of specific responsibilities that focus on the happiness of other family members also works well. One reader, for example, turned a 12-year-old liability into an asset by asking him to help guard against attractions that might frighten his 5-year-old sister.

Knowledge enhances anticipation and at the same time affords a level of comfort and control that helps kids understand the big picture. The more they feel in control, the less they will act out of control.

DISNEY, KIDS, AND SCARY STUFF

DISNEY ATTRACTIONS, BOTH RIDES AND SHOWS, are adventures. They focus on themes common to adventures: good and evil, life and death, beauty and the grotesque, fellowship and enmity. As you sample the attractions at Walt Disney World, you transcend the spinning and bouncing of midway rides to thought-provoking and emotionally powerful entertainment. All of the endings (except *Alien Encounter*) are happy, but the adventures' impact, given Disney's gift for special effects, often intimidates and occasionally frightens young children.

There are rides with menacing witches, burning towns, and ghouls popping out of their graves, all done with a sense of humor, provided you're old enough to understand the joke. And bones. There are bones everywhere: human bones, cattle bones, dinosaur bones, even whole skeletons. There's a stack of skulls at the headhunter's camp on the Jungle Cruise, a platoon of skeletons sailing ghost ships in Pirates of the Caribbean, and a haunting assemblage of skulls and skeletons in The Haunted Mansion. Skulls, skeletons, and bones punctuate Snow White's Scary Adventures, Peter Pan's Flight, and Big Thunder Mountain Railroad. In the Animal Kingdom, there's an entire children's playground made up exclusively of giant bones and skeletons.

Monsters and special effects at Disney-MGM Studios are more real and sinister than those in the other theme parks. If your child has difficulty coping with the witch in Snow

White's Scary Adventures, think twice about exposing him or her to machine-gun battles, earthquakes, and the creature from *Alien* at the Studios.

One reader tells of taking his preschool children on Star Tours:

> We took a 4-year-old and a 5-year-old, and they had the *^%#! scared out of them at Star Tours. We did this first thing in the morning, and it took hours of Tom Sawyer Island and Small World to get back to normal.
>
> Our kids were the youngest by far in Star Tours. I assume that other adults had more sense or were not such avid readers of your book. Preschoolers should start with Dumbo and work up to the Jungle Cruise in late morning, after being revved up and before getting hungry, thirsty, or tired. Pirates of the Caribbean is out for preschoolers. You get the idea.

At Walt Disney World, anticipate the almost inevitable emotional overload of your young children. Be sensitive, alert, and prepared for practically anything, even behavior that is out of character for your child at home. Most young children take Disney's macabre trappings in stride, and others are easily comforted by an arm around the shoulder or a squeeze of the hand. Parents who know that their children tend to become upset should take it slow and easy, sampling more benign adventures, gauging reactions, and discussing with the children how they felt about what they saw.

unofficial **TIP**
Be aware that 6- and 7-year-old children are especially prone to nightmares. Although this is a normal phase of childhood development, you can make their nights more peaceful by avoiding frightening attractions during the day.

Some Tips

1. START SLOW AND WARM UP While each major theme park offers several fairly unintimidating attractions that you can sample to determine your child's relative sensitivity, the Magic Kingdom is probably the best testing ground. At the Magic Kingdom, try Buzz Lightyear's Space Ranger Spin in Tomorrowland, Peter Pan in Fantasyland, and the Jungle Cruise in Adventureland to measure your child's reaction to unfamiliar sights and sounds. If your child takes these in stride, try Pirates of the Caribbean. Try the Astro Orbiter in Tomorrowland, the Mad Tea Party in Fantasyland, or Goofy's Barnstormer in Mickey's Toontown Fair to observe how your child tolerates certain ride speeds and motions.

Do not assume that because an attraction is a theater presentation it will not frighten your child. Trust us on this one. An attraction does not have to be moving to trigger unmitigated, panic-induced hysteria. Rides like the Big Thunder Mountain Railroad and Splash Mountain may look scary, but they do not have even one-fiftieth the potential for terrorizing children as do theater attractions like *Stitch's Great Escape.*

unofficial TIP
Before lining up for any attraction, be it a ride or a theater presentation, check out our description of it and see our Fright Factor list below.

2. BE ATTUNED TO PEER AND PARENT PRESSURE Sometimes young children will rise above their anxiety in an effort to please parents or siblings. This doesn't necessarily indicate a mastery of fear, much less enjoyment. If children leave a ride in apparently good shape, ask if they would like to go on it again (not necessarily now, but sometime). The response usually will indicate how much they actually enjoyed the experience. There's a big difference between having a good time and just mustering the courage to get through.

3. ENCOURAGE AND EMPATHIZE Evaluating a child's capacity to handle the visual and tactile effects of Walt Disney World requires patience, understanding, and experimentation. Each of us, after all, has our own demons. If a child balks at or is frightened by a ride, respond constructively. Let your children know that lots of people, adults and children, are scared by what they see and feel. Help them understand that it's OK if they get frightened and that their fear doesn't lessen your love or respect. Take pains not to compound the discomfort by making a child feel inadequate; try not to undermine self-esteem, impugn courage, or ridicule. Most of all, don't induce guilt by suggesting the child's trepidation might be ruining the family's fun. It is also sometimes necessary to restrain older siblings' taunting or teasing.

A visit to Walt Disney World is more than just an outing or an adventure for a young child. It's a testing experience, a sort of controlled rite of passage. If you help your little one work through the challenges, the time can be immeasurably rewarding and a bonding experience for you both.

The Fright Factor

Of course, each youngster is different, but there are seven attraction elements that alone or combined can push a child's buttons:

I. NAME OF THE ATTRACTION Young children will naturally be apprehensive about something called "The Haunted Mansion" or "The Tower of Terror."

2. VISUAL IMPACT OF THE ATTRACTION FROM OUTSIDE Big Thunder Mountain Railroad and Splash Mountain look scary enough to give even adults second thoughts, and they terrify many young children.

3. VISUAL IMPACT OF THE INDOOR QUEUING AREA Pirates of the Caribbean's caves and dungeons and The Haunted Mansion's "stretch rooms" can frighten kids even before they board the ride.

4. INTENSITY OF THE ATTRACTION Some attractions are overwhelming, inundating the senses with sights, sounds, movement, and even smell. Epcot's *Honey, I Shrunk the Audience* and *It's Tough to Be a Bug* in the Animal Kingdom (no pun intended), for example, combine loud sounds, lasers, lights, and 3-D cinematography to create a total sensory experience. For some preschoolers, this is two or three senses too many.

5. VISUAL IMPACT OF THE ATTRACTION ITSELF Sights in various attractions range from falling boulders to lurking buzzards, from grazing dinosaurs to attacking white blood cells. What one child calmly absorbs may scare the bejeebers out of another.

6. DARK Many Disney World attractions operate indoors in the dark. For some children, dark alone triggers fear. A child who is frightened on one dark ride (Snow White's Scary Adventures, for example) may be unwilling to try other indoor rides.

7. THE RIDE ITSELF; THE TACTILE EXPERIENCE Some rides are wild enough to cause motion sickness, to wrench backs, and to discombobulate patrons of any age.

Disney Orientation Course

We receive many tips from parents telling how they prepared their young children for the Disney experience. A common strategy is to acquaint children with the characters and stories behind the attractions by reading Disney books and watching Disney videos at home. A more direct approach is to watch Walt Disney World travel videos that show the attractions. Of the latter, a father from Arlington, Virginia, reports:

> My kids both loved The Haunted Mansion, with appropriate preparation. We rented a tape before going so they could see it, and then I told them it was all "Mickey Mouse Magic" and that Mickey was just "joking you," to put it in their terms, and that there weren't any real ghosts, and that Mickey wouldn't let anyone actually get hurt.

A Teaneck, New Jersey, mother adds:

> I rented movies to make my 5-year-old more comfortable with rides (Star Wars; Indiana Jones; Honey, I Shrunk the

Kids). *If kids are afraid of rides in the dark (like ours), buy a light-up toy and let them take it on the ride.*

If your video store doesn't rent Disney travel videos, you can order the free Walt Disney World Holiday Planning Video/DVD by calling Disney reservations at ☎ 407-824-8000. Ignore all prompts, and the phone system will assume you're on a rotary phone and patch you through to a live person (though you may be on hold a couple minutes). This video/DVD isn't as comprehensive as travelogues you might rent, but it's adequate for giving your kids a sense of what they'll see.

PREPARING YOUR CHILDREN TO MEET THE CHARACTERS

ALMOST ALL DISNEY CHARACTERS ARE quite large; several, like Brer Bear, are huge! Young children don't expect this, and can be intimidated if not terrified. Discuss the characters with your children before you go. If there is a high school or college with a costumed mascot nearby, arrange to let your kids check it out. If not, then Santa Claus or the Easter Bunny will do.

On the first encounter at Walt Disney World, don't thrust your child at the character. Allow the little one to deal with this big thing from whatever distance feels safe to him or her. If two adults are present, one should stay near the youngster while the other approaches the character and demonstrates that it's safe and friendly. Some kids warm to the characters immediately; some never do. Most take a little time and several encounters.

*un*official **TIP**
Tell children in advance that headpiece characters don't talk.

At Walt Disney World there are two kinds of characters: those whose costume includes a face-covering headpiece (animal characters and such humanlike characters as Captain Hook) and "face characters," those who resemble the characters, so no mask or headpiece is necessary. Face characters include Mary Poppins, Ariel, Jasmine, Aladdin, Cinderella, Belle, Snow White, Tarzan, Esmerelda, and Prince Charming.

Only face characters speak. Headpiece characters don't make noises of any kind. Because cast members couldn't possibly imitate the distinctive cinema voice of the character, Disney has determined that it's more effective to keep them silent. Lack of speech notwithstanding, headpiece characters are very warm and responsive, and communicate very effectively with gestures.

Some character costumes are cumbersome and give cast members very poor visibility. (Eye holes frequently are in the mouth of the costume or even on the neck or chest.) This means characters are somewhat clumsy and have limited sight. Children who approach the character from the back or side may not be noticed, even if the child touches the character. It's possible in this situation for the character to accidentally step on the child or knock him or her down. It's best for a child to approach a character from the front, but occasionally not even this works. Duck characters (Donald, Daisy, Uncle Scrooge), for example, have to peer around their bills.

It's okay for your child to touch, pat, or hug the character. Understanding the unpredictability of children, the character will keep his feet very still, particularly refraining from moving backward or sideways. Most characters will sign autographs or pose for pictures.

ROLE-PLAYING

ESPECIALLY FOR YOUNGER CHILDREN, role-playing is a great way to inculcate vital lessons concerning safety, contingency situations, and potential danger. Play "what would you do if" for a variety of scenarios, including getting lost, being approached by strangers, getting help if mommy is sick, and so on. Children have incredible recall when its comes to role-playing with siblings and parents, and are much more likely to respond appropriately in an actual situation than they will if the same information is presented in a lecture.

PHYSICAL PREPARATION

YOU'LL FIND THAT SOME PHYSICAL conditioning coupled with a realistic sense of the toll that Walt Disney World takes on your body will preclude falling apart in the middle of your vacation. As one of our readers put it, "If you pay attention to eat, heat, feet, and sleep, you'll be OK."

As you contemplate the stamina of your family, it's important to understand that somebody is going to run out of steam first, and when they do, the whole family will be affected. Sometimes a cold drink or a snack will revive the flagging member. Sometimes, however, no amount of cajoling or treats will work. In this situation it's crucial that you recognize that the child, grandparent, or spouse is at the end of his or her rope. The correct decision is to get them back to the hotel. Pushing the exhausted beyond their capacity will spoil the day for them—and you. Accept that stamina and energy levels vary and be prepared to administer to members of your family who poop out. One more thing: no guilt trips. "We've driven a thousand miles to take you to Disney World and now you're going to ruin everything!" is not an appropriate response.

THE AGONY OF THE FEET

HERE'S A LITTLE FACTOID TO CHEW ON: If you spend a day at Epcot and visit both sections of the park, you will walk five to nine miles! The walking, however, will be nothing like a five-mile hike in the woods. At Epcot (and the other Disney parks as well) you will be in direct sunlight most of the time, will have to navigate through huge jostling crowds, will be walking on hot pavement, and will have to endure waits in line between bursts of walking. The bottom line, if you haven't figured it out, is that Disney theme parks (especially in the summer) are not for wimps!

Though most children are active, their normal play usually doesn't condition them for the exertion of touring a Disney theme park. We recommend starting a program of family walks six weeks or more before your trip. A Pennsylvania mom who did just that offers the following:

> We had our 6-year-old begin walking with us a bit every day one month before leaving—when we arrived [at Walt Disney World] her little legs could carry her and she had a lot of stamina.

The first thing you need to do, immediately after making your hotel reservation, is to get thee to a footery. Take the whole family to a shoe store and buy each member the best pair of walking, hiking, or running shoes you can afford. Wear exactly the kind of socks to try on the shoes as you will wear when using them to hike. Do not under any circumstances attempt to tour Walt Disney World shod in sandals, flip-flops, loafers, or any kind of high heel or platform shoe.

Good socks are as important as good shoes. When you walk, your feet sweat like a mule in a peat bog, and moisture increases friction. To minimize friction, wear a pair of Smart Wool or CoolMax hiking socks available at most outdoor retailers (camping equipment) stores. To further combat moisture, dust your feet with some anti-fungal talcum powder.

unofficial **TIP**
If your children (or you, for that matter) do not consider it cool to wear socks, get over it! Bare feet, whether encased in Nikes, Weejuns, Docksiders, or Birkenstocks, will turn into lumps of throbbing red meat if you tackle a Disney park without socks.

All right, now you've got some good shoes and socks. The next thing to do is to break the shoes in. You can accomplish this painlessly by wearing the shoes in the course of normal activities for about three weeks.

Once the shoes are broken in, it's time to start walking. The whole family will need to toughen up their feet and build endurance. As you begin, remember that little people have little strides, and though your 6-year-old may create the appearance of running circles around you, consider that (1) he won't have the stamina to go at that pace very long, and (2) more to the point, he probably has to take two strides or so to every one of yours to keep up when you walk together.

Start by taking short walks around the neighborhood, walking on pavement, and increasing the distance about a quarter of a mile on each outing. Older children will shape up quickly. Younger children should build endurance more slowly and incrementally. Increase distance until you can manage a six- or seven-mile hike without requiring CPR. And remember, you're not training to be able walk six or seven miles just once; at Walt Disney World you will be hiking five to seven miles or more almost *every day*. So unless you plan to crash after the first day, you've got to prepare your feet to walk long distances for three to five consecutive days.

unofficial **TIP**
Be sure to give him or her adequate recovery time between walks (48 hours will usually be enough), however, or you'll make the problem worse.

Let's be honest and admit up front that not all feet are created equal. Some folks are blessed with really tough feet, whereas the feet of others sprout blisters if you look at them sideways. Assuming that there's nothing wrong with either shoes or socks, a few brisk walks will clue you in to what kind of feet your family have. If you have a tenderfoot in your family, walks of incrementally increased distances will usually toughen up his or her feet to some extent. For those whose feet refuse to toughen, your only alternative is preventive care. After several walks, you will know where your tenderfoot tends to develop blisters. If you can anticipate where blisters will develop, you can cover sensitive spots in advance with moleskin, a friction-resistant adhesive dressing.

When you initiate your walking program, teach your children to tell you if they feel a "hot spot" on their feet. This is the warning that a blister is developing. If your kids are too young, too oblivious, too preoccupied, or don't understand the concept, your best bet is to make regular foot checks. Have your children remove their shoes and socks and present their feet for inspection. Look for red spots and blisters, and ask if they have any places on their feet that hurt.

During your conditioning, and also at Walt Disney World, carry a foot emergency kit in your daypack or hip pack. The kit should contain gauze, Betadyne antibiotic ointment, moleskin or an assortment of Band-Aid Blister Bandages, scissors, a sewing needle or some such to drain blisters, as well as matches to sterilize the needle. An extra pair of dry socks and talc are optional.

If you discover a hot spot, dry the foot and cover the spot immediately with moleskin. Cut the covering large enough to cover the skin surrounding the hot spot. If

unofficial **TIP**
If your child is age 8 or younger, we recommend regular feet inspections whether he or she understands the hot spot idea or not. Even the brightest and most well-intentioned child will fail to sound off when distracted.

you find that a blister has already developed, first air out and dry the foot. Next, using your sterile needle, drain the fluid but do not remove the top skin. Clean the area with your Betadyne, and place a Band-Aid Blister Bandage over the blister. If you do not have moleskin or Band-Aid Blister Bandages, do not try to cover the hot spot or blister with regular Band-Aids. Regular Band-Aids slip and wad up.

unofficial **TIP**
If you have a child who will physically fit in a stroller, rent one, no matter how well conditioned your family is.

A stroller will provide the child the option of walking or riding, and, if he collapses, you won't have to carry him. Even if your child hardly uses the stroller at all, it serves as a convenient rolling depository for water bottles and other stuff you may not feel like carrying. Strollers at Walt Disney World are covered in detail on pages 155–157.

SLEEP, REST, AND RELAXATION

OK, WE KNOW THAT THIS SECTION is about physical preparation *before you go,* but this concept is so absolutely critical that we need to tattoo it on your brain right now.

Physical conditioning is important, but is *not* a substitute for adequate rest. Even marathon runners need recovery time. If you push too hard and try to do too much, you'll either crash or, at a minimum, turn what should be fun into an ordeal. Rest means plenty of sleep at night, naps during the afternoon on most days, and planned breaks in your vacation itinerary. And don't forget that the brain needs rest and relaxation as well as the body. The stimulation inherent in touring a Disney theme park is enough to put most children and many adults into system overload. It is imperative that you remove your family from this unremitting assault on the senses, preferably for part of each day, and do something relaxing and quiet like swimming or reading.

The theme parks are huge; don't try to see everything in one day. Tour in early morning and return to your hotel around 11:30 a.m. for lunch, a swim, and a nap. Even during off-season, when the crowds are smaller and the temperature more pleasant, the size of the major theme parks will exhaust most children under age 8 by lunchtime. Return to the park in late afternoon or early evening and continue touring. A family from Texas underlines the importance of naps and rest:

> Despite not following any of your "tours," we did follow the theme of visiting a specific park in the morning, leaving midafternoon for either a nap back at the room or a

trip to the Dixie Landings pool, and then returning to one of the parks in the evening. On the few occasions when we skipped your advice, I was muttering to myself by dinner. I can't tell you what I was muttering...

When it comes to naps, this mom does not mince words:

One last thing for parents of small kids—take the book's advice and get out of the park and take the nap, take the nap, TAKE THE NAP! Never in my life have I seen so many parents screaming at, ridiculing, or slapping their kids. (What a vacation!) Walt Disney World is overwhelming for kids and adults. Even though the rental strollers recline for sleeping, we noticed that most of the toddlers and preschoolers didn't give up and sleep until 5 p.m., several hours after the fun had worn off, and right about the time their parents wanted them to be awake and polite in a restaurant.

A mom from Rochester, New York, was equally adamant:

[You] absolutely must rest during the day. Kids went from 8 a.m. to 9 p.m. in the Magic Kingdom. Kids did great that day, but we were all completely worthless the next day. Definitely must pace yourself. Don't ever try to do two full days of park sightseeing in a row. Rest during the day. Go to a water park or sleep in every other day.

If you plan to return to your hotel in midday and would like your room made up, let housekeeping know.

ORGANIZATIONAL PREPARATION

ALLOW YOUR CHILDREN TO PARTICI-PATE in the planning of your time at Walt Disney World. Guide them diplomatically through the options, establishing advance decisions about what to do each day and how the day will be structured. Begin with your trip *to* Walt Disney World, deciding what time to depart, who sits by the window, whether to stop for meals or eat in the car, and so on. For the Walt Disney World part of your vacation, build consensus for

unofficial TIP
Before you leave home get each of your children a short haircut. Not only will they be cooler and more comfortable, but especially with your girls, you'll save them (and you) the hassle of tangles and about 20 minutes of foo-fooing a day.

unofficial TIP
Don't get obsesssed with any of the plans, especially the touring part. It's your vacation, after all, and you can amend (or even scrap) the plan if you want.

unofficial **TIP**
To keep your thinking fresh and to adequately cover all bases, develop your plan in a series of family meetings no longer than 30 minutes each. You'll discover that all members of the family will devote a lot of thought to the plan both in and between meetings. Don't try to anticipate every conceivable contingency or you'll end up with something as detailed and unworkable as the tax code.

wake-up call, bedtime, and building naps into the itinerary, and establish ground rules for eating, buying refreshments, and shopping. Determine the order for visiting the different theme parks and make a list of "must-see" attractions.

Generally it's better to just sketch in the broad strokes on the master plan. The detail of what to do when you actually arrive at the park can be decided the night before you go, or with the help of one of our touring plans once you get there. Above all, be flexible. One important caveat, however: Make sure you keep any promises or agreements that you make when planning. They may not seem important to you, but they will to your children, who will remember for a long, long time that you let them down.

The more you can agree to and nail down in advance, the less potential you'll have for disagreement and confrontation once you arrive. Because children are more comfortable with the tangible than the conceptual, and also because they sometimes have short memories, we recommend typing up all of your decisions and agreements and providing a copy to each child. Create a fun document, not a legalistic one. You'll find that your children will review it in anticipation of all the things they will see and do, will consult it often, and will even read it to their younger siblings.

By now you're probably wondering what one of these documents looks like, so here's a sample. Incidentally, this itinerary reflects the preferences of its creators, the Shelton family, and is not meant to be offered as an example of an ideal itinerary. It does, however, incorporate many of our most basic and strongly held recommendations, such as setting limits and guidelines in advance, getting enough rest, getting to the theme parks early, touring the theme parks in shorter visits with naps and swimming in between, and saving time and money by having a cooler full of food for breakfast. As you will see, the Sheltons go pretty much full-tilt without much unstructured time and will probably be exhausted by the time they get home, but that's their choice. One more thing—the Sheltons visited Walt Disney World in late June when all of the theme parks stay open late.

THE GREAT WALT DISNEY WORLD EXPEDITION

CO-CAPTAINS Mary and Jack Shelton

TEAM MEMBERS Lynn and Jimmy Shelton

EXPEDITION FUNDING The main Expedition Fund will cover everything except personal purchases. Each team member will receive $35 for souvenirs and personal purchases. Anything above $35 will be paid for by team members with their own money.

EXPEDITION GEAR Each team member will wear an official expedition T-shirt and carry a hip pack.

PRE-DEPARTURE Jack makes priority seating arrangements at Walt Disney World restaurants. Mary, Lynn, and Jimmy make up trail mix and other snacks for the hip packs.

Itinerary

DAY 1: FRIDAY

6:30 p.m.	Dinner
After dinner	Pack car
10 p.m.	Lights out

DAY 2: SATURDAY

7 a.m.	Wake up!
7:15 a.m.	Breakfast
8 a.m.	Depart Chicago for Hampton Inn, Chattanooga; Confirmation # DE56432; Lynn rides shotgun
About noon	Stop for lunch; Jimmy picks restaurant
7 p.m.	Dinner
9:30 p.m.	Lights out

DAY 3: SUNDAY

7 a.m.	Wake up!
7:30 a.m.	Breakfast
8:15 a.m.	Depart Chattanooga for Walt Disney World, Port Orleans Resort; Confirmation # L124532; Jimmy rides shotgun
About noon	Stop for lunch; Lynn picks restaurant
5 p.m.	Check in, buy park admissions, and unpack
6–7 p.m.	Mary and Jimmy shop for breakfast food for cooler
7:15 p.m.	Dinner at Boatwright's at Port Orleans
After dinner	Walk along Bonnet Creek
10 p.m.	Lights out

DAY 4: MONDAY

7 a.m.	Wake up! Cold breakfast from cooler in room
8 a.m.	Depart room to catch bus for Epcot
Noon	Lunch at Epcot
1 p.m.	Return to hotel for swimming and a nap
5 p.m.	Return to Epcot for touring, dinner, and *IllumiNations*
9:30 p.m.	Return to hotel
10:30 p.m.	Lights out

DAY 5: TUESDAY

7 a.m.	Wake up! Cold breakfast from cooler in room
7:45 a.m.	Depart room to catch bus for Disney-MGM Studios
Noon	Lunch at Studios
2:30 p.m.	Return to hotel for swimming and a nap
6 p.m.	Drive to dinner at cafe at Wilderness Lodge
7:30 p.m.	Return to Studios via car for touring and *Fantasmic!*
10 p.m.	Return to hotel
11 p.m.	Lights out

DAY 6: WEDNESDAY

ZZZZZZ!	Lazy morning—sleep in!
10:30 a.m.	Late-morning swim
Noon	Lunch at Port Orleans food court
1 p.m.	Depart room to catch bus for Animal Kingdom Tour until Animal Kingdom closes
8 p.m.	Dinner at Rainforest Cafe at Animal Kingdom
9:15 p.m.	Return to hotel via bus
10:30 p.m.	Lights out

DAY 7: THURSDAY

6 a.m.	Wake up! Cold breakfast from cooler in room
6:45 a.m.	Depart via bus for early entry at Magic Kingdom
11:30 a.m.	Return to hotel for lunch, swimming, and a nap
4:45 p.m.	Drive to Contemporary for dinner at Chef Mickey's
6:15 p.m.	Walk from the Contemporary to the Magic Kingdom for more touring, fireworks, and parade
11 p.m.	Return to Contemporary via walkway or monorail; get car and return to hotel
11:45 p.m.	Lights out

DAY 8: FRIDAY

8 a.m.	Wake up! Cold breakfast from cooler in room
8:40 a.m.	Drive to Blizzard Beach water park
Noon	Lunch at Blizzard Beach
1:30 p.m.	Return to hotel for nap and packing
4 p.m.	Revisit favorite park or do whatever we want
Dinner	When and where we decide
10 p.m.	Return to hotel
10:30 p.m.	Lights out

DAY 9: SATURDAY

7:30 a.m.	Wake up!
8:30 a.m.	After fast-food breakfast, depart for Executive Inn, Nashville; Confirmation # SD234; Lynn rides shotgun
About noon	Stop for lunch; Jimmy picks restaurant
7 p.m.	Dinner
10 p.m.	Lights out

DAY 10: SUNDAY

7 a.m.	Wake up!
7:45 a.m.	Depart for home after fast-food breakfast; Jimmy rides shotgun
About noon	Stop for lunch; Lynn picks restaurant for lunch
4:30 p.m.	Home Sweet Home!

Notice that the Sheltons' itinerary provides minimal structure and maximum flexibility. It specifies which park the family will tour each day without attempting to nail down exactly what the family will do there. No matter how detailed your itinerary is, be prepared for surprises at Walt Disney World, both good and bad. If an unforeseen event renders part of the plan useless or impractical, just roll with it. And always remember that it's your itinerary; you created it and you can change it. Just try to make any changes the result of family discussion and be especially careful not to scrap an element of the plan that your children perceive as something you promised them.

Routines That Travel

If when at home you observe certain routines—for example, reading a book before bed or having a bath first thing in the morning—try to incorporate these familiar activities into your vacation schedule. They will provide your children with a sense of security and normalcy.

Maintaining a normal routine is especially important with toddlers, as a mother of two from Lawrenceville, Georgia, relates:

> *The first day, we tried an early start so we woke the children (ages 2 & 4) and hurried them to get going. BAD IDEA with toddlers. This put them off schedule for naps and meals the rest of the day. It is best to let young ones stay on their regular schedule and see Disney at their own pace and you'll have much more fun.*

LOGISTIC PREPARATION

WHEN I RECENTLY LAUNCHED INTO MY SPIEL about good logistic preparation for a Walt Disney World vacation, a friend from Indianapolis said, "Wait, what's the big deal? You pack clothes, a few games for the car, then go!" So OK, I confess, that will work, but life can be sweeter and the vacation smoother (as well as less expensive) with the right gear.

CLOTHING

LET'S START WITH CLOTHES. WE RECOMMEND springing for vacation uniforms. Buy for each child several sets of jeans (or shorts) and T-shirts, all matching, and all the same. For a one-week trip, as an example, get each child three or so pair of khaki shorts, three or so light yellow T-shirts, three pairs of Smart Wool or CoolMax hiking socks. What's the point? First, you don't have to play fashion designer, coordinating a week's worth of stylish combos. Each morning the kids put on their uniform. It's simple, it's time-saving, and there are no decisions to make or arguments about what to wear. Second, uniforms make your children easier to spot and keep together in the theme parks. Third, the uniforms give your family, as well as the vacation itself, some added identity. If you're like the Shelton family who created the sample itinerary in the section on organizational planning, you might go so far as to create a logo for the trip to be printed on the shirts.

When it comes to buying your uniforms, we have a few suggestions. Purchase well-made, durable shorts or jeans that will serve your children well beyond the vacation. Active children can never have too many pairs of shorts or jeans. As far as the T-shirts go, buy short-sleeve shirts in light colors for warm weather, or long-sleeve, darker-colored T-shirts for cooler weather. We suggest that you purchase your colored shirts from a local T-shirt printing company. Cleverly listed under "T-shirts" (sometimes under "Screen Printing") in the Yellow Pages, these firms will be happy to sell you either printed T-shirts or unprinted T-shirts (called "blanks") with long or short sleeves. You can select from a wide choice of colors not generally available in retail clothing stores, and will not have to worry about finding the sizes you need. Plus, the shirts will cost a fraction of what a clothing retailer would charge. Most shirts come in the more durable 100% cotton or in the more wrinkle-resistant 50% cotton and 50% polyester (50/50s). The cotton shirts are a little cooler and more comfortable in hot, humid weather. The 50/50s dry a bit faster if they get wet.

LABELS A great idea, especially for younger children, is to attach labels with your family name, hometown, the name of your hotel, and the dates of your stay inside the shirt, for example:

Carlton Family of Frankfort, KY; Port Orleans; 5–12 May

Instruct your smaller children to show the label to an adult if they get separated from you. Elimination of the child's first name (which most children of talking age can articulate in any event) allows you to order labels that are all the same, that can be used by anyone in the family, and that can also be affixed to such easily lost items as caps, hats, jackets, hip packs, ponchos, and umbrellas. If fooling with labels sounds like too much of a hassle, check out "When Kids Get Lost" (pages 157–159) for some alternatives.

unofficial **TIP**
Consider affixing labels to the clothing of young children to help in the event they become separated from the family.

DRESSING FOR COOLER WEATHER Central Florida experiences temperatures all over the scale from November through March, so it could be a bit chilly if you visit during those months. Our suggestion is to layer: for example, a breathable, waterproof or water-resistant windbreaker over a light, long-sleeved polypro shirt over a long-sleeved T-shirt. As with the baffles of a sleeping bag or down coat, it is the air trapped between the layers that keeps you warm. If all the layers are thin, you won't be left with something bulky to cart around if you want to pull one or more off. Later in this section, we'll advocate wearing a hip pack. Each layer should be sufficiently compactible to fit easily in that hip pack along with whatever else is in it.

ACCESSORIES

I WANTED TO CALL THIS PART "Belts and Stuff," but the editor (who obviously spends a lot of time at Macy's) thought "Accessories" put a finer point on it. In any event, we recommend pants for your children with reinforced elastic waistbands that eliminate the need to wear a belt (one less thing to find when you're trying to leave). If your children like belts or want to carry an item suspended from their belts, buy them military-style 1½-inch-wide web belts at any army/navy surplus or camping equipment store. The belts weigh less than half as much as leather, are cooler, and are washable.

SUNGLASSES The Florida sun is so bright and the glare so blinding that we recommend sunglasses for each family member. For children and adults of all ages, a good accessory item is a polypro eyeglass strap for spectacles or sunglasses. The best models have a little device for adjusting the amount of slack in the strap. This allows your child to comfortably hang sunglasses from his or her neck when indoors or, alternately, to secure them fast to his or her head while experiencing a fast ride outdoors.

HIP PACKS AND WALLETS Unless you are touring with an infant or toddler, the largest thing anyone in your family should carry is a hip pack, or fanny pack. Each adult and child should have one. They should be large enough to carry at least a half-day's worth of snacks as well as other items deemed necessary (lip balm, bandanna, antibacterial hand gel, and so on) and still have enough room left to stash a hat, poncho, or light windbreaker. We recommend buying full-sized hip packs at outdoor retailers as opposed to small, child-sized hip packs. The packs are light; can be made to fit any child large enough to tote a hip pack; have slip-resistant, comfortable, wide belting; and will last for years.

Do not carry billfolds or wallets, car keys, Disney Resort IDs, or room keys in your hip packs. We usually give this advice because hip packs are vulnerable to thieves (who snip them off and run), but pickpocketing and theft are not all that common at Walt Disney World. In this instance, the advice stems from a tendency of children to inadvertently drop their wal-

unofficial **TIP** Unless you advise the front desk to the contrary, all Disney resort room keys can be used for park admission and as credit cards. They are definitely something you don't want to lose. Our advice is to void the charge privileges on your preteen children's cards and then collect them and put them together someplace safe when not in use.

let in the process of rummaging around in their hip packs for snacks and other items.

You should weed through your billfold and remove to a safe place anything that you will not need on your vacation (family photos, local library card, department store credit cards, business cards, movie rental ID cards, and so on). In addition to having a lighter wallet to lug around, you will decrease your exposure in the event that your wallet is lost or stolen. When we are working at Walt Disney World, we carry a small profile billfold with a driver's license, a credit card, our Disney Resort room key, and a small amount of cash. Think about it: you don't need anything else.

DAY PACKS We see a lot of folks at Walt Disney World carrying day packs (that is, small, frameless backpacks) and/or water bottle belts that strap around your waist. Day packs might be a good choice if you plan to carry a lot of camera equipment or if you need to carry baby supplies on your person. Otherwise, try to travel as light as possible. Packs are hot, cumbersome, not very secure, and must be removed every time you get on a ride or sit down for a show. Hip packs, by way of contrast, can simply be rotated around the waist from your back to your abdomen if you need to sit down. Additionally, our observation has been that the contents of one day pack can usually be redistributed to two or so hip packs (except in the case of camera equipment).

CAPS We do not recommend caps (or hats of any kind) for children unless they are especially sun sensitive. Simply put, kids pull caps on and off as they enter and exit attractions, restrooms, and restaurants, and . . . big surprise, they lose them. In fact, they lose them by the thousands. You could provide a ball cap for every Little Leaguer in America from the caps that are lost at Walt Disney World each summer.

If your children are partial to caps, there is a device sold at ski and camping supply stores that might increase the likelihood of the cap returning home with the child. Essentially, it's a short, light cord with little alligator clips on both ends. Hook one clip to the shirt collar and the other to the hat. It's a great little invention. I use one when I ski in case my ball cap blows off.

RAIN GEAR Rain in central Florida is a fact of life, although persistent rain day after day is unusual (it is the Sunshine State, after all!). Our suggestion is to check out the Weather Channel or weather forecasts on the Internet for three or so

> *unofficial* **TIP**
> Equip each child with a big bandanna. Although bandannas come in handy for wiping noses, scouring ice cream from chins and mouths, and dabbing sweat from the forehead, they can also be tied around the neck to protect from sunburn.

days before you leave home to see if there are any major storm systems heading for central Florida. Weather forecasting has improved to the extent that predictions concerning systems and fronts four to seven days out are now pretty reliable. If it appears that you might see some rough weather during your visit, you're better off bringing rain gear from home. If however, nothing big is on the horizon weatherwise, you can take your chances.

We at the *Unofficial Guide* usually do not bring rain gear. First, scattered thundershowers are more the norm than are prolonged periods of rain. Second, rain gear is pretty cheap at Walt Disney World, especially the ponchos for about $7 adults, $6 child, and is available in seemingly every retail shop. Third, in the theme parks, a surprising number of attractions and queuing areas are under cover. Fourth, we prefer to travel light.

If you do find yourself in a big storm, however, you'll want to have both a poncho and an umbrella. As one *Unofficial* reader put it, "Umbrellas make the rain much more bearable. When rain isn't beating down on your ponchoed head, it's easier to ignore."

An advantage of buying ponchos before you leave home is that you can choose the color. At Walt Disney World all the ponchos are clear, and it's quite a sight when 30,000 differently clad individuals suddenly transform themselves into what looks like an army of sumo maggots. If your family is wearing blue ponchos, they'll be easier to spot.

And consider this tip from a Memphis, Tennessee, mom: *Scotchgard your shoes. The difference is unbelievable.*

MISCELLANEOUS ITEMS

MEDICATION Some parents of hyperactive children on medication discontinue or decrease the child's normal dosage at the end of the school year. If you have such a child, be aware that Walt Disney World might overly stimulate him or her. Consult your physician before altering your child's medication regimen. Also, if your child has attention deficit disorder, remember that especially loud sounds can drive him or her right up the wall. Unfortunately, some Disney theater attractions are almost unbearably loud.

SUNSCREEN Overheating and sunburn are among the most common problems of younger children at Walt Disney World. Carry and use sunscreen of SPF 15 or higher. Be sure to put some on children in strollers, even if the stroller has a canopy. Some of the worst cases of sunburn we've seen were on the exposed foreheads and feet of toddlers and infants in strollers. Protect skin from overexposure. To avoid overheating, rest regularly in the shade or in an air-conditioned restaurant or show.

WATER BOTTLES Don't count on keeping young children hydrated with soft drinks and stops at water fountains. Long lines may hamper buying refreshments, and fountains may not be handy. Furthermore, excited children may not realize or tell you that they're thirsty or hot. We recommend renting a stroller for children ages 5 and younger and carrying plastic bottles of water. Plastic squeeze bottles with caps run about $3 in all major parks.

COOLERS AND MINI-FRIDGES If you drive to Walt Disney World, bring two coolers: a small one for drinks in the car, and a large one for the hotel room. If you fly and rent a car, stop and purchase a large Styrofoam cooler, which can be discarded at the end of the trip. If you will be without a car, rent a mini-fridge from your hotel. At Disney resorts, mini-refrigerators cost about $10 a day. Make sure you reserve one when you book your room. Refrigerators have either been placed or are in the process of being placed in all Disney Deluxe and Moderate resort rooms, free of charge to guests.

If you arrive at your room and there is no refrigerator, call housekeeping and request one. Along with free fridges, coffee makers have also been added in the rooms.

Coolers and mini-fridges allow you to have breakfast in your hotel room, store snacks and lunch supplies to take to the theme parks, and supplant expensive vending machines for snacks and beverages at the hotel. To keep the contents of your cooler cold, we suggest freezing a two-gallon milk jug full of water before you head out. In a good cooler, it will take the jug five or more days to thaw. If you buy a Styrofoam cooler in Florida, you can use bagged ice and ice from the ice machine at your hotel. Even if you have to rent a mini-fridge, you will save a bundle of cash as well as significant time by reducing dependence on restaurant meals and expensive snacks and drinks purchased from vendors.

FOOD PREP KIT If you plan to make sandwiches, bring along your favorite condiments and seasonings from home. A typical travel kit will include mayonnaise, ketchup, mustard, salt and pepper, and packets of sugar or artificial sweetener. Also throw in some plastic knives and spoons, paper napkins, plastic cups, and a box of Baggies. For breakfast you will need some plastic bowls for cereal. Of course, you can buy this stuff in Florida, but you probably won't consume it all, so why waste the money? If you drink bottled beer or wine, bring a bottle opener and corkscrew.

ENERGY BOOSTERS Kids get cranky when they're hungry, and when that happens your entire group has a problem. Like many parents you might, for nutritional reasons, keep a tight rein on snacks available to your children at home. At Walt Disney World, however, maintaining energy and equanimity trump between-meal snack discipline. For maximum zip and contentedness give your kids snacks containing complex carbohydrates (fruits, crackers, non-fat energy bars, etc.) *before* they get hungry or show signs of exhaustion. You should avoid snacks that are high in fats and proteins because these foods take a long time to digest and will tend to unsettle your stomach if it's a hot day.

ELECTRONICS Regardless of your childrens' ages, always bring a nightlight. Flashlights are also handy for finding stuff in a dark hotel room after the kids are asleep. If you are big coffee drinkers and if you drive, bring along a coffeemaker.

Walkmans and portable CD players with headphones as well as some electronic games are often controversial gear for a family outing. We recommend compromise. Headphones can allow kids to create their own space even when they're with others, and that can be a safety valve. That said, try to agree before the trip on some headphone parameters, so you don't begin to feel as if they're being used to keep other family members and the trip itself at a distance. If you're traveling by car, take turns choosing the radio station, CD, or audio tape for part of the trip.

An increasing number of readers stay in touch while on vacation by using walkie talkies. Here's what they have to say:

From a Roanoke, Virginia, family:

> *The single best purchase we made was to get the Motorola TalkAbout walkie-talkies. They have a two-mile range and are about the size of a deck of cards. We first started using them at the airport when I was checking the bags and she took the kids off to the gate. At the parks, the kids would invariably have diverse interests. With the walkie-talkies, however, we easily could split up and simply communicate with each other when we wanted to meet back up. At least half-dozen times, exasperated parents asked where they could rent/buy the walkie-talkies.*

If you go the walkie-talkie route, get a set that operates on multiple channels or opt for cellular phones as a Duluth, Georgia, family did:

> *I spoke with a woman who invested $100 in walkie-talkies. All day long all she could hear were other people's conversations as so many people are using them. My husband and I used our cellular phones and they worked beautifully. Even though I pay roaming charges on mine, there's no way I could use $100 worth!*

DON'T FORGET THE TENT This is not a joke and has nothing to do with camping. When my daughter was preschool age we about went crazy trying to get her to sleep in our shared hotel room. She was accustomed to having her own room at home and was hyperstimulated whenever we traveled. We tried makeshift curtains and room dividers and even rearranged the furniture in a few hotel rooms to create the illusion of a more private, separate space for her. It was all for naught. It wasn't until she was around 4 years old and we took her camping that we seized on an idea that had some promise. She liked the cozy, secure, womb-like feel of a backpacking tent, and quieted down much more readily than she ever had in hotel rooms. So, the next time we stayed in a hotel, we pitched our backpacking tent in the corner of the room. In she went, nested for a bit, and fell asleep.

Since the time of my daughter's childhood, there has been an astounding evolution in tent design. Responding to the needs of climbers and paddlers who often have to pitch tents on rocks (where it's impossible to drive stakes), tent manufactures developed a broad range of tents with self-supporting frames that can be erected virtually anywhere without ropes or stakes. Affordable and sturdy, many are as simple to put up as opening an umbrella. So, if your child is too young for a room of his or her own, or you can't afford a second hotel room, try pitching a small tent. Modern tents are self-contained, with floors and an entrance that can be zipped up (or not) for privacy but cannot be locked. Kids appreciate having their own space and enjoy the adventure of being in a tent, even one set up in the corner of a hotel room. Sizes range from children's "play tents" with a two- to three-foot base to models large enough to sleep two or three husky teens. Light and compact when stored, a two-adult-size tent in its own storage bag (called a "stuffsack") will take up about one-fifth or less of a standard overhead bin on a commercial airliner. Another option for infants and toddlers is to drape a sheet over a portable crib or playpen to make a tent.

THE BOX On one memorable Walt Disney World excursion when my children were younger, we started each morning with an immensely annoying, involuntary scavenger hunt. Invariably, seconds before our scheduled departure to the theme park, we discovered that some combination of shoes, billfolds, sunglasses, hip packs, or other necessities were unaccountably missing. For the next 15 minutes we would root through the room like pigs hunting truffles in an attempt to locate the absent items. Now I don't know about your kids, but when my kids lost a shoe or something, they always searched where it was easiest to look, as opposed to where the lost article was most likely to be. I would be jammed under a bed feeling around while my children stood in the middle of the room intently inspecting the ceiling. As my friends will tell you, I'm as open to a novel theory as the next guy, but we never did find any shoes on the ceiling. Not once. Anyway, here's what I finally did: I swung by a liquor store and mooched a big empty box. From then on, every time we returned to the room, I had the kids deposit shoes, hip packs, and other potentially wayward items in the box. After that the box was off limits until the next morning, when I doled out the contents.

PLASTIC GARBAGE BAGS There are two attractions, the Kali River Rapids raft ride in the Animal Kingdom, and Splash Mountain in the Magic Kingdom, where you are certain to get wet and possibly soaked. If it's really hot and you don't care, then fine. But if it's cool or you're just not up for a soaking, bring a large plastic trash bag to the park. By cutting holes in the top and on the sides you can fashion a sack poncho that will keep your clothes from getting wet. On the raft ride, you will also get your feet wet. If your not up for walking around in squishing, soaked shoes, bring a second, smaller plastic bag to wear over your feet while riding.

SUPPLIES FOR INFANTS AND TODDLERS

BASED ON RECOMMENDATIONS FROM hundreds of *Unofficial Guide* readers, here's what we suggest you carry with you when touring with infants and toddlers:

- A disposable diaper for every hour you plan to be away from your hotel room
- A plastic (or vinyl) diaper wrap with Velcro closures
- A cloth diaper or kitchen towel to put over your shoulder for burping
- Two receiving blankets: one to wrap the baby, one to lay the baby on or to drape over you when you nurse
- Ointment for diaper rash
- Moistened towelettes such as Handi Wipes
- Prepared formula in bottles if you are not breast-feeding
- A washable bib, baby spoon, and baby food if your infant is eating solids
- For toddlers, a small toy for comfort and to keep them occupied during attractions

Baby Care Centers at the theme parks will sell you just about anything that you forget or run out of. Like all things Disney, prices will be higher than elsewhere, but at least you won't need to detour to a drug store in the middle of your touring day.

▌ REMEMBERING *your* TRIP

1. Purchase a notebook for each child and spend some time each evening recording the events of the day. If your children have trouble getting motivated or don't know what to write about, start a discussion; otherwise, let them write or draw whatever they want to remember from the day's events.
2. Collect mementos along the way and create a treasure box in a small tin or cigar box. Months or years later, it's fun to look at postcards, seashells, or ticket stubs to jump-start a memory.
3. Add inexpensive postcards to your photographs to create an album, then write a few words on each page to accompany the images.

4. Give each child a disposable camera to record his or her version of the trip. One 5-year-old snapped an entire series of photos that never showed anyone above the waist—his view of the world (and the photos were priceless).

5. Nowadays, many families travel with a camcorder, though we recommend using one sparingly—parents end up viewing the trip through the lens rather than enjoying the sights. If you must, take it along, but only record a few moments of major sights (too much is boring anyway). And let the kids tape and narrate. On the topic of narration, speak loudly so as to be heard over the not insignificant background noise of the parks. Make use of lockers at all of the parks when the camcorder becomes a burden or when you're going to experience an attraction that might damage it or get it wet. Unless you've got a camcorder designed for underwater shots, leave it behind on Splash Mountain, the Kali River Rapids, and any other ride where water is involved.

6. Another inexpensive way to record memories is a palm-size tape recorder. Let all family members describe their experiences. Hearing a small child's voice years later is so endearing, and those recorded descriptions will trigger an album's worth of memories, far more focused than what many novices capture with a camcorder.

Finally, when it comes to taking photos and collecting mementos, don't let the tail wag the dog. You are not going to Walt Disney World to build the biggest scrapbook in history. Or as this Houston mom put it,

> *Tell your readers to get a grip on the photography thing. We were so busy shooting pictures that we kind of lost the thread. We had to get our pictures developed when we got home to see what all we did [while on vacation].*

◼ TRIAL RUN

IF YOU GIVE THOUGHTFUL CONSIDERATION to all areas of mental, physical, organizational, and logistical preparation discussed in this chapter, what remains is to familiarize yourself with Walt Disney World itself, and of course, to conduct your field test. Yep, that's right, we want you to take the whole platoon on the road for a day to see if you are combat ready. No joke, this is important. You'll learn who poops out first, who is prone to developing blisters, who has to pee every 11 seconds, and given the proper forum, how compatible your family is in terms of what you like to see and do.

For the most informative trial run, choose a local venue that requires lots of walking, dealing with crowds, and making decisions on how to spend your time. Regional theme parks and state fairs are your best bets, followed by large zoos and museums. Devote the whole day. Kick off the morning with an early start, just like you will at Walt Disney World, paying attention to who's organized and ready to go and who's dragging his or her butt and holding up the group. If you have to drive an hour or two to get to your test venue, no big deal. You'll have to do some commuting at Walt Disney World, too. Spend the whole day, eat a couple meals, stay late.

Don't bias the sample (that is, mess with the outcome) by telling everyone you are practicing for Walt Disney World. Everyone behaves differently when they know they are being tested or evaluated. Your objective is not to run a perfect drill, but to find out as much as you can about how the individuals in your family, as well as the family as a group, respond to and deal with everything they experience during the day. Pay attention to who moves quickly and who is slow; to who is adventuresome and who is reticent; to who keeps going and who needs frequent rest breaks; to who sets the agenda and who is content to follow; to who is easily agitated and who stays cool; to who tends to dawdle or wander off; to who is curious and who is bored; to who is demanding and who is accepting. You get the idea.

Discuss the findings of the test run with your spouse the next day. Don't be discouraged if your test day wasn't perfect; few (if any) are. Distinguish between problems that are remedial and problems that are intrinsic to your family's emotional or physical makeup (no amount of hiking, for example, will toughen up some people's feet).

Establish a plan for addressing remedial problems (further conditioning, setting limits before you go, trying harder to achieve family consensus, whatever) and develop strategies for minimizing or working around problems that are a fact of life (waking sleepyheads 15 minutes early, placing moleskin on likely blister sites before setting out, packing familiar food for the toddler who balks at restaurant fare). If you are an attentive observer, a fair diagnostician, and a creative problem solver, you'll be able to work out a significant percentage of the problems you're likely to encounter at Walt Disney World before you ever leave home.

PART FIVE

GET *in the* BOAT, MEN

THIS IS NOT A *JEOPARDY* ANSWER, but if it was, the question would be this: "What did George Washington say to his soldiers before they crossed the Delaware?" We share this interesting historic aside as our way of sounding the alarm, blowing the bugle, or whatever. It's time to move beyond preparation and practice and to leap into action. Walt Disney World here we come! Get in the boat, men!

READY, SET, TOUR! SOME TOURING CONSIDERATIONS

HOW MUCH TIME IS REQUIRED TO SEE EACH PARK?

THE MAGIC KINGDOM AND EPCOT offer such a large number of attractions and special live entertainment options that it is impossible to see everything in a single day, with or without a midday break. For a reasonably thorough tour of each, allocate a minimum of two days. The Animal Kingdom and the Disney-MGM Studios can each be seen in a day, although planning on a day and a half allows for a more relaxed visit.

WHICH PARK TO SEE FIRST?

THIS QUESTION IS LESS ACADEMIC than it appears. Children who see the Magic Kingdom first expect more of the same type of entertainment at the other parks. At Epcot, children are often disappointed by the educational orientation and more serious tone (as are many adults). Disney-MGM offers some pretty wild action, but the general presentation is educational and more mature. Though most children enjoy zoos, live animals can't be programmed to entertain. Thus, children may not find the Animal Kingdom as exciting as the Magic Kingdom or Disney-MGM.

First-time visitors should see Epcot first; you will be able to enjoy it fully without having been preconditioned to think of Disney entertainment as solely fantasy or adventure. Children will be more likely to enjoy Epcot on its own merits if they see it first, and they will be more relaxed and patient in their touring.

See the Animal Kingdom second. Like Epcot, it has an educational thrust, but it provides a change of pace because it features live animals. Next, see Disney-MGM Studios, which helps all ages make a fluid transition from the educational Epcot and Animal Kingdom to the fanciful Magic Kingdom. Also, because Disney-MGM Studios is smaller, you won't walk as much or stay as long. Save the Magic Kingdom for last.

OPERATING HOURS

DISNEY CAN'T BE ACCUSED OF BEING inflexible regarding operating hours at the parks. They run a dozen or more schedules each year, making it advisable to call ☎ 407-824-4321 for the exact hours before you arrive. In the off-season, parks may be open for as few as eight hours (from 10 a.m. to 6 p.m.). By contrast, at busy times (particularly holidays), they may be open from 8 a.m. until 2 a.m. the next morning.

Usually, hours approximate the following: From September through mid-March, excluding holiday periods, the Magic Kingdom is open from 9 a.m. to 7, 8, or 9 p.m. During the same period, Epcot is open from 9 a.m. to 9 p.m., and Disney-MGM Studios is open from 9 a.m. to 7 or 8 p.m. The Animal Kingdom is open from 9 a.m. until 6 or 7 p.m. During summer, expect the Animal Kingdom to remain open until 8 p.m. Epcot and Disney-MGM Studios are normally open until 9 or 10 p.m., with the Magic Kingdom sometimes open as late as 1 a.m.

OFFICIAL OPENING VERSUS REAL OPENING

THE OPERATING HOURS YOU'RE QUOTED when you call are "official hours." The parks sometimes open earlier. Many visitors, relying on information disseminated by Disney Guest Relations, arrive at the official opening time and

Walt Disney World

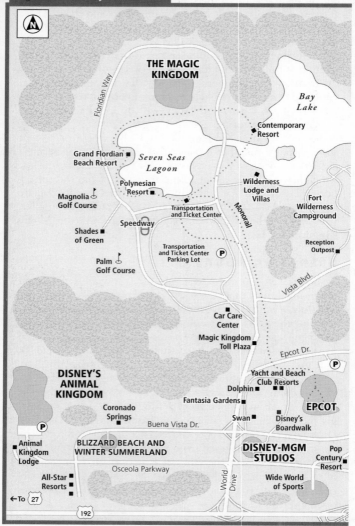

THE MAGIC
KINGDOM

Bay
Lake

Contemporary
Resort

Floridian Way

Grand Floridian ■
Beach Resort

Seven Seas
Lagoon

Polynesian
Resort ■

Wilderness
Lodge and
Villas

Fort
Wilderness
Campground

Magnolia ⛳
Golf Course

Transportation
and Ticket Center

Monorail

Reception
Outpost ■

Speedway

Shades ■
of Green

Transportation
and Ticket Center
Parking Lot (P)

Palm ⛳
Golf Course

Vista Blvd.

Car Care
Center ■

Magic Kingdom
Toll Plaza ■

Epcot Dr.

(P)

DISNEY'S
ANIMAL
KINGDOM

Yacht and Beach
Club Resorts

Dolphin ■

Coronado
Springs ■

Fantasia Gardens ■

EPCOT

(P)

Buena Vista Dr.

Swan ■

Disney's
Boardwalk

Animal
Kingdom
Lodge ■

BLIZZARD BEACH AND
WINTER SUMMERLAND

DISNEY-MGM
STUDIOS

Pop
Century ■
Resort

Osceola Parkway

World Drive

All-Star ■
Resorts ■

Wide World
of Sports

←To (27)

(192)

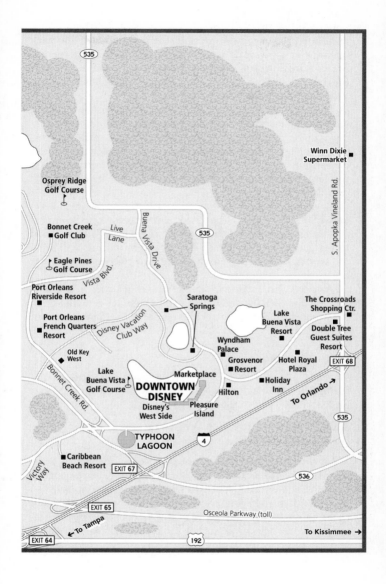

find the park packed with people. If the official hours are 9 a.m. to 9 p.m., for example, Main Street in the Magic Kingdom open at 8 or 8:30 a.m. with the remainder of the park opening at 8:30 or 9 a.m. If the official opening for the Magic Kingdom is 8 a.m. and you're eligible for early entry (if you are staying in a Disney resort), you sometimes are able to enter the park as early as 6:30 a.m.

Disney publishes hours of operation well in advance but reserves the flexibility to react daily to gate conditions. Disney traffic controllers survey local hotel reservations, estimate how many visitors they should expect on a given day, and open the theme parks early to avoid bottlenecks at parking facilities and ticket windows and to absorb the crowds as they arrive.

If you're a Disney resort guest and want to take advantage of Extra Magic Hours early entry, arrive one hour and 20 minutes before the early-entry park is scheduled to open to the general public. Buses, boats, and monorails will initiate service to the early-entry park about two hours before it opens to the general public.

At day's end, rides and attractions shut down at approximately the official closing time. Main Street remains open 30 minutes to an hour after the rest of the Magic Kingdom has closed.

THE RULES

SUCCESSFUL TOURING OF THE MAGIC KINGDOM, the Animal Kingdom, Epcot, or Disney-MGM Studios hinges on five rules:

1. Determine in Advance What You Really Want to See

What rides and attractions appeal most to you? Which additional rides and attractions would you like to experience if you have some time left? What are you willing to forgo?

To help you set your touring priorities, we describe each theme park and their attractions later in this book. In each description, we include the author's evaluation of the attraction and the opinions of Walt Disney World guests expressed as star ratings. Five stars is the best possible rating.

Finally, because attractions range from midway-type rides and horse-drawn trolleys to colossal, high-tech extravaganzas, we have developed a hierarchy of categories to pinpoint attractions' magnitude:

SUPER HEADLINERS The best attractions the theme park has to offer. Mind-boggling in size, scope, and imagination.

Represents the cutting edge of modern attraction technology and design.

HEADLINERS Full-blown, multimillion-dollar, full-scale themed adventures and theater presentations. Modern in technology and design and employing a complete range of special effects.

MAJOR ATTRACTIONS Themed adventures on a more modest scale, but incorporating state-of-the-art technologies. Or, larger-scale attractions of older design.

MINOR ATTRACTIONS Midway-type rides, small "dark" rides (cars on a track, zigzagging through the dark), small theater presentations, transportation rides, and elaborate walk-through attractions.

DIVERSIONS Exhibits, both passive and interactive. Includes playgrounds, video arcades, and street theater.

Though not every Walt Disney World attraction fits neatly into these descriptions, the categories provide a comparison of attractions' size and scope. Remember that bigger and more elaborate doesn't always mean better. Peter Pan's Flight, a minor attraction in the Magic Kingdom, continues to be one of the park's most beloved rides. Likewise, for many young children, no attraction, regardless of size, surpasses Dumbo.

2. Arrive Early! Arrive Early! Arrive Early!

This is the single most important key to efficient touring and avoiding long lines. There are no lines and fewer people first thing in the morning. The same four rides you can experience in one hour in early morning can take as long as three hours to see after 10:30 a.m. Have breakfast before you arrive so you won't waste prime touring time sitting in a restaurant.

The earlier a park opens, the greater the potential advantage. This is because most vacationers won't make the sacrifice to rise early and get to a theme park before it opens. Fewer people are willing to be on hand for an 8 a.m. opening than for a 9 a.m. opening. On those rare occasions when a park opens at 10 a.m., almost everyone arrives at the same time, so it's almost impossible to get a jump on the crowd. If you're a Disney resort guest and have early-entry privileges, arrive as early as early entry allows (6:30 a.m. if the park opens to the public at 8 a.m., or 7:30 a.m. if the park opens to the public at 9 a.m.). If you are visiting during midsummer, arrive at non-early-entry parks 40 minutes before the official opening time. During holiday periods, arrive at non-early-entry parks 50 minutes before the official opening.

3. Avoid Bottlenecks

Crowd concentrations and/or faulty crowd management cause bottlenecks. Avoiding bottlenecks involves being able to predict where, when, and why they occur. Concentrations of hungry people create bottlenecks at restaurants during lunch and dinner. Concentrations of people moving toward the exit at closing time create bottlenecks in gift shops en route to the gate. Concentrations of visitors at new and popular rides and at rides slow to load and unload create bottlenecks and long lines. To help you get a grip on which attractions cause bottlenecks, we have developed a Bottleneck Scale with a range of one to ten. If an attraction ranks high on the Bottleneck Scale, try to experience it during the first two hours the park is open. The scale is included in each attraction profile in Parts Six through Nine.

4. Go Back to Your Hotel for a Rest in the Middle of the Day

You may think we're beating the dead horse with this midday nap thing, but if you plug away all day at the theme parks, you'll understand how the dead horse feels. No joke; resign yourself to going back to the hotel in the middle of the day for swimming, reading, and a snooze.

5. Let Off Steam

Time at a Disney theme park is extremely regimented for younger children. Often held close for fear of losing them, they are ushered from line to line and attraction to attraction throughout the day. After a couple of hours of being on such a short leash, it's not surprising that they're in need of some physical freedom and an opportunity to discharge that pent-up energy. As it happens, each of the major theme parks offers some sort of elaborate, creative playground perfect for such a release. At the Magic Kingdom it's Tom Sawyer Island, at the Animal Kingdom it's the Boneyard, and at the Disney-MGM Studios it's the "Honey, I Shrunk the Kids" Adventure Set. Epcot's play area, the Fitness Fairground in the Wonders of Life Pavilion, is a little anemic in comparison to the other parks' playgrounds, and is open only seasonally. Because Epcot has such large pedestrian plazas, however, there are several places where children can cut loose without making nuisances of themselves. Be advised that each playground (or plaza) is fairly large, and it's pretty easy to misplace a child while they're exploring. All children's playgrounds except the Fitness Fairgrounds, however, have only one exit, so although your kids might get lost within the playground, they cannot wander off into the rest of the park without passing through the single exit (usually staffed by a Disney cast member).

YOUR DAILY ITINERARY

PLAN EACH DAY IN THREE BLOCKS:

1. Early morning theme-park touring
2. Midday break
3. Late afternoon and evening theme-park touring

Choose the attractions that interest you most, and check their bottleneck ratings along with what time of day we recommend you visit. If your children are 8 years old or younger, review the attraction's fright potential rating. Using the theme park maps in this guide, work out a step-by-step plan and write it down. Experience attractions with a high bottleneck rating as early as possible, transitioning to attractions with bottleneck ratings of six to eight around midmorning. Plan on departing the park for your midday break by 11:30 a.m. or so.

For your late afternoon and evening touring block, you do not necessarily have to return to the same theme park. If you have purchased one of the Disney admission options that allow you to "park hop," that is, visit more than one theme park on a given day, you may opt to spend the afternoon/evening block somewhere different. In any event, as you start your afternoon/evening block, see attractions with low bottleneck ratings until about 5 p.m. After 5 p.m., any attraction with a rating of one to seven is fair game. If you stay into the evening, try attractions with ratings of eight to ten during the hour just before closing.

In addition to attractions, each theme park offers a broad range of special live entertainment events. In the morning block, concentrate on the attractions. For the record, we regard live shows that offer five or more daily performances a day (except for street entertainment) as attractions. Thus, *Indiana Jones* at the Disney-MGM Studios is an attraction, as is *Festival of the Lion King* at the Animal Kingdom. *IllumiNations* at Epcot or the parades at the Magic Kingdom, on the other hand, are live entertainment events. A schedule of live performances is listed on the handout park map available at the entrance

unofficial **TIP**
We strongly recommend deferring special parades, stage shows, and other productions until the afternoon/evening block.

of each park. When planning your day, also be aware that major live events draw large numbers of guests from the attraction lines. Thus, a good time to see an especially popular attraction is during a parade or other similar event.

FASTPASS

In 1999, Disney launched a new system to moderate the waiting time for popular attractions. Called FASTPASS, it was originally tried at the Animal Kingdom and then subsequently expanded to cover attractions at the other parks. Here's how it works:

Your handout park map, as well as signage at respective attractions, will tell you which attractions are included. Attractions operating FASTPASS will have a regular line and a FASTPASS line. A sign at the entrance will tell you how long the wait is in the regular line. If the wait is acceptable to you, hop in line. If the wait seems too long, you can insert your park admission pass into a special FASTPASS machine and receive an appointment time to come back and ride later in the day. When you return at the appointed time, you will enter the FASTPASS line and proceed directly to the attraction's preshow or boarding area with no further wait. This procedure, pioneered by Universal Studios Hollywood many years ago, works well and can save a lot of time standing in line. There is no extra charge to use FASTPASS.

The effort to accommodate FASTPASS holders makes anyone in the regular line feel like an illegal immigrant. As a telling indication of their status, guests in the regular lines are referred to as "standby guests."

unofficial **TIP**
FASTPASS works remarkably well, primarily because Disney provides preferential treatment for FASTPASS holders.

However, FASTPASS doesn't eliminate the need to arrive at the theme park early. Because each park offers a limited number of FASTPASS attractions, you still need to get an early start if you want to see as much as possible in a single day. Plus, as we'll discuss later, there is a limited supply of FASTPASSes available for each attraction on a given day. If you don't arrive until the middle of the afternoon, you might find that all the FASTPASSes have been distributed to other guests. FASTPASS does make it possible to see more with less waiting than ever before, and it also allows you to postpone wet rides, like Kali River Rapids at the Animal Kingdom or Splash Mountain at the Magic Kingdom, until the warmer part of the day.

UNDERSTANDING THE FASTPASS SYSTEM The basic purpose of the FASTPASS system is to reduce the waiting time for designated attractions by more equally distributing the arrival of guests at those attractions over the course of the day. This is accomplished by providing an incentive, namely a shorter wait in line, for guests who are willing to postpone experiencing the attraction until later in the day. The system also, in effect, imposes a penalty (i.e., being relegated to standby status) on those who opt not to use it.

When you insert your admission pass into a FASTPASS time clock, the machine spits out a small slip of paper about two-thirds the size of a credit card—small enough to fit in your wallet but also small enough to lose easily. Printed on the paper is the name of the attraction and a specific one-hour time window, for example 1:15–2:15 p.m., during which you can return to ride. Also printed on the paper is the time you'll be eligible to obtain another FASTPASS.

*un*official **TIP**
Each person in your party must have his or her own FASTPASS.

When you report back to the attraction during your one-hour window, you'll enter a line marked "FASTPASS Return" that will route you more or less directly to the boarding or preshow area. Each person in your party must be ready to show a FASTPASS to the Disney cast member at the entrance of the FASTPASS Return line. Before you enter the boarding area or theater, another cast member will collect your FAST-PASS.

You may show up at any time during the period printed on your FASTPASS, and from our observation, no specific time within the window is better or worse. This holds true because cast members are instructed to minimize waits for FASTPASS holders. Thus, if the FASTPASS Return line is suddenly inundated, cast members rapidly intervene to reduce the FAST-PASS line by admitting as many as 25 FASTPASS holders for each standby guest until the FASTPASS line is reduced to an acceptable length. Although FASTPASS will eliminate as much as 80% of the wait you'd experience in the regular line, you can still expect a short wait, but it's usually less than 20 minutes. Often the FASTPASS will be accepted if you arrive at an attraction after the return window has expired.

*un*official **TIP**
As a rule of thumb, the earlier in the day you secure a FAST-PASS, the shorter the interval between time of issue and your one-hour return window.

You can obtain a FASTPASS anytime after a park opens, but the FASTPASS Return lines do not begin operating until about 45 minutes after opening. Whenever you obtain a FASTPASS, you can be assured of a period of time between when you receive your FASTPASS and when you can report back. The interval can be as short as 20 minutes or as long as three to seven hours, depending on park attendance, the popularity of the attraction, and the attraction's hourly capacity.

To more effectively distribute guests over the course of a day, the FASTPASS machines bump the one-hour return period back five minutes for a set number of passes issued (usually the number is equal to about 6% of the attraction's hourly capacity). For example, when Splash Mountain opens at 9 a.m., the first 125 people to obtain a FASTPASS will get a 9:40–10:40 a.m. return window. The next 125 guests are issued FASTPASSes with a 9:45–10:45 a.m. window. If an attraction is exceptionally popular and/or its hourly capacity is relatively small, the return window might be pushed back all the way to park closing time. When this happens the FASTPASS machines simply shut down and a sign is posted saying FASTPASSes are all gone for the day. It's not unusual for Test Track at Epcot or Winnie the Pooh at the Magic Kingdom to distribute an entire day's allocation of FASTPASSes by 1 p.m.

unofficial **TIP**
With very few exceptions, using the standby line at theater attractions requires less time than using FASTPASS.

Rides routinely exhaust their daily FASTPASS supply, but shows almost never do. FASTPASS machines at theaters try to balance attendance at each show so that the audience of any given performance is divided about evenly between standby and FASTPASS guests. Consequently, standby guests for shows are not discriminated against to the degree experienced by standby guests for rides. In practice, FAST-PASS diminishes the wait for standby guests.

WHEN TO USE FASTPASS Except as discussed below, there's no reason to use FASTPASS during the first 30–40 minutes a park is open. Lines for most attractions are quite manageable during this period, and this is the only time of day when FAST-PASS attractions exclusively serve those in the regular line. Using FASTPASS requires two trips to the same attraction: one to obtain the pass and another to use it. This means you must invest time to secure the pass (sometimes there are lines at the FASTPASS machines!) and then later inter-

unofficial **TIP**
Regardless of time of day, if the wait in the regular line at a FASTPASS attraction is 25–30 minutes or less, we recommend joining the regular line.

rupt your touring and backtrack in order to use your FAST-PASS. And don't forget that even in the FASTPASS line you must endure some waiting.

Six attractions in the Disney parks build lines so quickly in the early morning that failing to queue up within the first six or so minutes of operation will mean a long wait. The attractions are Soarin' and Test Track at Epcot, Kilimanjaro Safaris and Expedition Everest (opens 2006) at the Animal Kingdom, Space Mountain at the Magic Kingdom, and Rock 'n' Roller Coaster at Disney-MGM Studios. With these attractions, you can either be present when the park opens and race directly to the attraction or opt for a FASTPASS. Another six FASTPASS attractions, including Splash Mountain, Winnie the Pooh, Peter Pan's Flight, and Jungle Cruise in the Magic Kingdom and Tower of Terror at Disney-MGM Studios, and Mission: Space at Epcot develop long lines within 20–40 minutes of park opening. If you can get to one or more of these before the wait becomes intolerable, all the better. Otherwise, your options are FASTPASS or a long wait.

FASTPASS Guidelines

- Don't mess with FASTPASS if it can't save you 30 minutes or more.

- If you arrive after a park opens, obtain a FASTPASS for your preferred FASTPASS attraction first thing.

- Do not obtain a FASTPASS for a theater attraction until you have experienced all the FASTPASS rides on your itinerary (using FASTPASS at theater attractions usually requires more time than using the standby line).

- Always check the return period before obtaining a FASTPASS.

- Obtain FASTPASSes for Rock 'n' Roller Coaster at MGM-Studios, Soarin' and Test Track at Epcot, and Winnie the Pooh, Peter Pan's Flight, Space Mountain, and Splash Mountain at the Magic Kingdom as early in the day as practicable.

- Try to obtain FASTPASSes for remaining rides by 1 p.m.

- Don't depend on FASTPASSes being available for rides after 2 p.m. during busier times of year.

- Make sure everyone in your party has his or her own FASTPASS.

- Be mindful that you can obtain a second FASTPASS as soon as you enter the return period for your first FASTPASS or at the time printed at the bottom of your FASTPASS, whichever comes first.

There are a number of attractions where the time gap between issuance and return can be three to seven hours. If you think you might want to use FASTPASS on the following attractions, try to secure it before 11 a.m.:

MAGIC KINGDOM	EPCOT	DISNEY-MGM STUDIOS
Winnie the Pooh	Test Track	Rock 'n' Roller Coaster
Peter Pan's Flight	Soarin'	
Space Mountain		
Splash Mountain		

VARIABLES THAT AFFECT HOW MUCH YOU'LL SEE

HOW QUICKLY YOU MOVE FROM ONE RIDE to another; when and how many refreshment and restroom breaks you take; when, where, and how you eat meals; and your ability (or lack thereof) to find your way around will all have an impact on how much you'll see. Smaller groups almost always move faster than larger groups, and families with older children and teens generally can cover more ground than families with young children. Switching off (see pages 133–135), among other things, prohibits families with little ones from moving expeditiously among attractions. Plus, some children simply cannot conform to the "arrive early!" rule.

A mom from Nutley, New Jersey, writes:

> [Although you] advise getting to parks at opening, we just couldn't burn the candle at both ends. Our kids (10, 7, and 4) would not go to sleep early and couldn't be up at dawn and still stay relatively sane. It worked well for us to let them sleep a little later, go out and bring breakfast back to the room while they slept, and still get a relatively early start by not spending time on eating breakfast out. We managed to avoid long lines with an occasional early morning, and hitting popular attractions during parades, mealtimes, and late evenings.

Finally, if you have young children in your party, be prepared for character encounters. The appearance of a Disney character is usually sufficient to stop your family dead in its tracks. What's more, although some characters continue to stroll the parks, it is becoming more the rule to assemble characters in some specific venue (like the Hall of Fame at Mickey's Toontown Fair) where families must line up for photos and autographs. Meeting characters, posing for photos, and collecting autographs can burn hours. If your kids are into character autograph collecting, you will need to anticipate these interruptions to your touring and negotiate some understanding with your children about when you will tour and when you will collect autographs. The only time-efficient way to collect autographs is to line up at the character greeting areas first thing in the morning. Because this is also the best time to experience popular attractions, you may have some tough decisions to make.

While we realize that starting early and going full-tilt through the morning might not be consistent with your idea of a vacation, it's still the best way to see the most popular attractions without long waits. We recommend, therefore, continuous, expeditious touring until around 11 a.m. or so. After that point, breaks and diversions won't affect your touring significantly.

Other variables that can profoundly affect your progress are beyond your control. Chief among these are the manner and timing in which a ride is brought to capacity. For example, Big Thunder Mountain Railroad, a roller coaster in the Magic Kingdom, has five trains. On a given morning it may begin operation with two of the five, then add the other three if and when needed. If the waiting line builds rapidly before operators decide to go to full capacity, you could have a long wait, even in the early morning.

Another variable relates to the time you arrive for a theater performance. Usually, your wait will be the length of time from your arrival to the end of the presentation in progress. Thus, if *Country Bear Jamboree* is 15 minutes long and you arrive one minute after a show has begun, your wait for the next show will be 14 minutes. Conversely, if you arrive as the show is wrapping up, your wait will be only a minute or two.

A WORD ABOUT DISNEY THRILL RIDES

READERS OF ALL AGES SHOULD ATTEMPT to be open-minded about the so-called Disney "thrill rides." In comparison with rides at other theme parks, the Disney thrill attractions are quite tame, with more emphasis on sights, atmosphere, and special effects than on the motion, speed, or feel of the ride itself. While we suggest you take Disney's preride warnings seriously, we can tell you that guests of all ages report enjoying rides such as Tower of Terror, Big Thunder Mountain, and Splash Mountain.

A reader from Washington sums up the situation well:

> Our boys and I are used to imagining typical amusement
> park rides when it comes to roller coasters. So, when we
> thought of Big Thunder Mountain and Space Mountain,
> what came to mind was gigantic hills, upside-down loops,
> huge vertical drops, etc. I actually hate roller coasters, espe-
> cially the unpleasant sensation of a long drop, and I have
> never taken a ride that loops you upside down.
>
> In fact, the Disney [rides] are all tame in comparison.
> There are never any long and steep hills (except Splash
> Mountain, and it is there for anyone to see, so you have
> informed consent going on the ride). I was able to build up
> courage to go on all of them, and the more I rode them the
> more I enjoyed them—the less you tense up expecting a big
> long drop, the more you enjoy the special effects and even
> swinging around curves. Swinging around curves is really
> the primary motion challenge of Disney roller coasters.

Disney, recognizing that it needs more attractions that appeal to the youth and young adult markets, has added some
roller coasters to its parks. The Rock 'n' Roller Coaster at the
Disney-MGM Studios, for example, incorporates at least
some of the features our Washington reader seeks to avoid.

A WORD ABOUT HEIGHT REQUIREMENTS

A NUMBER OF ATTRACTIONS REQUIRE CHILDREN to
meet minimum height and age requirements, usually 44
inches tall to ride with an adult, or 44 inches and 7 years of
age to ride alone. If you have children too short or too young
to ride, you have several options, including switching off
(described on pages 133–135). Although the alternatives
may resolve some practical and logistic issues, be forewarned
that your smaller children might nonetheless be resentful of
their older (or taller) siblings who qualify to ride. A mom
from Virginia bumped into just such a situation, writing:

> You mention height requirements for rides but not the in-
> tense sibling jealousy this can generate. Frontierland was a
> real problem in that respect. Our very petite 5-year-old, to
> her outrage, was stuck hanging around while our 8-year-old
> went on Splash Mountain and [Big] Thunder Mountain
> with Grandma and Granddad, and the nearby alternatives
> weren't helpful [too long a line for rafts to Tom Sawyer Is-
> land, etc.]. If we had thought ahead, we would have left the
> younger kid back in Mickey's Toontown with one of the
> grownups for another roller coaster ride or two and then
> met up later at a designated point. The best areas had a play-

ground or other quick attractions for short people near the rides with height requirements, like the Boneyard near the dinosaur ride at the Animal Kingdom.

The reader makes a valid point, though in practical terms splitting the group and meeting later can be more complicated that she might imagine. If you choose to split up, ask the Disney greeter at the entrance to the attraction(s) with height requirements how long the wait is. Tack five minutes for riding onto the anticipated wait, and then add five or so minutes to exit and reach the meeting point for an approximate sense of how long the younger kids (and their supervising adult) will have to do other stuff. Our guess is that even with a long line for the rafts, the reader would have had more than sufficient time to take her daughter to Tom Sawyer Island while the sibs rode Splash Mountain and Big Thunder Mountain with the grandparents. For sure she had time to tour the Swiss Family Treehouse in adjacent Adventureland.

WAITING-LINE STRATEGIES FOR ADULTS WITH YOUNG CHILDREN

CHILDREN HOLD UP BETTER THROUGH the day if you minimize the time they spend in lines. Arriving early and using our touring plans immensely reduces waiting. Here are additional ways to reduce stress for children:

1. LINE GAMES Wise parents anticipate restlessness in line and plan activities to reduce the stress and boredom. In the morning, have waiting children discuss what they want to see and do during the day. Later, watch for and count Disney characters or play simple guessing games like 20 Questions. Lines move continuously, so games requiring pen and paper are impractical. The holding area of a theater attraction, however, is a different story. Here, tic-tac-toe, hangman, drawing, and coloring make the time fly by.

ATTRACTIONS YOU CAN USUALLY ENTER AT THE LAST MINUTE	
Magic Kingdom	
Liberty Square	*The Hall of Presidents*
	Liberty Square Riverboat
Epcot	
Future World	*The Circle of Life* (except during mealtimes)
World Showcase	*Reflections of China*
	The American Adventure
	O Canada!
Disney-MGM Studios	*Sounds Dangerous*
	Backlot Tour
Animal Kingdom	*Flights of Wonder*

2. LAST-MINUTE ENTRY If an attraction can accommodate an unusually large number of people at once, it's often unnecessary to stand in line. The Magic Kingdom's *Liberty Square* Riverboat is a good example. The boat holds about 450 people, usually more than are waiting in line. Instead of standing uncomfortably in a crowd, grab a snack and sit in the shade until the boat arrives and loading is under way. After the line is almost gone, join it.

At large-capacity theaters like that for Epcot's *The American Adventure,* ask the entrance greeter how long it will be until guests are admitted for the next show. If it's 15 minutes or more, take a restroom break or get a snack, returning a few minutes before the show starts. You aren't allowed to carry food or drink into the attraction, so make sure you have time to finish your snack.

ATTRACTIONS WHERE YOU CAN USUALLY COMPLETE A HAIL MARY PASS	
Magic Kingdom	
Adventureland	Swiss Family Treehouse
Frontierland	*Country Bear Jamboree*
Fantasyland	Mad Tea Party
	Snow White's Scary Adventures
	Dumbo the Flying Elephant
	Cinderella's Golden Carousel
	Peter Pan's Flight
Epcot	
Future World	Spaceship Earth
	Living with the Land
Disney-MGM Studios	
Sounds Dangerous	*Indiana Jones Epic Stunt Spectacular!*
Animal Kingdom	
DinoLand U.S.A.	TriceraTop Spin

3. THE HAIL MARY PASS Certain lines are configured to allow you and your smaller children to pass under the rail to join your partner just before actual boarding or entry. This technique allows children and one adult to rest, snack, or go to the potty while another adult or older sibling stands in line. Other guests are very understanding about this strategy when used for young children. You're likely to meet hostile opposition, however, if you try to pass older children or more than one adult under the rail. To preempt hostility, tell the folks behind you in line what you are doing and why.

4. SWITCHING OFF (A.K.A. THE BABY SWAP) Several attractions have minimum height and/or age requirements, usually 40 to 48 inches tall to ride with an adult, or age 7 *and* 40 inches to ride alone. Some couples with children too small or too young forgo these attractions, while others take turns to ride. Missing some of Disney's best rides is an unnecessary sacrifice, and waiting in line twice for the same ride is a tremendous waste of time.

Instead, take advantage of the "switching off" option, also called "The Baby Swap." To switch off, there must be at least two adults. Everybody waits in line together, adults and children. When you reach an attendant (called a "greeter"), tell him or her that you want to switch off. The greeter will allow everyone, including the young children, to enter the

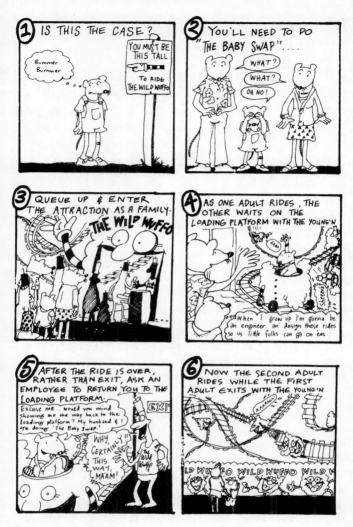

attraction. When you reach the loading area, one adult rides while the other stays with the kids. Then the riding adult disembarks and takes charge of the children while the other adult rides. A third adult in the party can ride twice, once with each of the switching off adults, so that the switching off adults don't have to experience the attraction alone.

Most rides with age and height minimums load and unload in the same area, facilitating switching off. An exception is Space Mountain, where the first adult at the conclusion of the

ATTRACTIONS WHERE SWITCHING OFF IS COMMON	
Magic Kingdom	
Tomorrowland	Space Mountain
Frontierland	Splash Mountain
	Big Thunder Mountain Railroad
Epcot	
Future World	Body Wars
	Test Track
	Mission: Space
Disney-MGM Studios	
Star Tours	*The Twilight Zone* Tower of Terror
Rock 'n' Roller Coaster	
Animal Kingdom	
DinoLand U.S.A.	Dinosaur
Asia	Kali River Rapids
	Primeval Whirl

ride must also inform the unloading attendant that he or she is switching off. The attendant will admit the first adult to an internal stairway that goes back to the loading area.

Attractions at which switching off is practiced are oriented to more mature guests. Sometimes it takes a lot of courage for a child just to move through the queue holding dad's hand. In the boarding area, many children suddenly fear abandonment as one parent leaves to experience the attraction. Unless your children are prepared for switching off, you might have an emotional crisis on your hands. A mom from Edison, New Jersey, advises:

> Once my son came to understand that the switch-off would not leave him abandoned, he did not seem to mind. I would recommend to your readers that they practice the switch off on some dry runs at home, so that their child is not concerned that he will be left behind. At the very least, the procedure could be explained in advance so that the little ones know what to expect.

Finally, a mother from Ada, Michigan, who discovered that the procedure for switching off varies from attraction to attraction, offered this suggestion:

> Parents need to tell the very first attendant they come to that they would like to switch off. Each attraction has a different procedure for this. Tell every other attendant too, because they forget quickly.

5. HOW TO RIDE TWICE IN A ROW WITHOUT WAITING Many young children like to ride a favorite attraction two or more times in succession. Riding the second time often gives them a feeling of mastery and accomplishment. Unfortunately, even in the early morning, repeat rides can be time consuming. If you ride Dumbo as soon as the Magic Kingdom opens, for instance, you will wait only a minute or two for your first ride. When you come back for your second, the wait will be about 12 minutes. If you want to ride a third time, count on 20 minutes or longer.

The best way to get your child on the ride twice (or more) without blowing your morning is to use the "Chuck Bubba Relay" (named in honor of a Kentucky reader):

a. Mom and little Bubba enter the waiting line.

b. Dad lets a specific number of people go in front of him (24 at Dumbo), then gets in line.

c. As soon as the ride stops, mom exits with Bubba and passes him to dad to ride the second time.

d. If everybody is really getting into this, mom can hop in line again, no fewer than 24 people behind dad.

The Chuck Bubba Relay won't work on every ride, because waiting areas are configured differently (that is, it's impossible in some cases to exit the ride and make the pass). For those rides (all in Fantasyland) where the Bubba Relay works, here are the numbers of people to count off:

Mad Tea Party: 53	Snow White's Scary Adventures: 52
Dumbo the Flying Elephant: 24	Cinderella's Golden Carousel: 75
Peter Pan's Flight: 64	Magic Carpets of Aladdin: 48

If you're the second adult in the relay, you'll reach a place in line where it's easiest to make the hand-off, often where those exiting the ride pass closest to those waiting to board. In any event, you'll know it when you see it. If you reach it before the first parent arrives with Bubba, let those behind you pass until Bubba shows up.

6. LAST-MINUTE COLD FEET If your young child gets cold feet just before boarding a ride where there is no age or height requirement, you usually can arrange with the loading attendant for a switch off. This is common at Pirates of the Caribbean, where children lose their courage while winding through the dungeon-like waiting area. Additionally, no law says you *have* to ride. If you reach the boarding area and someone is unhappy, tell an attendant you've changed your mind and you'll be shown the way out.

7. ELEVATOR SHOES FOR THE SHORT AND THE BRAVE If you have a child who is begging to go on the rides with height requirements but who is a little too short, slip heel lifts into his Nikes before he reaches the measuring point. Be sure to leave the heel lifts in, because he may be measured again before boarding.

A Huntsville, Alabama, mom has worked out all the details on the heel lift problem:

> Knowing my wild child 3-year-old as I do, I was interested in your comment regarding shoe lifts. I don't know about other places, but in the big city of Huntspatch where we live, one has to have a prescription for lifts. Normal shoe repair places don't make them. I couldn't think of a material with which to fashion a homemade lift that would be comfortable enough to stand on while waiting in line. I ended up purchasing some of those painfully ugly two-inch chunky-heeled sandals at my local 'mart where they carried these hideous shoes in unbelievably tiny sizes ($12). Since they didn't look too comfortable, we popped them on her right before we entered the ride lines. None of the height checkers ever asked her to remove them and she clip-clopped onto Splash Mountain, Big Thunder Railroad (Dat BIG Choo-Choo), Star Wars, and The Tower of Terror—twice! However, the same child became so terrified at the Tiki Bird show that we were forced to leave—go figure! For adventuresome boys, I would suggest purchasing some of those equally hideous giant-heeled cowboy boots.

Similarly, a Long Pond, Pennsylvania, mom had this to offer:

> Tower of Terror, Star Tours, and Body Wars have 40-inch requirements. Being persistent with a 39½-inch child, we tried these several times. She got on Tower of Terror two of three times, Body Wars one of one time, and Star Tours one of two tries. She wore elevator shoes and a bun hair style to increase height.

Note that boosting your child's height by an inch or two with a heel lift or the like will not compromise his safety on the ride.

8. CATCH-22 AT TOMORROWLAND SPEEDWAY Though Tomorrowland Speedway is a great treat for young children, they're required to be 52 inches tall in order to drive unassisted. Few children ages 6 and younger measure up, so the ride is essentially withheld from the very age group that would most enjoy it. To resolve this catch-22, go on the ride with your small child. The attendants will assume that you will drive. After getting into the car, shift your child over behind the steering wheel. From your position, you will still be able to control the foot pedals. Children will feel like they're really driving, and because the car travels on a self-guiding track, there's no way they can make a mistake while steering.

CHARACTER ANALYSIS

THE LARGE AND FRIENDLY COSTUMED versions of Mickey, Minnie, Donald, Goofy, and others—known as "Disney characters"—provide a link between Disney animated films and the theme parks. To people emotionally invested, the characters in Disney films are as real as next-door neighbors, never mind that they're just drawings on plastic. In recent years, theme park personifications of the characters also have become real to us. It's not just a person in a mouse costume we see; it is Mickey himself. Similarly, meeting Goofy or Snow White in Fantasyland is an encounter with a celebrity, a memory to be treasured.

While there are hundreds of Disney animated film characters, only about 250 have been brought to life in costume. Of these, a relatively small number (less than a fifth) are "greeters" (characters who mix with patrons). The remaining characters perform in shows or parades. Originally confined to the Magic Kingdom, characters are now found in all the major theme parks and Disney hotels.

unofficial **TIP**
If your children can't enjoy things until they see Mickey, ask a cast member where to find him. If the cast member doesn't know right away, he or she can find out quickly. Cast members have a number they can call to learn exactly where the characters are at any time.

CHARACTER WATCHING Character watching has become a pastime. Families once were content to meet characters only occasionally and by chance. They now pursue them relentlessly, armed with autograph books and cameras. Because some characters are only rarely seen, character watching has become character collecting. (To cash in on character collecting, Disney sells autograph books throughout the World.) Mickey, Minnie, and Goofy are a snap to bag; they seem to be everywhere. But Winnie the Pooh seldom comes out. Other characters appear regularly, but only in a location consistent with their starring role. Cinderella, predictably, reigns at Cinderella Castle in Fantasyland, while Brer Fox and Brer Bear frolic in Frontierland near Splash Mountain.

A Brooklyn dad thinks the character autograph–hunting craze has gotten out of hand, complaining:

> Whoever started the practice of collecting autographs from the characters should be subjected to Chinese water torture! We went to Walt Disney World 11 years ago, with an 8-year-old and an 11-year-old. We would bump into characters, take pictures, and that was it. After a while, our children noticed that some of the other children were getting autographs. We managed to avoid joining in during our first day at the Magic Kingdom and our first day at Epcot, but by day three our children were collecting autographs. However, it did not get too out of hand, since it was limited to accidental character meeting.
>
> This year when we took our youngest child (who is now age 8), he had already seen his siblings' collection, and was determined to outdo them. However, rather than random meetings, the characters are now available practically all day long at different locations, according to a printed schedule, which our son was old enough to read. We spent more time standing in line for autographs than we did for the most popular rides!

A family from Birmingham, Alabama, found some benefit in their children's relentless pursuit of characters, writing:

> We had no idea we would be caught up in this madness, but after my daughters grabbed your guidebook to get Pocahontas to sign it (we had no blank paper), we quickly bought a Disney autograph book and gave in. It was actually the highlight of their trip, and my son even got into the act by helping get places in line for his sisters. They LOVED looking for characters (I think it has all been planned by Kodak to sell film). The possibility of seeing a new character revived my 7-year-old's energy on many occasions. It was an amazing, totally unexpected part of our visit.

"THEN SOME CONFUSION HAPPENED" Young children sometimes become lost at character encounters. Usually, there's a lot of activity around a character, with both adults and children touching it or posing for pictures. Most commonly, Mom and Dad stay in the crowd while Junior approaches to meet the character. In the excitement and with people milling and the character moving around, Junior heads off in the wrong direction to look for Mom and Dad. In the words of a Salt Lake City mom: "Milo was shaking hands with Dopey one minute, then some confusion happened and [Milo] was gone." Families with several young children and parents

unofficial **TIP**
Our advice for parents with preschoolers is to stay with the kids when they meet characters, stepping back only to take a quick picture.

who are busy with cameras can lose track of a youngster in a heartbeat.

MEETING CHARACTERS FOR FREE

YOU CAN *SEE* DISNEY CHARACTERS IN live shows at all the theme parks and in parades at the Magic Kingdom and Disney-MGM Studios. Consult your daily entertainment schedule for times. If you want to *meet* the characters, get autographs, and take photos, consult the free *Times Guide*.

AT THE MAGIC KINGDOM Characters are encountered more frequently here than anywhere else in Walt Disney World. There almost always will be a character next to City Hall on Main Street and usually one or more in Town Square or near the railroad station. If it's rainy, look for characters on the veranda of Tony's Town Square Restaurant. Characters appear in all the lands but are more plentiful in Fantasyland and Mickey's Toontown Fair. At Mickey's Toontown Fair, you can meet Mickey privately in his Judge's Tent. Characters actually work shifts at the Toontown Hall of Fame next to Mickey's Country House. Here, you can line up to meet three different assortments of characters. Each assortment has its own greeting area and, of course, its own line. One group, variously labeled Mickey's Pals or Famous Friends or something similar, will include Minnie, Pluto, Goofy, Donald, and sometimes Chip and Dale, Daisy, and Uncle Scrooge. The other two assortments vary and are more ambiguously defined. The 100 Acre Wood Friends are mostly Winnie the Pooh characters, while Fairy Tale Friends include Snow White, assorted dwarfs, Sleeping Beauty, the Beast, Belle, Cinderella, Prince Charming, and so on. Sometimes, however, it's Villains (Captain Hook, Cruella DeVil, Jabar, et al.) and Princesses (Sleeping Beauty, Mary Poppins, yada, yada, yada). Cinderella regularly greets diners at Cinderella's Royal Table in the castle. Also look for characters in the central hub and by Splash Mountain in Frontierland.

Characters are featured in afternoon and evening parades and also play a major role in Castle Forecourt shows (at the entrance to the castle on the moat side) and at the Galaxy Palace Theater in Tomorrowland. Find performance times for shows and parades in the park's daily entertainment schedule. Sometimes characters stay to greet the audience after shows.

AT EPCOT At first Disney didn't think characters would be appropriate for the more serious, educational style of Epcot. Later, in response to criticism that Epcot lacked warmth and humor, characters were imported. To integrate them thematically, new and often bizarre costumes were created. Goofy roams Future World in a metallic silver cape reminiscent of Buck Rogers. Mickey greets guests at the American Adventure dressed like Ben Franklin.

Although chance encounters with characters are less frequent at Epcot than at the other parks, Epcot compensates by periodically bringing in characters by the busload, literally. Several times each day, a whole platoon of characters pile onto a British double-decker bus and set out for one of the countries arrayed around the World Showcase Lagoon. When the bus stops, all of the characters hop off and mingle with the crowd, posing for pictures and signing autographs. Mickey, Minnie, Goofy, Chip and Dale, and Pluto are almost always on the bus, frequently accompanied by Ballou, Tigger, Eyeore, the Genie from Aladdin, Jasmine, Mushu, Timor, and Snow White. The bus is dispatched about eight to ten times a day. Specific times and stops are listed in the Epcot handout park map. In fact, the bus offers the easiest access to the most characters in one place in all of Walt Disney World. Once the crowd in the immediate area gets the drift, however, the characters are mobbed.

> *unofficial* **TIP**
> Position yourself at a scheduled stop a couple of minutes before the bus arrives so you can score a bunch of photos and autographs before everyone else figures out what's going on.

Characters may be rarer at Epcot, but they're often easier to meet. A father from Effingham, Illinois, writes:

> *Trying to get autographs and pictures with Disney characters in the Magic Kingdom was a nightmare. Every character we saw was mobbed by kids and adults. Our kids had no chance. But at Epcot and Disney-MGM, things were much better. We got autographs, pictures, and more involvement. Our kids danced with several characters and received a lot of personal attention.*

AT DISNEY-MGM STUDIOS Characters are likely to turn up anywhere at the Studios but are most frequently found in front of the Animation Building, along Mickey Avenue (leading to the soundstages), and at the end of Streets of America on the backlot. Mickey and his "friends" pose for keepsake photos (about $14 each) on Hollywood Boulevard, Sunset Boulevard, and Streets of America. Characters are also prominent in shows, with *Voyage of the Little Mermaid* running almost continuously and an abbreviated version of

Beauty and the Beast performed several times daily at the Theater of the Stars. Check the *Times Guide* for show times.

AT THE ANIMAL KINGDOM Camp Minnie-Mickey in the Animal Kingdom is a special location designed specifically for meeting characters. There are four designated character greeting "trails" where you can meet Mickey, Minnie, and various characters from *The Jungle Book* and *The Lion King*. Also at Camp Minnie-Mickey are two stage shows featuring characters from *The Lion King* and *Pocahontas*.

Responding to requests, each theme park has added a lot of information about characters to its handout *Times Guide*. The *Times Guide* lists where and when certain characters will be available and provides information on character dining.

> *unofficial* **TIP**
> Lines for face characters move m-u-c-h more slowly than do lines for nonspeaking characters. Because face characters are allowed to talk, they often engage children in lengthy conversations, much to the dismay of families still in the queue.

Disney has taken several initiatives intended to satisfy guests' inexhaustible desire to meet the characters. Most important, Disney assigned Mickey and a number of other characters to all-day duty in Mickey's Toontown Fair in the Magic Kingdom and Camp Minnie-Mickey in the Animal Kingdom. Although making the characters more available has taken the guesswork out of finding them, it has robbed encounters of much of their spontaneity. Instead of chancing on a character, it's much more common now to wait in line to meet the character.

DINING

FOR EFFICIENCY AND ECONOMY, WE recommend eating breakfast in your hotel room. Even if you roll out to Denny's or eat breakfast at your hotel, however, finish early enough to arrive at the theme park prior to opening. For lunch it's cheaper and more relaxed to eat out of the parks during your midday break. If you elect not to take a midday break, you won't have any trouble finding something your children will eat. Hamburgers, fries, hot dogs, or pizza can be had within 50 yards of any attraction. Plan on spending about twice what you would pay at a Hardee's or McDonald's. Portions are often large enough to split.

No matter how formal or imposing a Disney full-service restaurant appears, rest assured that the staff is accustomed

RECOMMENDED COUNTER-SERVICE RESTAURANTS	
MAGIC KINGDOM	
Tomorrowland Terrace Noodle Station	Cosmic Ray's
Pecos Bill's Tall Tale Inn and Cafe	The Plaza Pavilion
EPCOT	
Rose and Crown Pub	Sunshine Seasons (The Land)
Sommerfest	Yakitori House
DISNEY-MGM STUDIOS	
ABC Commissary	Backlot Express
Studio Catering Company	
ANIMAL KINGDOM	
Flame Tree Barbecue	

to wiggling, impatient, and often boisterous children. The bottom line: young children are the rule, not the exception, at Disney restaurants. Almost all Disney restaurants offer a child's menu, and all have booster seats and high chairs. Because the waitstaff understands how tough it can be for children to sit still for an extended period, they will supply your little ones with crackers and rolls and serve your dinner much faster than in comparable restaurants elsewhere. And if your children raise the roof? No problem, the other diners will be too preoccupied with their own kids to notice.

CHARACTER DINING

FRATERNIZING WITH CHARACTERS HAS BECOME so popular that Disney offers character breakfasts, brunches, and dinners where families can dine in the presence of Mickey, Minnie, Goofy, and other costumed versions of animated celebrities. Besides grabbing customers from Denny's and Hardee's, character meals provide a familiar, controlled setting in which young children can warm gradually to characters. Though we mention only the featured character(s) in the following descriptions, all meals are attended by several characters. Adult prices apply to persons ages 12 or older, children's prices to ages 3 to 11. Little ones under age 3 eat free.

Character Dining: What to Expect

Character meals are bustling affairs held in hotels' or theme parks' largest full-service restaurants. Character breakfasts offer a buffet or a fixed menu served family-style. The typical family-style breakfast includes scrambled eggs; bacon, sausage, and ham; hash browns; waffles or French toast; biscuits, rolls, or pastries; and fruit. The meal is served in large skillets or platters at your table. If you run out of something, you can order seconds (or thirds) at no additional charge. Buffets offer much the same fare, but you have to fetch it yourself.

Character dinners range from a set menu served family-style to buffets or ordering off the menu. The character dinner at the Liberty Tree Tavern in the Magic Kingdom, for example, is served family-style and consists of turkey, ham, marinated flank steak, salad, mashed potatoes, green vegetables, and, for kids, macaroni and cheese. Dessert is extra. Character dinner buffets, such as those at 1900 Park Fare at the Grand Floridian and Chef Mickey's at the Contemporary Resort, offer separate adults' and children's serving lines. Typically, the children's buffet includes hamburgers, hot dogs, pizza, fish sticks, fried chicken nuggets, macaroni and cheese, and peanut butter and jelly sandwiches. Selections at the adult buffet usually include prime rib or other carved meat, baked or broiled Florida seafood, pasta, chicken, an ethnic dish or two, vegetables, potatoes, and salad.

At both breakfasts and dinners, characters circulate around the room while you eat. During your meal, each of the three to five characters present will visit your table, arriving one at a time to cuddle with the kids (and sometimes the adults), pose for photos, and sign autographs. Keep autograph books (with pens) and loaded cameras handy.

unofficial **TIP**
For the best photos, adults should sit across the table from their children. Always seat the children where characters can reach them most easily, such as on the aisle rather than against the wall.

Disney people don't rush you to leave after you've eaten. You can get seconds on coffee or juice and stay as long as you wish to enjoy the characters. Remember, however, that there are lots of eager children and adults waiting not so patiently to be admitted.

When to Go

Though a number of character breakfasts are offered around Walt Disney World, attending them usually prevents you from arriving at the theme parks in time for opening. Because early morning is best for touring the parks and you don't want to burn daylight lingering over breakfast, we suggest:

1. Substitute a character breakfast for lunch. Have juice or coffee and a roll or banana from room service or from your cooler first thing in the morning to tide you over. Then tour the theme park for an hour or two before breaking off around 10:15 a.m. to go to the character breakfast of your choice.

Make a big brunch of your character breakfast and skip lunch. You should be fueled until dinner.

2. Go on your arrival or departure day. The day you arrive and check in is usually good for a character dinner. Settle in at your hotel, swim, then dine with the characters. This strategy has the added benefit of exposing your children to the characters before chance encounters at the parks. Some children, moreover, won't settle down to enjoy the parks until they have seen Mickey. Departure days also are good for a character meal. Schedule a character breakfast on your check-out day before you head for the airport or begin your drive home.

3. Go on a rest day. If you plan to stay five or more days, you probably will take a day off from touring to rest or do something else in the Orlando area. These are perfect days for a character meal.

4. Go for lunch or dinner instead of breakfast. A character dinner in late afternoon or evening won't conflict with your touring schedule.

How to Choose a Character Meal

We receive a lot of mail asking for advice about character meals. This question from a Waterloo, Iowa mom is typical:

> Are all character breakfasts pretty much the same or are some better than others? How should I go about choosing one?

In fact, some are better than others, sometimes much better. Here's what we look for when we evaluate character meals.

1. THE CHARACTERS The various meals offer a diverse assortment of Disney characters. Selecting a meal that features your children's special favorites is a good first step. Check the Character Meal Hit Parade chart (pages 150–151) to see which characters are assigned to each meal. With the exception of 1900 Park Fare at the Grand Floridian, most restaurants stick with the same characters from year to year. Even so, it's wise to check the character lineup when you phone to make your advance reservations, as this mom from Austin, Texas attests:

> We went to two character meals at 1900 Park Fare. We ate dinner there the night we arrived, unaware that the characters would all be villains. My 4-year-old was a little scared of the witch from Snow White but amazingly kept his cool! Cruella DeVil, Captain Hook and Prince John (from Robin Hood) were also there. My son asked the next morning if that witch was going to be at the theme parks

too. Needless to say, we did not ride the Snow White ride in the Magic Kingdom! (The character breakfast was kinder and gentler.)

A family from Michigan, unfortunately did not fare as well:

Our character meal at the 1900 Park Fare was a DISASTER! Please warn other readers that have younger children that when they make advance reservations, and the characters are "villians," they may want to rethink their options. We went for my daughters fifth birthday and she was scared to death. The Queen of Hearts chased her sobbing and screaming down the hallway. Most young children we saw at dinner were very frightened. Captain Hook and Prince John were laid back but Governor Ratcliff (Pocahontas) and the Queen were amazingly rude and intimidating. I was very disappointed in our meal and the characters.

The villains have been replaced by princesses. The moral of the story, however, remains the same: Always confirm which characters will attend before you make your advance reservations.

2. ATTENTION FROM THE CHARACTERS In all character meals the characters circulate among the guests hugging children, posing for pictures, and signing autographs. How much time a character spends with you and your children depends primarily on the ratio of characters to guests. The more characters and fewer guests the better. Because many character meals never fill to capacity, the Character to Guest Ratios in our Character Meal Hit Parade chart were adjusted to reflect an average attendance as opposed to a sell-out crowd. Even so, there's quite a range. The best character to guest ratio is at Cinderella's Royal Table, where there is approximately 1 character to every 26 guests. The worst ratio can be found at the Garden Grove Café at the Swan Resort. Here there is only 1 character for every 216 guests. What this means in practical terms is that your family will get eight times more attention from the characters at Cinderella's Royal Table than from those at the Garden Grove Café. As an aside, many children particularly enjoy meals with characters such as Snow White, Belle, Jasmine, Cinderella, Aladdin, etc. These so-called "face characters" speak and are thus able to engage children in a way not possible for the mute animal characters.

3. THE SETTING Some character meals are staged in quite exotic settings, while for others moving the venue to an elementary school cafeteria would be an improvement.Our chart rates the setting of each character meal with the familiar five-star scale. Two restaurants, Cinderella's Royal Table in the Magic Kingdom, and the Garden Grill in the Land Pavilion at Epcot, deserve special mention. Cinderella's Royal Table is situated on the first and second floors of Cinderella Castle in Fantasyland, offering guests a look at the inside of the castle. The Garden Grill is a revolving restaurant that overlooks several scenes from the "Living With the Land" boat ride attraction. Although Chef Mickey's at the Contemporary Resort is rather sterile and cold in appearance, it affords a great view of the monorail running through the interior of the hotel. The respective themes and settings of the remaining character meal venues, while apparent to adults, are lost on children.

4. THE FOOD Although some food served at character meals is quite good, most is average, in other words palatable but nothing to get excited about. In terms of variety, consistency, and quality, restaurants generally do a better job with breakfast than with lunch or dinner (if served). Some restaurants offer a buffet while others opt for "one skillet," family-style service where all the hot items on the bill of fare are served from the same pot or skillet. A few restaurants offer more traditional table service, where a waiter serves a pre-set meal to each guest individually. This last-mentioned type of service provides for dishes that are fresher than those that languish under buffet heat lamps or dry out in metal skillets and pots. This, however, like most generalizations, has its exceptions. In our chart, to help you sort it out, we rate the food at each character meal using the tried and true five-star scale.

5. THE PROGRAM Some of the larger restaurants stage modest performances where the characters dance, head up a parade or conga line around the room, or lead songs and cheers. For some guests these productions lend a celebratory air to the proceedings, while for others they turn what was already mayhem into absolute chaos. In either event, the antics consume time that the characters could be spending with families at their table.

6. NOISE If you want to eat in peace, character meals are a bad choice. That having been said, some are much noisier than others. Once again, our chart gives you some idea of what to expect.

7. WHICH MEAL? Although character breakfasts seem to be the most popular, character lunches and dinners are usually more practical because they do not interfere with your early morning touring. During hot weather months especially, a character lunch at midday can be heavenly.

8. COST Dinners cost more than lunches, and lunches more than breakfasts. Prices for any given meal vary only about $3 from the least expensive to the most expensive restaurant. Breakfasts run $17–$20 for adults, $8–$11 for children ages 3–9. For character lunches, expect to pay $18–$24 for adults, $10–$13 for kids. Dinners range from $21–$24 for adults and $10–$11 for children. Little ones ages 2 and under eat free.

9. RESERVATIONS The Disney dining reservations system makes advance reservations for character meals up to 90 days prior to the day you wish to dine. An advance reservation for most character meals are easy to obtain, even if you forget to call until a couple of weeks before you leave home. Breakfasts at Cinderella's Royal Table are another story. To get a breakfast table at Cinderella's, you'll need our strategy (explained below) as well as the help of Congress and the Pope.

10. NO RESERVATIONS Character meals at the Gulliver's Grill at the Swan Resort do not participate in the advance reservations program. All of their business is walk-in (groups of ten or more should call ahead). Waits to be seated almost never exceed 20 minutes, even at the busiest times of year. Gulliver's Grill serves an outstanding buffet, but has only one character on duty at a time.

11. ODDITIES Character meals are odd affairs at best, with the name "character meal" rather implying that you eat the characters. Yet although we have seen characters savagely gnawed, we've not seen one devoured. Semantics aside, the oddities we refer to are ones that may confuse or disappoint you. In the confusion department, the Garden Grove Café at the Swan Resort changes its name to Gulliver's Grill for dinner. If you ask, Garden Grove Café/Gulliver's Grill will tell you that two characters attend each meal. What you need to know, however, is that they work alternating 30 minute shifts, so there is usually only one character present at a time.

Many who fail to obtain advance reservations for the character breakfast at Cinderella's Royal Table reserve a table for a character lunch. Unfortunately, dinner is not a character meal. Although Cinderella and Snow White have been known to make impromptu appearances during dinner, there's no guarantee. Finally, 1900 Park Fare at the Grand Floridian Resort trots out five characters for dinner but only four for breakfast. Conversely, the Crystal Palace features four characters for breakfast but only three for lunch and dinner.

Getting an Advance Reservation at Cinderella's Royal Table

Cinderella's Royal Table, situated in Cinderella Castle in the Magic Kingdom, hosts the obsessively popular character breakfast starring Cinderella and a number of other Disney princesses. Admittedly, the toughest ticket at Disney World is an advance reservation for this character meal. Why? Cinderella's Royal Table is Disney's tiniest character meal restaurant, accommodating only about 130 diners at a time. Demand so outdistances supply for this event that Walt Disney World visitors go to unbelievable lengths to secure an advanced reservation. After decades of guests complaining and beating their chests over their inability to get a table, Disney finally is offering a noon to 2 p.m. character lunch with the same cast of characters.

This frustrated reader from Golden, Colorado, complains:

> I don't know what you have to do to get an advance reservation for Cinderella's [Royal] Table in the castle. I called Disney Dining every morning at 7 [a.m.], which was 5 [a.m.] where I live! It was like calling into one of those radio shows where the first person to call wins a prize. Every time I finally got through, all the tables were gone. I am soooo frustrated and mad I could spit. What do you have to do to get a table for Cinderella's breakfast?

The only way to get a table is to obtain an advance reservation through Disney reservations. You must call ☎ 407-WDW-DINE at 7 a.m. EST exactly 90 days before the day you want to eat at Cinderella's. Reservations can be made 90 days in advance.

Here's how it works. It's 6:50 a.m. EST and all the Disney dining reservationists are warming up their computers to begin filling available seats at 7 a.m. As the clock strikes seven, Disney dining is blasted with an avalanche of calls, all trying to make advance reservations for the character meals at Cinderella's Royal Table. There are more than 100 reservationists on duty, and most advance reservations can be assigned in two minutes or less. Thus, the coveted seats go quickly, selling out as early as 7:02 a.m. on many days.

To be among the fortunate few who score an advance reservation, try the following. First, call on the correct morning. Use a calendar and count backward exactly 90 days from (but not including) the day you wish to dine. (The computer doesn't understand months, so you can't, for example, call on February 1st to make an advance reservation for May 1st because that's fewer than 90 days.) If you want to eat on May 1st, for example, begin your 90-day

Character Meal Hit Parade

1. CINDERELLA'S ROYAL TABLE	**2. AKERSHUS PRINCESS STORYBOOK BREAKFAST**	**3. CHEF MICKEY'S**
RANK 1	RANK 2	RANK 3
LOCATION Magic Kingdom	LOCATION Epcot	LOCATION Contemporary
MEALS SERVED Breakfast/Lunch	MEALS SERVED Breakfast/Lunch/Dinner	MEALS SERVED Breakfast/Dinner
CHARACTERS Cinderella, Snow White, Belle, Jasmine, Aladdin	CHARACTERS 4–6 characters chosen from Belle, Mulan, Snow White, Sleeping Beauty, Esmeralda, Mary Poppins, Jasmine, Pocahontas	CHARACTERS *Breakfast:* Minnie, Mickey, Chip, Pluto, Goofy *Dinner:* Mickey, Pluto, Chip, Dale, Goofy
SERVED Daily	SERVED Daily	SERVED Daily
SETTING ★★★★★	SETTING ★★★★	SETTING ★★★
SERVICE Buffet/Family style	SERVICE Family style	SERVICE Buffet
FOOD VARIETY AND QUALITY ★★★	FOOD VARIETY AND QUALITY ★★★½	FOOD VARIETY AND QUALITY ★★★ (breakfast) ★★★½ (dinner)
NOISE LEVEL Quiet	NOISE LEVEL Quiet	NOISE LEVEL Loud
CHARACTER TO GUEST RATIO 1 to 26	CHARACTER TO GUEST RATIO 1 to 54	CHARACTER TO GUEST RATIO 1 to 56

7. LIBERTY TREE TAVERN	**8. RESTURANTOSAURUS**	**9. CAPE MAY CAFE**
RANK 7	RANK 8	RANK 9
LOCATION Magic Kingdom	LOCATION Animal Kingdom	LOCATION Beach Club
MEALS SERVED Dinner	MEALS SERVED Breakfast	MEALS SERVED Breakfast
CHARACTERS Minnie, Pluto, Donald Duck, Meeko, Chip and/or Dale	CHARACTERS Mickey, Donald, Pluto, Goofy	CHARACTERS Goofy, Chip, Dale, Pluto
SERVED Daily	SERVED Daily	SERVED Daily
SETTING ★★★½	SETTING ★★★	SETTING ★★★
SERVICE Family style	SERVICE Buffet	SERVICE Buffet
FOOD VARIETY AND QUALITY ★★★	FOOD VARIETY AND QUALITY ★★★	FOOD VARIETY AND QUALITY ★★½
NOISE LEVEL Moderate	NOISE LEVEL Very loud	NOISE LEVEL Moderate
CHARACTER TO GUEST RATIO 1 to 26	CHARACTER TO GUEST RATIO 1 to 112	CHARACTER TO GUEST RATIO 1 to 67

4. CRYSTAL PALACE	5. 1900 PARK FARE	6. GARDEN GRILL
RANK 4	RANK 5	RANK 6
LOCATION Magic Kingdom	LOCATION Grand Floridian	LOCATION Epcot
MEALS SERVED Breakfast/Lunch/Dinner	MEALS SERVED Breakfast/Dinner	MEALS SERVED Lunch/Dinner
CHARACTERS *Breakfast:* Pooh, Tigger, Eeyore, Piglet *Dinner:* Pooh, Tigger, Eeyore	CHARACTERS *Breakfast:* Mary Poppins and friend *Dinner:* Cinderella and friends	CHARACTERS Chip, Dale, Mickey, Pluto
SERVED Daily	SERVED Daily	SERVED Daily
SETTING ★★★	SETTING ★★★	SETTING ★★★★½
SERVICE Buffet	SERVICE Buffet	SERVICE Family style
FOOD VARIETY AND QUALITY ★★½ (breakfast) ★★★ (dinner)	FOOD VARIETY AND QUALITY ★★★ (breakfast) ★★★½ (dinner)	FOOD VARIETY AND QUALITY ★★½
NOISE LEVEL Very loud	NOISE LEVEL Moderate	NOISE LEVEL Very quiet
CHARACTER TO GUEST RATIO 1 to 67 (breakfast) 1 to 89 (dinner)	CHARACTER TO GUEST RATIO 1 to 54 (breakfast) 1 to 44 (dinner)	CHARACTER TO GUEST RATIO 1 to 46

10. OHANA	11. GULLIVER'S GRILL	12. GARDEN GROVE CAFE
RANK 10	RANK 11	RANK 12
LOCATION Polynesian Resort	LOCATION Swan	LOCATION Swan
MEALS SERVED Breakfast	MEALS SERVED Dinner	MEALS SERVED Breakfast
CHARACTERS Mickey, Goofy, Chip, Dale	CHARACTERS Goofy and Pluto or Rafiki and Timon	CHARACTERS Goofy and Pluto
SERVED Daily	SERVED Daily	SERVED Saturday and Sunday
SETTING ★★	SETTING ★★★	SETTING ★★★
SERVICE Family style	SERVICE Buffet/Menu	SERVICE Buffet/Menu
FOOD VARIETY AND QUALITY ★★½	F FOOD VARIETY AND QUALITY ★★★½	FOOD VARIETY AND QUALITY ★★★½
NOISE LEVEL Moderate	NOISE LEVEL Moderate	NOISE LEVEL Moderate
CHARACTER TO GUEST RATIO 1 to 57	CHARACTER TO GUEST RATIO 1 to 198	CHARACTER TO GUEST RATIO 1 to 198

backward count on April 30th. If you count correctly, you'll find that the correct morning to call is January 31st. If you don't feel like counting days, call ☎ 407-WDW-DINE, and the Disney folks will calculate it for you. Call them during the afternoon when they're less busy, about 100 days before your trip. Let them know when you'd like your advance reservation, and they'll tell you the morning to call.

To get a table, you must dial at almost exactly 7 a.m. EST. Disney does not calibrate its clock with the correct time as determined by the U.S. Naval Observatory or the National Institute of Standards and Technology, but we conducted synchronizing tests and determined that Disney reservation system clocks are accurate to within one to three seconds. Several Internet sites will give you the exact time. Our favorite is **www.atomictime.net,** which offers the exact time in displays that show hours, minutes, and seconds. Once the Atomic Time home page is up, click on "html multizone continuous" and look for the Eastern Time Zone. Using this site or your local "Time of Day" number from the phone directory, synchronize your watch TO THE SECOND. About 18 to 20 seconds before 7 a.m., dial ☎ 407-WDW-DINE, waiting to dial the final "E" in "DINE" until 7 seconds before the hour.

Hang up and redial until your call is answered. When it is, you will hear one of two recorded messages:

1. "Thank you for calling the Disney Reservation Center. Our office is closed . . . " If you get this message, hang up the instant you hear the words "Our office" and hit redial.

OR

2. You'll get a recording with a number of prompts. The prompts change periodically. Call a few mornings before the day you actually make your reservation to learn what prompts are being used. Once you know the prompts, you can determine which numbers on your touch-tone phone to press in order to work through the prompts at warp speed. Some prompts begin with "If," others may request info such as your phone number or resort reservation number. Do not listen to the entire prompt. Immediately press the appropriate numbered key(s) as determined by your previous trial run.

Your call will be answered momentarily by a Disney Reservations Center (DRC) agent. Don't get nervous if you're on hold for a bit. The worst thing you can do now is hang up and try again.

As soon as a live DRC agent comes on the line, interrupt immediately and say, "I need Cindy's breakfast (lunch), for May 1st, for four people, any available time" (substituting your own breakfast (lunch) dates, of course). Don't engage in "good mornings" or other pleasantries. Time is of the essence. You can apologize later to the DRC agent for your momentary rudeness if you feel the need, but she already knows what's going on. Don't try and pick a specific time. Even two seconds to ask for a specific time will seriously diminish your chances of getting an advance reservation.

If the atomic clock thing seems too complicated (not to mention anal), start dialing ☎ 407-WDW-DINE about 50 seconds before 7 a.m. If the reservation center isn't open yet, you'll get a recorded message saying so. When this happens, hang up and call back immediately. If you have a redial button on your phone, use it to speed the dialing process. Continue hanging up and redialing as fast as you can until you get the recording with the prompts. This recording verifies that your call has been placed in the service queue in the order in which it was received. If you were among the first to get through, a reservationist will normally pick up in 3 to 20 seconds. What happens next depends on how many others got through ahead of you, but chances are good that you'll be able to get an advance reservation. Bear in mind that while you're talking, other agents are confirming advance reservations for other guests, so you want the transaction to go down as fast as possible. Flexibility on your part counts. It's much harder to get a seating for a large group; give some thought to breaking your group into numbers that can be accommodated at tables for four or even tables for two.

All advance reservations for Cinderella's Royal Table character meals require a credit-card deposit (not guarantee) of $10 per adult and $5 per child at the time of the booking. The name on the booking can't be changed after the advance reservation is made. Advance reservations may be canceled with the deposit refunded in full by calling ☎ 407-WDW-DINE at least 24 hours before the seating time.

While many readers have been successful using our strategies, some have not:

[Regarding] reservations for breakfast at Cinderella's castle. I did exactly what you suggested, five days in a row, and was unable to get through to an actual person until after 7:15 each day (although I was connected and put on hold at exactly 7 a.m. each time). Of course, by then, all reservations were gone (this was for the first week in May, not a peak time).

On most days, a couple of hundred calls slam Disney's automated call queuing system within milliseconds of one another. With this call volume, 1/20 of a second or less can make the difference between getting and not getting a table. As it happens, there are variables beyond your control. When you hit the first digit of a long-distance number, your phone system leaps into action. As you continue entering digits, your phone system is already searching for the best path to the number you're calling. According to federal regulation, a phone system must connect the call to the target number within 20 seconds of your entering the last digit. In practice, most systems make the connection much faster, but your system could be pokey. How fast your call is connected, therefore, depends on your local phone system's connection speed, and even this varies according to traffic volume and available routing paths for individual calls. Distance counts too, although we're talking milliseconds. Thus, it takes just a bit longer for a call to reach Disney World from Chicago than from Atlanta, and longer yet if you're calling from San Francisco.

unofficial **TIP**
It's often easier to get through to reservations if you call on Saturday or Sunday. Presumably, folks don't mind calling at the break of dawn if they're up getting ready for work but object to interrupting their beauty rest on weekends.

So, if you're having trouble getting an advance reservation at Cinderella's Royal Table using the strategies outlined earlier, here are our suggestions. Make a test call to ☎ 407-WDW-DINE at 7 a.m. EST a couple of days before you call in earnest. Using a stopwatch or the stopwatch function on your watch, time the interval between entering the last digit of the number and when the phone starts to ring. This exercise will provide a rough approximation of the call connection speed at that time from your area, taking into account both speed of service and distance. For most of you, the connection interval will be very short. Some of you, however, might discover that your problem in getting through is because of slow service. Either way, factor in the connection interval in timing your call to Disney. Phone traffic is heavier on weekdays than weekends, so if you plan to call reservations on a weekday, conduct your test on a weekday. Finally, don't use a cell phone to make the call. The connection time will usually be slower and certainly less predictable.

Though this is one of the most widely used sections in this guidebook, we're amazed that anyone would go to this much trouble to eat with Cinderella . . . atomic clocks, split-second timing, test calls . . . yikes!

IF YOU CAN'T GET AN ADVANCE RESERVATION If you insist on a meal at Cinderella's but can't get an advance reservation, go to the restaurant on the day you wish to dine and try for a table as a walk-in. This is a long shot, though possible during the least busy times of year. There's also a fair shot at success on cold or rainy days when there's an above-average probability of no-shows. If you try to walk in, your chances are best during the last hour of serving.

Dinner at Cinderella's is not a character meal, but Cinderella or Snow White sometimes look in (no guarantees). Landing an advance reservation for dinner is a snap. If you're unable to lock up a table for breakfast or lunch, a dinner reservation will at least get your children inside the castle. Even without characters, a meal in the castle costs a bundle, as this Snellville, Georgia, mom points out:

> We ate [dinner] at Cinderella's Castle to fulfill my longtime dream. The menu was very limited and expensive. For three people, no appetizers or dessert, the bill was $100.

And no alcoholic beverages, either. Alcohol isn't served in the Magic Kingdom.

Character Campfire

A campfire sing-along is held nightly at 7 or 8 p.m. (depending on the season) near the Meadow Trading Post and Bike Barn at Fort Wilderness Campground. Chip and Dale lead the songs, and a full-length Disney film follows. The program is free and open to resort guests. For a schedule, call ☎ 407-824-2788.

STROLLERS

STROLLERS ARE AVAILABLE FOR A MODEST daily rental fee at all four major theme parks. If you rent a stroller at the Magic Kingdom and decide to go to Epcot, the Animal Kingdom, or Disney-MGM Studios, turn in your Magic Kingdom stroller and keep your receipt to present at the next park. You'll be issued another stroller without additional charge.

Strollers are a must for infants and toddlers, but we have observed many sharp parents renting strollers for somewhat older children (up to age 5 or so). The stroller prevents parents from having to carry children when they sag and provides a convenient place to carry water and snacks.

unofficial **TIP**
When you enter a show or board a ride, you must park your stroller, usually in an open area. Bring a cloth or towel to dry it if it rains before you return.

unofficial **TIP**
Rental strollers are too large for all infants and many toddlers. If you plan to rent a stroller for your infant or toddler, bring pillows, cushions, or rolled towels to buttress him in.

A family from Tulsa, Oklahoma, recommends springing for a double stroller:

We rent a double for baggage room or in case the older child gets tired of walking.

If you go to your hotel for a break and intend to return to the park, leave your rental stroller by an attraction near the park entrance, marking it with something personal, such as a bandanna. When you return, your stroller will be waiting.

Bringing your own stroller is permitted. However, only collapsible strollers are allowed on monorails, parking-lot trams, and buses. Your stroller is unlikely to be stolen, but mark it with your name.

Having her own stroller was indispensable to a Mechanicsville, Virginia, mother of two toddlers:

How I was going to manage to get the kids from the parking lot to the park was a big worry for me before I made the trip. I didn't read anywhere that it was possible to walk to the entrance of the parks instead of taking the tram, so I wasn't sure I could do it.

I found that for me personally, since I have two kids aged 1 and 2, it was easier to walk to the entrance of the park from the parking lot with the kids in [my own] stroller than to take the kids out of the stroller, fold the stroller (while trying to control the two kids and associated gear), load the stroller and the kids onto the tram, etc. . . . No matter where I was parked I could always just walk to the entrance . . . it sometimes took awhile but it was easier for me.

An Oklahoma mom, however, reports a bad experience with bringing her own stroller:

The first time we took our kids we had a large stroller (big mistake). It is so much easier to rent one in the park. The large [personally owned] strollers are nearly impossible to get on the buses and are a hassle at the airport. I remember feeling dread when a bus pulled up that was even semifull of people. People look at you like you have a cage full of live chickens when you drag heavy strollers onto the bus.

STROLLER WARS Sometimes strollers disappear while you're enjoying a ride or show. Disney staff will often rearrange strollers parked outside an attraction. This may be done to tidy up or to clear a walkway. Don't assume your stroller is stolen because it isn't where you left it. It may be neatly arranged a few feet away.

Sometimes, however, strollers are taken by mistake or ripped off by people not wanting to spend time replacing one that's missing. Don't be alarmed if yours disappears. You won't have to buy it, and you'll be issued a new one.

WHEN KIDS *get* LOST

IF ONE OF YOUR CHILDREN GETS SEPARATED from you, don't panic. All things considered, Walt Disney World is about the safest place to get lost we can think of. Disney cast members are trained to watch for seemingly lost kids, and because children become detached from parents so frequently in the theme parks, cast members know exactly what to do.

If you lose a child in the Magic Kingdom, report it to a Disney employee, then check at the Baby Center and at City Hall, where lost-children logs are kept. At Epcot, report the loss, then check at Baby Services near the Odyssey Center. At Disney-MGM Studios, report the situation at the Guest Relations Building at the entrance end of Hollywood Boulevard. At Animal Kingdom, go to the Baby Center in Discovery Island. Paging isn't used, but in an emergency an "all points bulletin" can be issued throughout the park(s) via internal communications. If a Disney employee encounters a lost child, he or she will immediately take the child to the park's guest relations center or its baby-care center.

As comforting as this knowledge is, however, it's nevertheless scary when a child turns up missing. Fortunately, circumstances surrounding a child becoming lost are fairly predictable and, for the most part, preventable.

For starters, consider how much alike children dress, especially in warm climates where shorts and T-shirts are the norm. Throw your children in with 10,000 other kids the same size and suddenly that "cute little outfit" turns into theme-park camouflage. It's also smart to sew a label into each child's shirt that states his or her name, your family name, your hometown, and the name of your hotel. The same thing can be accomplished by writing the information on a strip of masking tape. Hotel security professionals suggest the information be printed in small letters and the tape be affixed to the outside of the child's shirt, five inches

unofficial **TIP**
We suggest that children younger than age 8 be color-coded by dressing them in "vacation uniforms" with distinctively colored T-shirts or equally eye-catching apparel.

below the armpit. Also, special name tags can be obtained at the major theme parks.

Other than just blending in, children tend to become separated from their parents under remarkably similar circumstances:

1. PREOCCUPIED SOLO PARENT In this situation, the party's only adult is preoccupied with something like buying refreshments, loading the camera, or using the restroom. Junior is there one second and gone the next.

2. THE HIDDEN EXIT Sometimes parents wait on the sidelines while two or more young children experience a ride together. Parents expect the kids to exit in one place and, lo and behold, the youngsters pop out somewhere else. Exits from some attractions are distant from the entrances. Make sure you know exactly where your children will emerge before letting them ride by themselves.

3. AFTER THE SHOW At the end of many shows and rides, a Disney staffer will announce, "Check for personal belongings and take small children by the hand." When dozens, if not hundreds, of people leave an attraction simultaneously, it's surprisingly easy for parents to lose contact with their children unless they have them directly in tow.

4. RESTROOM PROBLEMS Mom tells 6-year-old Tommy, "I'll be sitting on this bench when you come out of the restroom." Three possibilities: One, Tommy exits through a different door and becomes disoriented (Mom may not know there is another door). Two, Mom decides she also will use the restroom, and Tommy emerges to find her gone. Three, Mom pokes around in a shop while keeping an eye on the bench, but misses Tommy when he comes out.

If you can't be with your child in the restroom, make sure there's only one exit. The restroom on a passageway between Frontierland and Adventureland in the Magic Kingdom is the all-time worst for disorienting visitors. Children and adults alike have walked in from the Adventureland side and walked out on the Frontierland side (and vice versa). Adults realize quickly that something is wrong. Young children, however, sometimes fail to recognize the problem. Designate a meeting spot more distinctive than a bench, and be thorough in your instructions: "I'll meet you by this flagpole. If you get out first, stay right here." Have your child repeat the directions back to you.

5. PARADES There are many parades and shows at which the audience stands. Children tend to jockey for a better view.

By moving a little this way and that, the child quickly puts distance between you before either of you notices.

6. MASS MOVEMENTS Be on guard when huge crowds disperse after fireworks or a parade, or at park closing. With 20,000 to 40,000 people at once in an area, it's very easy to get separated from a child or others in your party. Use extra caution after the evening parade and fireworks in the Magic Kingdom, *Fantasmic!* at the Disney-MGM Studios, or *Illumi-Nations* at Epcot. Families should have specific plans for where to meet if they get separated.

7. CHARACTER GREETINGS Activity and confusion are common when the Disney characters appear, and children can slip out of sight. See "Then Some Confusion Happened" (pages 139–140).

8. GETTING LOST AT THE ANIMAL KINGDOM It's especially easy to lose a child at the Animal Kingdom, particularly in the Oasis entryway, on the Maharaja Jungle Trek, and on the Gorilla Falls Exploration Trail. Mom and Dad will stop to observe an animal. Junior stays close for a minute or so, and then, losing patience, wanders to the other side of the exhibit or to a different exhibit.

9. LOST . . . IN THE OZONE More often than you'd think, kids don't realize they're lost. They are so distracted that they sometimes wander around for quite a while before they notice that their whole family has mysteriously disappeared. Fortunately, Disney cast members are trained to look out for kids who have zoned out and will either help them find their family or deposit them at the Lost Child Center. There are times, however, when parents panic during the interval in which these scenarios play out. If you lose a child and he doesn't turn up at the Lost Child Center right away, take a deep breath. He's probably lost in the ozone.

10. TEACH YOUR KIDS WHO THE GOOD GUYS ARE On your very first day in the parks, teach your kids how to recognize a Disney cast member by pointing out the Disney name tags that they all wear. Instruct your children to find someone with such a name tag if they get separated from you.

AT THE MAGIC KINGDOM, STROLLER and wheelchair rentals are to the right of the train station, and lockers are on the station's ground floor. On your left as you enter Main Street is City Hall, the center for information, lost and found, guided tours, and entertainment schedules.

If you don't already have a handout park map, get one at City Hall. The handout lists all attractions, shops, and eateries; provides helpful information about first aid, baby care, and assistance for the disabled; and gives tips for good photos. It also lists times for the day's special events, live entertainment, Disney character parades, concerts, and other activities. Additionally, it tells when and where to find Disney characters.

Main Street ends at a central hub from which branch the entrances to five other sections of the Magic Kingdom: Adventureland, Frontierland, Liberty Square, Fantasyland, and Tomorrowland. Mickey's Toontown Fair doesn't connect to the central hub—it is wedged like a dimple between the cheeks of Fantasyland and Tomorrowland.

In this and the following three chapters we rate the individual attractions at each of the four major Disney theme parks. The author's rating as well as ratings according to age group are given on a scale of zero to five stars—the more stars, the better the attraction. The author's rating is from the perspective of an adult. The author, for example, might rate a ride such as Dumbo much lower than the age group for which the ride is intended, in this case, children. His rating, therefore, will more closely approximate how another adult will experience the attraction than how your children will like it. The bottleneck rating ranges from one to ten; the higher the rating, the more congested the attraction. In general, try to experience attractions with a high bottleneck rating early in the morning (that is, between 8 and 10 a.m.) before the park gets crowded or late in the day when the crowd has diminished.

MAIN STREET, U.S.A.

Walt Disney World Railroad

APPEAL BY AGE	PRESCHOOL ★★★★	GRADE SCHOOL ★★½	TEENS ★★★
YOUNG ADULTS ★★★		OVER 30 ★★	SENIORS ★★★

What it is Scenic railroad ride around perimeter of the Magic Kingdom, and transportation to Frontierland and Mickey's Toontown Fair. **Scope and scale** Minor attraction. **Fright potential** Not frightening in any respect. **Bottleneck rating** 6. **When to go** Anytime. **Special comments** Main Street is usually the least congested station. **Author's rating** Plenty to see; ★★½. **Duration of ride** About 20 minutes for a complete circuit. **Average wait in line per 100 people ahead of you** 8 minutes. **Assumes** 2 or more trains operating. **Loading speed** Moderate.

ADVENTURELAND

THE FIRST LAND TO THE LEFT OF MAIN STREET, Adventureland combines an African safari theme with an old New Orleans/Caribbean atmosphere.

Swiss Family Treehouse

APPEAL BY AGE	PRESCHOOL ★★★	GRADE SCHOOL ★★★½	TEENS ★★★
YOUNG ADULTS ★★★		OVER 30 ★★★	SENIORS ★★★

What it is Outdoor walk-through tree house. **Scope and scale** Minor attraction. **Fright potential** Not frightening in any respect. **Bottleneck rating** 6. **When to go** Before 11:30 a.m. or after 5 p.m. **Special comments** Requires climbing a lot of stairs. **Author's rating** A visual delight; ★★★. **Duration of tour** 10–15 minutes. **Average wait in line per 100 people ahead of you** 7 minutes. **Loading speed** Doesn't apply.

Jungle Cruise (FASTPASS)

APPEAL BY AGE	PRESCHOOL ★★★½	GRADE SCHOOL ★★★½	TEENS ★★½
YOUNG ADULTS ★★★		OVER 30 ★★★	SENIORS ★★★

What it is Outdoor safari-themed boat ride adventure. **Scope and scale** Major attraction. **Fright potential** Moderately intense, some macabre

Magic Kingdom

Frontierland

Liberty Square

Adventureland

Main Street, U.S.A.

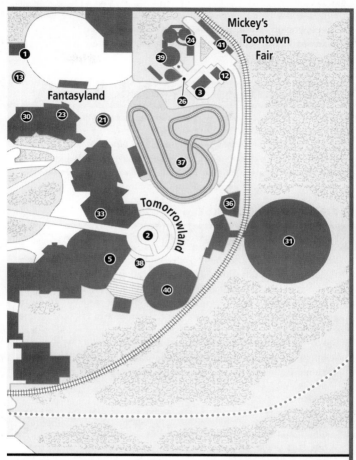

sights; a good test attraction for little ones. **Bottleneck rating** 10. **When to go** Before 10 a.m. or 2 hours before closing. **Author's rating** A long-enduring Disney masterpiece; ★★★. **Duration of ride** 8–9 minutes. **Average wait in line per 100 people ahead of you** 3½ minutes. **Assumes** 10 boats operating. **Loading speed** Moderate.

Magic Carpets of Aladdin

APPEAL BY AGE	PRESCHOOL ★★★★½		GRADE SCHOOL ★★★★
TEENS ★½	YOUNG ADULTS ★½	OVER 30 ★½	SENIORS ★½

What it is Elaborate midway ride. **Scope and scale** Minor attraction. **Fright potential** Much like Dumbo; a favorite of most younger children. **Bottleneck rating** 10. **When to go** Before 10 a.m. or in the hour before park closing. **Author's rating** An eye-appealing children's ride; ★★★. **Duration of ride** 1½ minutes. **Average wait in line per 100 people ahead of you** 16 minutes. **Loading speed** Slow.

Pirates of the Caribbean

APPEAL BY AGE	PRESCHOOL ★★★	GRADE SCHOOL ★★★★★	TEENS ★★★★
YOUNG ADULTS ★★★★		OVER 30 ★★★★½	SENIORS ★★★★½

What it is Indoor pirate-themed adventure boat ride. **Scope and scale** Headliner. **Fright potential** Slightly intimidating queuing area; intense boat ride with gruesome (though humorously presented) sights and a short, unexpected slide down a flume. **Bottleneck rating** 7. **When to go** Before noon or after 5 p.m. **Special comments** Frightens some young children. **Author's rating** Disney audio-animatronics at its best; not to be missed; ★★★★★. **Duration of ride** About 7½ minutes. **Average wait in line per 100 people ahead of you** 1½ minutes. **Assumes** Both waiting lines operating. **Loading speed** Fast.

Enchanted Tiki Birds

APPEAL BY AGE	PRESCHOOL ★★★★	GRADE SCHOOL ★★★½	TEENS ★★★
YOUNG ADULTS ★★★		OVER 30 ★★★	SENIORS ★★★

What it is Audio-animatronic Pacific island musical theater show. **Scope and scale** Minor attraction. **Fright potential** A thunderstorm momentarily surprises very young children. **Bottleneck rating** 4. **When to go** Before 11 a.m. or after 3:30 p.m. **Special comments** Frightens some preschoolers. **Author's rating** Very, very unusual; ★★★½. **Duration of presentation** 15½ minutes. **Preshow entertainment** Talking birds. **Probable waiting time** 15 minutes.

▮ FRONTIERLAND

FRONTIERLAND ADJOINS ADVENTURELAND as you move clockwise around the Magic Kingdom. The focus is on the Old West, with stockade-type structures and pioneer trappings.

Splash Mountain (FASTPASS)

APPEAL BY AGE	PRESCHOOL †	GRADE SCHOOL ★★★★★	TEENS ★★★★★
YOUNG ADULTS ★★★★★		OVER 30 ★★★★★	SENIORS ★★★★★

† Many preschoolers are too short to meet the height requirement, and others are visually intimidated when they see the ride from the waiting line. Among preschoolers who actually ride, most give the attraction high marks (★★★–★★★★★ stars).

What it is Indoor/outdoor water-flume adventure ride. **Scope and scale** Super headliner. **Fright potential** Visually intimidating from outside, with moderately intense visual effects. The ride, culminating in a 52-foot plunge down a steep chute, is somewhat hair-raising for all ages. **Bottleneck rating** 10. **When to go** As soon as the park opens, during afternoon or evening parades, just before closing, or use FASTPASS. **Special comments** Must be 40 inches tall to ride; children younger than 7 must ride with an adult. Switching-off option provided (pages 133–135). **Author's rating** A wet winner; not to be missed; ★★★★★. **Duration of ride** About 10 minutes. **Average wait in line per 100 people ahead of you** 3½ minutes. **Assumes** Operating at full capacity. **Loading speed** Moderate.

Big Thunder Mountain Railroad (FASTPASS)

APPEAL BY AGE	PRESCHOOL ★★★	GRADE SCHOOL ★★★★	TEENS ★★★★
YOUNG ADULTS ★★★★		OVER 30 ★★★★	SENIORS ★★★

What it is Tame, Western-mining-themed roller coaster. **Scope and scale** Headliner. **Fright potential** Visually intimidating from outside, with moderately intense visual effects; the roller coaster is wild enough to frighten many adults, particularly seniors. **Bottleneck rating** 9. **When to go** Before 10 a.m., in the hour before closing, or use FASTPASS. **Special comments** Must be 40 inches tall to ride; children younger than age 7 must ride with an adult. Switching-off option provided (pages 133–135). **Author's rating** Great effects; relatively tame ride; not to be missed; ★★★★. **Duration of ride** Almost 3½ minutes. **Average wait in line per 100 people ahead of you** 2½ minutes. **Assumes** 5 trains operating. **Loading speed** Moderate to fast.

Country Bear Jamboree

APPEAL BY AGE	PRESCHOOL ★★★	GRADE SCHOOL ★★★	TEENS ★★½
YOUNG ADULTS ★★★		OVER 30 ★★★	SENIORS ★★★

What it is Audio-animatronic country hoedown theater show. **Scope and scale** Major attraction. **Fright potential** Not frightening in any respect. **Bottleneck rating** 8. **When to go** Before 11:30 a.m., before a parade, or during the 2 hours before closing. **Special comments** Shows change at Christmas. **Author's rating** A Disney classic; ★★★. **Duration of presentation** 15 minutes. **Preshow entertainment** None. **Probable waiting time** This attraction is moderately popular but has a comparatively small capacity. **Probable waiting time** between noon and 5:30 p.m. on a busy day will average 15–45 minutes.

Tom Sawyer Island and Fort Langhorn

APPEAL BY AGE	PRESCHOOL ★★★★★	GRADE SCHOOL ★★★★★	TEENS ★★
YOUNG ADULTS ★★		OVER 30 ★★	SENIORS ★★

What it is Outdoor walk-through exhibit/rustic playground. **Scope and scale** Minor attraction. **Fright potential** Not frightening in any respect. **Bottleneck rating** 4. **When to go** Midmorning through late afternoon. **Special comments** Closes at dusk. **Author's rating** The place for rambunctious kids; ★★★.

Frontierland Shootin' Arcade

APPEAL BY AGE	PRESCHOOL ★★★	GRADE SCHOOL ★★★★	TEENS ★★★
YOUNG ADULTS ★★		OVER 30 ★★	SENIORS ★★

What it is Electronic shooting gallery. **Scope and scale** Diversion. **When to go** Whenever convenient. **Special comments** Costs 50 cents per play. **Author's rating** Very nifty shooting gallery; ★½.

LIBERTY SQUARE

LIBERTY SQUARE RE-CREATES COLONIAL AMERICA at the time of the American Revolution. The architecture is Federal or Colonial. A real, 130-year-old live oak (dubbed the "Liberty Tree") lends dignity and grace to the setting.

The Hall of Presidents

APPEAL BY AGE	PRESCHOOL ★	GRADE SCHOOL ★★½	TEENS ★★★
YOUNG ADULTS ★★★½		OVER 30 ★★★★	SENIORS ★★★★

What it is Audio-animatronic historical theater presentation. **Scope and scale** Major attraction. **Fright potential** Not frightening in any respect. **Bottleneck rating** 4. **When to go** Anytime. **Author's rating** Impressive and moving; ★★★. **Duration of presentation** Almost 23

minutes. **Preshow entertainment** None. **Probable waiting time**
Lines for this attraction look awesome but are usually swallowed up as
the theater exchanges audiences. Your wait will probably be the
remaining time of the show that's in progress when you arrive. Even
during the busiest times, waits rarely exceed 40 minutes.

Liberty Square Riverboat

APPEAL BY AGE	PRESCHOOL ★★★½	GRADE SCHOOL ★★★	TEENS ★★½
YOUNG ADULTS ★★★		OVER 30 ★★★	SENIORS ★★★

What it is Outdoor scenic boat ride. **Scope and scale** Major
attraction.   **Fright potential** Not frightening in any respect.
Bottleneck rating 4. **When to go** Anytime. **Author's rating** Slow,
relaxing, and scenic; ★★½. **Duration of ride** About 16 minutes.
Average wait to board 10–14 minutes.

The Haunted Mansion (FASTPASS)

APPEAL BY AGE	PRESCHOOL [varies]	GRADE SCHOOL ★★★★★	TEENS ★★★★
YOUNG ADULTS ★★★★		OVER 30 ★★★★	SENIORS ★★★★

What it is Haunted-house dark ride. **Scope and scale** Major attraction.
Fright potential The name raises anxiety, as do the sounds and sights of
the wiating area. An intense attraction with humorously presented
macabre sights, the ride itself is gentle. **Bottleneck rating** 8. **When to
go** Before 11:30 a.m., or use FASTPASS after 8 p.m. **Special comments**
Frightens some very young children. **Author's rating** Some of Walt Disney World's best special effects; not to be missed; ★★★★. **Duration of
ride** 7-minute ride plus a 1½-minute preshow. **Average wait in line per
100 people ahead of you** 2½ minutes. **Assumes** Both "stretch rooms"
operating. **Loading speed** Fast.

FANTASYLAND

FANTASYLAND IS THE HEART OF THE Magic Kingdom, a
truly en-chanting place spread gracefully like a miniature
Alpine village beneath the lofty towers of the Cinderella Castle.

It's a Small World

APPEAL BY AGE	PRESCHOOL ★★★½	GRADE SCHOOL ★★★	TEENS ★★½
YOUNG ADULTS ★★½		OVER 30 ★★½	SENIORS ★★★

What it is World brotherhood–themed indoor boat ride. **Scope and
scale** Major attraction. **Fright potential** Not frightening in any
respect. **Bottleneck rating** 6. **When to go** Anytime. **Author's rating**
Exponentially "cute"; ★★★. **Duration of ride** Approximately 11
minutes. **Average wait in line per 100 people ahead of you** 1¾

minutes. **Assumes** Busy conditions with 30 or more boats operating. **Loading speed** Fast.

Peter Pan's Flight (FASTPASS)

APPEAL BY AGE	PRESCHOOL ★★★½	GRADE SCHOOL ★★★½	TEENS ★★★½
YOUNG ADULTS ★★★½		OVER 30 ★★★½	SENIORS ★★★½

What it is Indoor track ride. **Scope and scale** Minor attraction. **Fright potential** Not frightening in any respect. **Bottleneck rating** 8. **When to go** Before 10 a.m., or use FASTPASS after 6 p.m. **Author's rating** Happy, mellow, and well done; ★★★★. **Duration of ride** A little over 3 minutes. **Average wait in line per 100 people ahead of you** 5½ minutes. **Loading speed** Moderate to slow.

Mickey's PhilharMagic (FASTPASS)

APPEAL BY AGE	PRESCHOOL ★★★½	GRADE SCHOOL ★★★★½	TEENS ★★★★
YOUNG ADULTS ★★★★		OVER 30 ★★★★	SENIORS ★★★★

What it is 3-D movie. **Scope and scale** Major attraction. **Special comments** Not to be missed. **When to go** Before 11 a.m., during parades, or use FASTPASS. **Author's rating** ★★★★. A masterpiece **Duration of presentation** About 20 minutes. **Probable waiting time** 12–30 minutes.

Cinderella's Golden Carousel

APPEAL BY AGE	PRESCHOOL ★★★★	GRADE SCHOOL ★★½	TEENS —
YOUNG ADULTS —		OVER 30 —	SENIORS —

What it is Merry-go-round. **Scope and scale** Minor attraction. **Fright potential** Not frightening in any respect. **Bottleneck rating** 9. **When to go** Before 11 a.m. or after 8 p.m. **Special comments** Adults enjoy the beauty and nostalgia of this ride. **Author's rating** A beautiful children's ride; ★★★. **Duration of ride** About 2 minutes. **Average wait in line per 100 people ahead of you** 5 minutes. **Loading speed** Slow.

The Many Adventures of Winnie the Pooh (FASTPASS)

APPEAL BY AGE	PRESCHOOL ★★★★½	GRADE SCHOOL ★★★★	TEENS ★★★
YOUNG ADULTS ★★★		OVER 30 ★★★	SENIORS ★★★

What it is Indoor track ride. **Scope and scale** Minor attraction. **Fright potential** Not frightening in any respect. **Bottleneck rating** 8. **When to go** Before 10 a.m., in the 2 hours before closing, or use FASTPASS. **Author's rating** Cute as the Pooh-bear himself: ★★★½. **Duration of ride** About 4 minutes. **Average wait in line per 100 people ahead of you** 4 minutes. **Loading speed** Moderate.

Snow White's Scary Adventures

APPEAL BY AGE	PRESCHOOL ★	GRADE SCHOOL ★★½	TEENS ★★
YOUNG ADULTS ★★½		OVER 30 ★★½	SENIORS ★★½

What it is Indoor track ride. **Scope and scale** Minor attraction. **Fright potential** Moderately intense spook-house-genre attraction with some grim characters. Terrifies many preschoolers. **Bottleneck rating** 8. **When to go** Before 11 a.m. or after 6 p.m. **Special comments** Terrifying to many young children. **Author's rating** Worth seeing if the wait isn't long; ★★½. **Duration of ride** Almost 2½ minutes. **Average wait in line per 100 people ahead of you** 6¼ minutes. **Loading speed** Moderate to slow.

Ariel's Grotto

APPEAL BY AGE	PRESCHOOL ★★★★★	GRADE SCHOOL ★★★★★
TEENS ★★	YOUNG ADULTS ★	OVER 30 ★	SENIORS ★

What it is Interactive fountain and character-greeting area. **Scope and scale** Minor attraction. **Fright potential** Not frightening in any respect. **Bottleneck rating** 9. **When to go** Before 10 a.m. or after 9 p.m. **Author's rating** One of the most elaborate of the character-greeting venues; ★★★. **Average wait in line per 100 people ahead of you** 30 minutes.

Dumbo the Flying Elephant

APPEAL BY AGE	PRESCHOOL ★★★★★	GRADE SCHOOL ★★★★	TEENS ★½
YOUNG ADULTS ★½		OVER 30 ★½	SENIORS ★½

What it is Disneyfied midway ride. **Scope and scale** Minor attraction. **Fright potential** A tame midway ride; a great favorite of most young children. **Bottleneck rating** 10. **When to go** Before 10 a.m. or after 9 p.m. **Author's rating** An attractive children's ride; ★★★. **Duration of ride** 1½ minutes. **Average wait in line per 100 people ahead of you** 20 minutes. **Loading speed** Slow.

Mad Tea Party

APPEAL BY AGE	PRESCHOOL ★★★★	GRADE SCHOOL ★★★★	TEENS ★★★★
YOUNG ADULTS ★★★★		OVER 30 ★★	SENIORS ★★

What it is Midway-type spinning ride. **Scope and scale** Minor attraction. **Fright potential** Low, but this type of ride can induce motion sickness in all ages. **Bottleneck rating** 9. **When to go** Before 11 a.m. or after 5 p.m. **Special comments** You can make the teacups spin faster by turning the wheel in

Motion Sickness

WARNING!

the center of the cup. **Author's rating** Fun, but not worth the wait; ★★. **Duration of ride** 1½ minutes. **Average wait in line per 100 people ahead of you** 7½ minutes. **Loading speed** Slow.

▌ MICKEY'S TOONTOWN FAIR

MICKEY'S TOONTOWN FAIR IS THE ONLY NEW "land" to be added to the Magic Kingdom since its opening and the only land that doesn't connect to the central hub. Attractions include an opportunity to meet Mickey Mouse, tour Mickey's and Minnie's houses, and ride a child-sized roller coaster.

Mickey's Country House and Judge's Tent

APPEAL BY AGE	PRESCHOOL ★★★½	GRADE SCHOOL ★★★	TEENS ★★½
YOUNG ADULTS ★★½		OVER 30 ★★½	SENIORS ★★½

What it is Walk-through tour of Mickey's house and meeting with Mickey. **Scope and scale** Minor attraction. **Fright potential** Not frightening in any respect. **Bottleneck rating** 9. **When to go** Before 11:30 a.m. or after 4:30 p.m. **Author's rating** Well done; ★★★. **Duration of tour** 15–30 minutes (depending on the crowd). **Average wait in line per 100 people ahead of you** 20 minutes. **Touring speed** Slow.

Minnie's Country House

APPEAL BY AGE	PRESCHOOL ★★★	GRADE SCHOOL ★★★★	TEENS ★★½
YOUNG ADULTS ★★½		OVER 30 ★★½	SENIORS ★★½

What it is Walk-through exhibit. **Scope and scale** Minor attraction. **Fright potential** Not frightening in any respect. **Bottleneck rating** 9. **When to go** Before 11:30 a.m. or after 4:30 p.m. **Author's rating** Great detail; ★★. **Duration of tour** About 10 minutes. **Average wait in line per 100 people ahead of you** 12 minutes. **Touring speed** Slow.

Toontown Hall of Fame

APPEAL BY AGE	PRESCHOOL ★★★★	GRADE SCHOOL ★★★★★	TEENS
★★	YOUNG ADULTS ★★	OVER 30 ★★	SENIORS ★★

What it is Character-greeting venue. **Scope and scale** Minor attraction. **Fright potential** Not frightening in any respect. **Bottleneck rating** 10. **When to go** Before 10:30 a.m. or after 5:30 p.m. **Author's rating** You want characters? We got 'em! ★★. **Duration of greeting** About 7–10 minutes. **Average wait in line per 100 people ahead of you** 35 minutes. **Touring speed** Slow.

The Barnstormer at Goofy's Wiseacres Farm

| APPEAL BY AGE | PRESCHOOL ★★★★ | GRADE SCHOOL ★★★ | TEENS ★★½ |
| YOUNG ADULTS ★★½ | | OVER 30 ★★½ | SENIORS ★★ |

What it is Small roller coaster. **Scope and scale** Minor attraction. **Fright potential** A children's coaster; frightens some preschoolers. **Bottleneck rating** 9. **When to go** Before 10:30 a.m., during parades, or in the evening just before the park closes. **Special comments** Must be 35 inches or taller to ride. **Author's rating** Great for little ones, but not worth the wait for adults; ★★. **Duration of ride** About 53 seconds. **Average wait in line per 100 people ahead of you** 7 minutes. **Loading speed** Slow.

Donald's Boat

| APPEAL BY AGE | PRESCHOOL ★★★★ | GRADE SCHOOL ★★½ |
| TEENS ★ | YOUNG ADULTS ★½ | OVER 30 ★½ | SENIORS ★½ |

What it is Playground and (when the water is running) interactive fountain. **Scope and scale** Diversion. **Fright potential** Not frightening in any respect. **Bottleneck rating** 3. **When to go** Anytime. **Author's rating** A favorite of the 5-and-under set; ★★½.

■ TOMORROWLAND

TOMORROWLAND IS A MIX OF RIDES AND experiences relating to the technological development of humankind and what life will be like in the future. An exhaustive renovation of Tomorrowland was completed in 2000.

Astro Orbiter

| APPEAL BY AGE | PRESCHOOL ★★★★ | GRADE SCHOOL ★★★ | TEENS ★★½ |
| YOUNG ADULTS ★★½ | | OVER 30 ★★ | SENIORS ★ |

What it is Buck Rogers–style rockets revolving around a central axis. **Scope and scale** Minor attraction. **Fright potential** Visually intimidating waiting area for a relatively tame ride. **Bottleneck rating** 10. **When to go** Before 11 a.m. or after 5 p.m. **Special comments** This attraction, formerly StarJets, is not as innocuous as it appears. **Author's rating** Not worth the wait; ★★. **Duration of ride** 1½ minutes. **Average wait in line per 100 people ahead of you** 13½ minutes. **Loading speed** Slow.

Buzz Lightyear's Space Ranger Spin (FASTPASS)

APPEAL BY AGE	PRESCHOOL ★★★★	GRADE SCHOOL ★★★★★	TEENS ★★★★½
YOUNG ADULTS ★★★★		OVER 30 ★★★★	SENIORS ★★★★

What it is Whimsical space travel–themed indoor ride. **Scope and scale** Minor attraction. **Fright potential** Dark ride with cartoonlike aliens may frighten some preschoolers. **Bottleneck rating** 5. **When to go** Before 10:30 a.m., after 6 p.m., or use FASTPASS. **Author's rating** A real winner! ★★★★. **Duration of ride** About 4½ minutes. **Average wait in line per 100 people ahead of you** 3 minutes. **Loading speed** Fast.

Space Mountain (FASTPASS)

APPEAL BY AGE	PRESCHOOL †	GRADE SCHOOL ★★★★★	TEENS ★★★★★
YOUNG ADULTS ★★★★½		OVER 30 ★★★★	SENIORS †

† Some preschoolers loved Space Mountain; others were frightened. The sample size of senior citizens who experienced this ride was too small to develop an accurate rating.

What it is Roller coaster in the dark. **Scope and scale** Super headliner. **Fright potential** Very intense roller coaster in the dark; the Magic Kingdom's wildest ride and a scary roller coaster by any standard. **Bottleneck rating** 10. **When to go** When the park opens, between 6 and 7 p.m., during the hour before closing, or use FASTPASS. **Special comments** Great fun and action; much wilder than Big Thunder Mountain Railroad. Must be 44 inches tall to ride; children younger than age 7 must be accompanied by an adult. Switching-off option provided (pages 133–135). **Author's rating** An unusual roller coaster with excellent special effects; not to be missed; ★★★★. **Duration of ride** Almost 3 minutes. **Average wait in line per 100 people ahead of you** 3 minutes. **Assumes** Two tracks, one dedicated to FASTPASS riders, dispatching at 21-second intervals. **Loading speed** Moderate to fast.

Tomorrowland Indy Speedway

APPEAL BY AGE	PRESCHOOL ★★★★		GRADE SCHOOL ★★★
TEENS ★	YOUNG ADULTS ½	OVER 30 ½	SENIORS ½

What it is Drive-'em-yourself miniature cars. **Scope and scale** Major attraction. **Fright potential** Not frightening in any respect. **Bottleneck rating** 9. **When to go** Before 11 a.m. or after 5 p.m. **Special comments** Must be 52 inches tall to drive unassisted. **Author's rating** Boring for adults (★); great for preschoolers **Duration of ride** About 4¼ minutes. **Average wait in line per 100 people ahead of you** 4½ minutes. **Assumes** 285-car turnover every 20 minutes. **Loading speed** Slow.

Tomorrowland Transit Authority

APPEAL BY AGE PRESCHOOL ★★★½	GRADE SCHOOL ★★★	TEENS ★★½
YOUNG ADULTS ★★½	OVER 30 ★★½	SENIORS ★★★

What it is Scenic tour of Tomorrowland. **Scope and scale** Minor attraction. **Fright potential** Not frightening in any respect. **Bottleneck rating** 3. **When to go** During hot, crowded times of day (11:30 a.m.–4:30 p.m.). **Special comments** A good way to check out the FASTPASS line at Space Mountain. **Author's rating** Scenic, relaxing, informative; ★★★. **Duration of ride** 10 minutes. **Average wait in line per 100 people ahead of you** 1½ minutes. **Assumes** 39 trains operating. **Loading speed** Fast.

Walt Disney's Carousel of Progress (open seasonally)

APPEAL BY AGE PRESCHOOL ★★	GRADE SCHOOL ★★½	TEENS ★★½
YOUNG ADULTS ★★★	OVER 30 ★★★	SENIORS ★★★½

What it is Audio-animatronic theater production. **Scope and scale** Major attraction. **Fright potential** Not frightening in any respect. **Bottleneck rating** 4. **When to go** Anytime. **Author's rating** Nostalgic, warm, and happy; ★★★. **Duration of presentation** 18 minutes. **Preshow entertainment** Documentary on the attraction's long history. **Probable waiting time** Less than 10 minutes.

The Timekeeper (open seasonally)

APPEAL BY AGE PRESCHOOL ★★	GRADE SCHOOL ★★★½	TEENS ★★★★
YOUNG ADULTS ★★★★	OVER 30 ★★★★	SENIORS ★★★★

What it is Time-travel movie adventure. **Scope and scale** Major attraction. **When to go** Anytime. **Special comments** Audience must stand throughout entire presentation. **Author's rating** Outstanding; not to be missed; ★★★★. **Duration of presentation** About 20 minutes. **Preshow entertainment** Robots, lasers, and movies. **Probable waiting time** 8–15 minutes.

Stitch's Great Escape

APPEAL BY AGE	PRESCHOOL —	GRADE SCHOOL ★★★	TEENS ★★★
YOUNG ADULTS ★★★		OVER 30 ★★	SENIORS ★★

What it is Theater-in-the-round sci-fi adventure show. **Scope and scale** Major attraction. **When to go** Before 11 a.m. or after 6 p.m.; try during parades. **Special comments** Frightens children of all ages. 40-inch minimum height requirement. **Author's rating** A cheap coat of paint on a broken car; ★★. **Duration of presentation** About 12 minutes. **Preshow entertainment** About 6 minutes. **Probable waiting time** 12–35 minutes.

PARADES

AN AFTERNOON PARADE ALWAYS TAKES PLACE. When the park is open past 8 p.m., there are also evening parades and fireworks. The best viewing spots for the parades are in Liberty Square, while the best viewing spot for the fireworks is the veranda of The Plaza Pavilion restaurant in Tomorrowland. For parade and fireworks times, consult the daily entertainment schedule on the back of the park handout map or the *Times Guide*.

PART SEVEN

EPCOT

EDUCATION, INSPIRATION, AND CORPORATE imagery are the focus at Epcot, the most adult of the Walt Disney World theme parks. What it gains in taking a futuristic, visionary, and technological look at the world, it loses, just a bit, in warmth, happiness, and charm. Some people find the attempts at education to be superficial; others want more entertainment and less education. Most visitors, however, are in between, finding plenty of amusement and information alike.

Epcot's theme areas are distinctly different. Future World combines Disney creativity and major corporations' technological resources to examine where humankind has come from and where we're going. World Showcase features landmarks, cuisine, and culture from almost a dozen nations and is meant to be a sort of permanent World's Fair.

Most Epcot services are concentrated in Future World's Entrance Plaza, near the main gate. The Baby Center is on the World Showcase side of the Odyssey Center, between World Showcase and Future World.

◼ FUTURE WORLD

Spaceship Earth

APPEAL BY AGE	PRE-SCHOOL ★★★	GRADE SCHOOL ★★★★	TEENS ★★★½
YOUNG ADULTS ★★★½	OVER 30 ★★★★		SENIORS ★★★★

What it is Educational dark ride through past, present, and future. **Scope and scale** Headliner. **Fright potential** Dark and imposing persentation intimidates a few preschoolers. **Bottleneck rating** 7. **When to go** Before 10 a.m. or after 4 p.m. **Special comments** If lines are long when you arrive, try again after 4 p.m. **Author's rating** One of Epcot's best; not to be missed; ★★★★. **Duration of ride** About 16

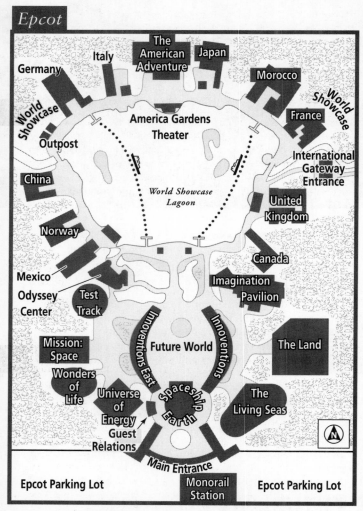

Epcot

Germany
Italy
The American Adventure
Japan
Morocco
World Showcase
France
World Showcase
Outpost
America Gardens Theater
International Gateway Entrance
China
World Showcase Lagoon
United Kingdom
Norway
Canada
Mexico
Imagination Pavilion
Odyssey Center
Test Track
Innoventions East
Future World
Innoventions
The Land
Mission: Space
Wonders of Life
Universe of Energy
Spaceship Earth
The Living Seas
Guest Relations
Main Entrance
Epcot Parking Lot
Monorail Station
Epcot Parking Lot

minutes. **Average wait in line per 100 people ahead of you** 3 minutes. **Loading speed** Fast.

Innoventions

APPEAL BY AGE	PRE-SCHOOL ★½	GRADE SCHOOL ★★★½	TEENS ★★★
YOUNG ADULTS ★★★½		OVER 30 ★★★	SENIORS ★★★

What it is Static and hands-on exhibits relating to products and technologies of the near future. **Scope and scale** Major diversion. **Fright potential** Not frightening in any respect. **Bottleneck rating** 8.

When to go On your second day at Epcot or after seeing all major attractions. **Special comments** Most exhibits demand time and participation to be rewarding; not much gained here by a quick walk-through. **Author's rating** Vastly improved; ★★★½.

The Living Seas

APPEAL BY AGE	PRE-SCHOOL ★★★	GRADE SCHOOL ★★★	TEENS ★★★
YOUNG ADULTS ★★★		OVER 30 ★★★	SENIORS ★★★★

What it is A huge saltwater aquarium, plus exhibits on oceanography, ocean ecology, and sea life. **Scope and scale** Major attraction. **Fright potential** Not frightening in any respect. **Bottleneck rating** 7. **When to go** Before 11:30 a.m. or after 5 p.m. **Author's rating** An excellent marine exhibit; ★★★½. **Average wait in line per 100 people ahead of you** 3½ minutes. **Loading speed** Fast.

THE LAND PAVILION

THE LAND IS A HUGE PAVILION CONTAINING three attractions and several restaurants. It was extensively reno-vated in the 1990s, and its three attractions were updated and improved. The original emphasis was on farming, but it now focuses on environmental concerns.

Living with the Land (FASTPASS)

APPEAL BY AGE	PRE-SCHOOL ★★½†	GRADE SCHOOL ★★★	TEENS ★★★½
YOUNG ADULTS ★★★★		OVER 30 ★★★★	SENIORS ★★★★

What it is Indoor boat-ride adventure through the past, present, and future of U.S. farming and agriculture. **Scope and scale** Major attraction. **Fright potential** Not frightening in any respect, but loud. **Bottleneck rating** 5. **When to go** Before 11 a.m., or use FASTPASS. **Special comments** Take the ride early in the morning, but save other Land attractions for later in the day. It's located on the pavilion's lower level. **Author's rating** Interesting and fun; not to be missed; ★★★★. **Duration of ride** About 12 minutes. **Average wait in line per 100 people ahead of you** 3 minutes. **Assumes** 15 boats operating. **Loading speed** Moderate.

Soarin' (FASTPASS)

APPEAL BY AGE	PRE-SCHOOL —	GRADE SCHOOL ★★★★★	TEENS ★★★★½
YOUNG ADULTS ★★★★★		OVER 30 ★★★★★	SENIORS ★★★★

What it is Flight simulation ride. **Scope and scale** Super headliner. **Fright potential When to go** First 30 minutes the park is open or use FASTPASS. **Special comments** Entrance on the lower level of The Land pavilion. May induce motion sickness; 40-inch minimum-height requirement; switching off available (see pages 133–135). **Author's rating** Exciting and mellow at the same time; ★★★★½. Not to be missed. **Duration of ride** 5½ minutes. **Average wait in line per 100 people ahead of you** 4 minutes. **Assumes** 2 concourses operating. **Loading speed** Moderate.

The Circle of Life

APPEAL BY AGE	PRE-SCHOOL ★★½	GRADE SCHOOL ★★★	TEENS ★★½
YOUNG ADULTS ★★★		OVER 30 ★★★	SENIORS ★★★

What it is Film exploring man's relationship with his environment. **Scope and scale** Minor attraction. **Fright potential** Not frightening in any respect. **Bottleneck rating** 5. **When to go** Before 11 a.m. or after 2 p.m. **Author's rating** Highly interesting and enlightening; ★★★½. **Duration of presentation** About 12½ minutes. **Preshow entertainment** None. **Probable waiting time** 10–15 minutes.

IMAGINATION PAVILION

THIS MULTIATTRACTION PAVILION IS SITUATED on the west side of Innoventions West and down the walk from The Land. Outside is an "upside-down waterfall" and one of our favorite Future World landmarks, the "jumping water," a fountain that hops over the heads of unsuspecting passersby.

Journey into Imagination with Figment

APPEAL BY AGE	PRE-SCHOOL ★★	GRADE SCHOOL ★★	TEENS ★★
YOUNG ADULTS ★★★		OVER 30 ★★★	SENIORS ★★★

What it is Dark fantasy-adventure ride. **Scope and scale** Major attraction wannabe. **Fright potential** Frightens a small percentage of preschoolers. **When to go** Anytime. **Author's rating** ★★½. **Duration of ride** About 6 minutes. **Average wait in line per 100 people ahead of you** 2 minutes. **Loading speed** Fast.

Honey, I Shrunk the Audience (FASTPASS)

APPEAL BY AGE PRE-SCHOOL ★★★½	GRADE SCHOOL ★★★★½	TEENS ★★★★½
YOUNG ADULTS ★★★★½	OVER 30 ★★★★½	SENIORS ★★★★

What it is 3-D film with special effects. **Scope and scale** Headliner. **Fright potential** Extremely intense visual effects and loudness frighten many young children. **Bottleneck rating** 10. **When to go** Before 11:30 a.m., after 6 p.m., or use FASTPASS. **Special comments** Adults should not be put off by the sci-fi theme. The loud, intense show with tactile effects frightens some young children. **Author's rating** An absolute hoot! Not to be missed; ★★★★½. **Duration of presentation** About 17 minutes. **Preshow entertainment** 8 minutes. **Probable waiting time** 12 minutes (at suggested times).

Test Track Ride (FASTPASS)

APPEAL BY AGE	PRE-SCHOOL ★★★★	GRADE SCHOOL ★★★★	TEENS ★★★★
YOUNG ADULTS ★★★★		OVER 30 ★★★★	SENIORS ★★★★

What it is Automobile test-track simulator ride. **Scope and scale** Super headliner. **Fright potential** Intense thrill ride may frighten guests of any age. Switching-off option provided. **Bottleneck rating** 10. **When to go** First 30 minutes the park is open, just before closing, or use FASTPASS. **Special comments** 40-inch height minimum. **Author's rating** Not to be missed; ★★★½. **Duration of ride** About 4 minutes. **Average wait in line per 100 people ahead of you** 4½ minutes. **Loading speed** Moderate to fast.

WONDERS OF LIFE PAVILION (open seasonally)

THIS MULTIFACETED PAVILION DEALS with the human body, health, and medicine. Housed in a 100,000-square-foot, gold-domed structure, Wonders of Life focuses on the capabilities of the human body and the importance of keeping fit.

Body Wars

APPEAL BY AGE	PRE-SCHOOL ★★★	GRADE SCHOOL ★★★★	TEENS ★★★★
YOUNG ADULTS ★★★★		OVER 30 ★★★½	SENIORS ★★½

Motion Sickness WARNING!

What it is Flight-simulator ride through the human body. **Scope and scale** Headliner. **Fright potential** Very intense, with frightening visual effects. Ride may cause motion sickness in riders of all ages. Switching-off option provided. **Bottleneck rating** 9. **When to go** Anytime. **Special comments** Not recommended for pregnant women or people prone to motion sickness; 40-inch height minimum. **Author's rating** Anatomy made fun; not to be missed; ★★★★. **Duration of ride** 5 minutes. **Average wait in line per 100 people ahead of you** 4 minutes. **Assumes** All simulators operating. **Loading speed** Moderate to fast.

Cranium Command

APPEAL BY AGE	PRE-SCHOOL ★★	GRADE SCHOOL ★★★★	TEENS ★★★★
YOUNG ADULTS ★★★★½		OVER 30 ★★★★½	SENIORS ★★★★½

What it is Audio-animatronic theater show about the brain. **Scope and scale** Major attraction. **Fright potential** Not frightening in any respect. **Bottleneck rating** 5. **When to go** Before 11 a.m. or after 3 p.m. **Author's rating** Funny, outrageous, and educational; not to be missed; ★★★★½. **Duration of presentation** About 20 minutes. **Preshow entertainment** Explanatory lead-in to feature presentation. **Probable waiting time** Less than 10 minutes at times suggested.

The Making of Me

APPEAL BY AGE	PRE-SCHOOL ★½	GRADE SCHOOL ★★★½	TEENS ★★½
YOUNG ADULTS ★★★		OVER 30 ★★★	SENIORS ★★★

What it is Humorous movie about human conception and birth. **Scope and scale** Minor attraction. **Fright potential** Not frightening in any respect. **Bottleneck rating** 10. **When to go** Early in the morning or after 4:30 p.m. **Author's rating** Sanitized sex education; ★★★. **Duration of presentation** 14 minutes. **Preshow entertainment** None. **Probable waiting time** 25 minutes or more, unless you go at suggested times.

Mission: Space (FASTPASS)

APPEAL BY AGE	PRE-SCHOOL —	GRADE SCHOOL ★★★★½	TEENS ★★★★½
YOUNG ADULTS ★★★★½		OVER 30 ★★★★	SENIORS ★★★½

What it is Space flight simulation ride. **Scope and scale** Super headliner. **Fright potential** Intense thrill ride may frighten guests of any age. Switching-off option provided. **Bottleneck rating** 10. **When to go** First 30 minutes the park is open, or use FASTPASS. **Special comments** Not recommended for pregnant women or people prone to motion sickness; 44-inch minimum-height requirement. **Author's rating** Impressive; ★★★★. **Duration of ride** About 5 minutes plus pre-show. **Average wait in line per 100 people ahead of you** 4 minutes.

Universe of Energy: Ellen's Energy Adventure

APPEAL BY AGE	PRE-SCHOOL ★★★	GRADE SCHOOL ★★★★	TEENS ★★★½
YOUNG ADULTS ★★★★		OVER 30 ★★★★	SENIORS ★★★★

What it is Combination ride/theater presentation about energy. **Scope and scale** Major attraction. **Fright potential** Dinosaur segment frightens some preschoolers; visually intense, with some intimidating effects. **Bottleneck rating** 8. **When to go** Before 11:15 a.m. or after 4:30 p.m. **Special comments** Don't be dismayed by long lines; 580 people enter the pavilion each time the theater changes audiences. **Author's rating** The most unique theater in Walt Disney World; ★★★★. **Duration of presentation** About 26½ minutes. **Preshow entertainment** 8 minutes. **Probable waiting time** 20–40 minutes.

The "Mom, I Can't Believe It's Disney!" Fountain

APPEAL BY AGE	PRE-SCHOOL ★★★★	GRADE SCHOOL ★★★★★	TEENS ★★★★
YOUNG ADULTS ★★★★		OVER 30 ★★★★	SENIORS ★★★★★

What it is Combination fountain and shower. **Fright potential** Not frightening in any respect. **When to go** When it's hot. **Scope and scale** Diversion. **Special comments** Secretly installed by Martians during *IllumiNations*. **Author's rating** Yes!! ★★★★. **Duration of Experience** Indefinite. **Probable waiting time** None.

■ WORLD SHOWCASE

WORLD SHOWCASE, EPCOT'S SECOND THEME AREA, is an ongoing World's Fair encircling a picturesque, 40-acre lagoon. The cuisine, culture, history, and architecture of almost a dozen countries are permanently displayed in individual national pavilions spaced along a 1.2-mile promenade. Pavilions replicate familiar landmarks and street scenes from the host countries.

IllumiNations

APPEAL BY AGE	PRE-SCHOOL ★★★		GRADE SCHOOL ★★★★	TEENS
★★★★	YOUNG ADULTS ★★★★	OVER 30 ★★★★		SENIORS ★★★★

What it is Nighttime fireworks and laser show at World Showcase Lagoon. **Scope and scale** Super headliner. **Fright potential** Not frightening in any respect. **When to go** Stake out viewing position 20–40 minutes before showtime. **Special comments** Showtime is listed in the daily entertainment schedule on the handout park map. Audience stands during performance. **Author's rating** Epcot's most impressive entertainment event; ★★★★. **Duration of presentation** About 14 minutes.

MEXICO PAVILION

El Río del Tiempo

APPEAL BY AGE	PRE-SCHOOL ★★	GRADE SCHOOL ★★	TEENS ★½
YOUNG ADULTS ★★		OVER 30 ★★	SENIORS ★½

What it is Indoor scenic boat ride. **Scope and scale** Minor attraction. **Fright potential** Not frightening in any respect. **Bottleneck rating** 5. **When to go** Before 11 a.m. or after 3 p.m. **Author's rating** Light and relaxing; ★★. **Duration of ride** About 7 minutes (plus 1½-minute wait to disembark). **Average wait in line per 100 people ahead of you** 4½ minutes. **Assumes** 16 boats in operation. **Loading speed** Moderate.

NORWAY PAVILION

Maelstrom (FASTPASS)

APPEAL BY AGE	PRE-SCHOOL ★★★½	GRADE SCHOOL ★★★½	TEENS ★★★
YOUNG ADULTS ★★★		OVER 30 ★★★	SENIORS ★★★

What it is Indoor adventure boat ride. **Scope and scale** Major attraction. **Fright potential** Dark, visually intense in parts. Ride ends with a plunge down a 20-foot flume. **Bottleneck rating** 9. **When to**

go Before noon, after 4:30 p.m., or use FASTPASS. **Author's rating** Too short, but has its moments; ★★★. **Duration of ride** 4½ minutes, followed by a 5-minute film with a short wait in between; about 14 minutes for the whole show. **Average wait in line per 100 people ahead of you** 4 minutes. **Assumes** 12 or 13 boats operating. **Loading speed** Fast.

CHINA PAVILION

Reflections of China

APPEAL BY AGE	PRE-SCHOOL ★★	GRADE SCHOOL ★★½	TEENS ★★★
YOUNG ADULTS ★★★½		OVER 30 ★★★★	SENIORS ★★★★

What it is Film about the Chinese people and country. **Scope and scale** Major attraction. **Fright potential** Not frightening in any respect. **Bottleneck rating** 5. **When to go** Anytime. **Special comments** Audience stands throughout performance. **Author's rating** This beautifully produced film was introduced in 2003; ★★★½. **Duration of presentation** About 14 minutes. **Preshow entertainment** None. **Probable waiting time** 10 minutes.

GERMANY PAVILION

THE GERMANY PAVILION DOES NOT HAVE attractions. The main focus is the Biergarten, a full-service (priority seating required) restaurant serving German food and beer. Yodeling, folk dancing, and oompah-band music are regularly performed during mealtimes. Be sure to check out the large, elaborate model railroad located just beyond the restrooms as you walk from Germany toward Italy.

ITALY PAVILION

ONCE AGAIN, THERE ARE NO ATTRACTIONS in this section, though it neighbors *The American Adventure*. The entrance to Italy is marked by a 105-foot-tall campanile (bell tower) intended to mirror the tower in St. Mark's Square in Venice. Left of the campanile is a replica of the 14th-century Doge's Palace.

UNITED STATES PAVILION

The American Adventure

APPEAL BY AGE	PRE-SCHOOL ★★	GRADE SCHOOL ★★★	TEENS ★★★
YOUNG ADULTS ★★★★		OVER 30 ★★★★½	SENIORS ★★★★★

What it is Patriotic mixed-media and audio-animatronic theater presentation on U.S. history. **Scope and scale** Headliner. **Fright potential** Not frightening in any respect. **Bottleneck rating** 6. **When**

to go Anytime. **Author's rating** Disney's best historic/patriotic attraction; not to be missed; ★★★★. **Duration of presentation** About 29 minutes. **Preshow entertainment** Voices of Liberty chorale singing. **Probable waiting time** 16 minutes.

JAPAN PAVILION

THE FIVE-STORY, BLUE-ROOFED PAGODA, inspired by a 17th-century shrine in Nara, sets this pavilion apart. A hill garden behind it encompasses waterfalls, rocks, flowers, lanterns, paths, and rustic bridges. There are no attractions.

MOROCCO PAVILION

THE BUSTLING MARKET, WINDING STREETS, lofty minarets, and stuccoed archways re-create the romance and intrigue of Marrakesh and Casablanca. Attention to detail makes Morocco one of the most exciting World Showcase pavilions, but there are no attractions.

FRANCE PAVILION

Impressions de France

APPEAL BY AGE	PRE-SCHOOL ★½	GRADE SCHOOL ★★½	TEENS ★★★
YOUNG ADULTS ★★★★		OVER 30 ★★★★	SENIORS ★★★★

What it is Film essay on the French people and country. **Scope and scale** Major attraction. **Fright potential** Not frightening in any respect. **Bottleneck rating** 8. **When to go** Anytime. **Author's rating** Exceedingly beautiful film; not to be missed; ★★★½. **Duration of presentation** About 18 minutes. **Preshow entertainment** None. **Probable waiting time** 12 minutes (at suggested times).

UNITED KINGDOM PAVILION

A BLEND OF ARCHITECTURE ATTEMPTS to capture Britain's city, town, and rural atmospheres. One street alone has a thatched-roof cottage, four-story timber-and-plaster building, pre-Georgian plaster building, formal Palladian dressed stone exterior, and a city square with a Hyde Park bandstand (whew!). There are no attractions.

CANADA PAVILION

O Canada!

APPEAL BY AGE	PRE-SCHOOL ★★	GRADE SCHOOL ★★½	TEENS ★★★
YOUNG ADULTS ★★★½		OVER 30 ★★★★	SENIORS ★★★★

What it is Film essay on the Canadian people and their country. **Scope and scale** Major attraction. **Fright potential** Not frightening in any respect. **Bottleneck rating** 6. **When to go** Anytime. **Special comments** Audience stands during performance. **Author's rating** Makes you want to catch the first plane to Canada! ★★★½. **Duration of presentation** About 18 minutes. **Preshow entertainment** None. **Probable waiting time** 10 minutes.

PART EIGHT

THE ANIMAL KINGDOM

WITH ITS LUSH FLORA, WINDING STREAMS, meandering paths, and exotic setting, the Animal Kingdom is a stunningly beautiful theme park. The landscaping alone conjures images of rain forest, veldt, and even formal gardens. Add to this loveliness a population of more than 1,000 animals, replicas of Africa's and Asia's most intriguing architecture, and a diverse array of singularly original attractions, and you have the most unique of all Walt Disney World theme parks. The Animal Kingdom's six sections, or "lands," are the Oasis, Discovery Island, DinoLand U.S.A., Camp Minnie-Mickey, Africa, and Asia.

At the entrance plaza, ticket kiosks front the main entrance. To your right before the turnstiles, you'll find the kennel and an ATM. Passing through the turnstiles, wheelchair and stroller rentals are to your right. Guest Relations, the park headquarters for information, handout park maps, entertainment schedules, missing persons, and lost and found, is to the left.

The park is arranged somewhat like the Magic Kingdom. The lush, tropical Oasis serves as Main Street, funneling visitors to Discovery Island at the center of the park. Discovery Island is the park's retail and dining center. From Discovery Island, guests can access the respective theme areas: Africa, Camp Minnie-Mickey, Asia, and DinoLand U.S.A.

DISCOVERY ISLAND

DISCOVERY ISLAND IS AN ISLAND OF tropical greenery and whimsical equatorial African architecture, executed in

Disney's Animal Kingdom

Africa

Camp Minnie-Mickey

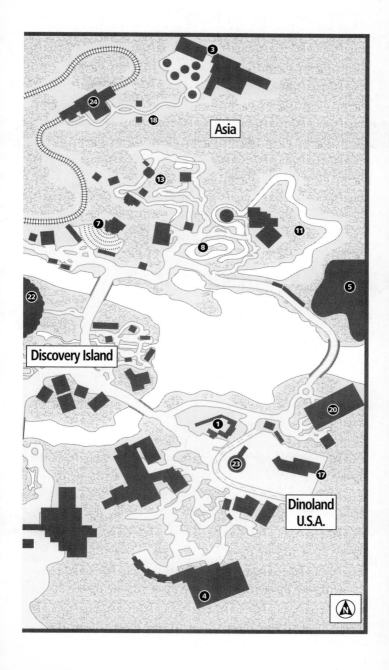

vibrant hues of teal, yellow, red, and blue. Connected to the other lands by bridges, the island is the hub from which guests can access the park's various theme areas. In addition to several wildlife exhibits, Discovery Island's Tree of Life hosts the film *It's Tough to Be a Bug*.

The Tree of Life/It's Tough to Be a Bug! (FASTPASS)

APPEAL BY AGE	PRESCHOOL ★★★½	GRADE SCHOOL ★★★½	TEENS ★★★½
YOUNG ADULTS ★★★		OVER 30 ★★★	SENIORS ★★★

What it is 3-D theater show. **Scope and scale** Major attraction. **Fright potential** Very intense and loud, with special effects that startle viewers of all ages and potentially terrify young children. **Bottleneck rating** 9. **When to go** Before 10:30 a.m., after 4 p.m., or use FASTPASS. **Special comments** The theater is inside the tree. **Author's rating** Zany and frenetic; ★★★★. **Duration of presentation** Approximately 7½ minutes. **Probable waiting time** 12–30 minutes.

CAMP MINNIE-MICKEY

THIS LAND IS DESIGNED TO BE THE DISNEY characters' Animal Kingdom headquarters. A small land, Camp Minnie-Mickey is about the size of Mickey's Toontown Fair but has a rustic and woodsy theme like a summer camp. In addition to a character meeting and greeting area, Camp Minnie-Mickey is home to two live stage productions featuring Disney characters.

Character Trails

Characters can be found at the end of each of several "character trails" named Jungle, Forest, or some such, and Mickey and Minnie. Each trail has its own private reception area and, of course, its own queue.

Festival of the Lion King

APPEAL BY AGE	PRESCHOOL ★★★★	GRADE SCHOOL ★★★★½	TEENS ★★★★
YOUNG ADULTS ★★★★		OVER 30 ★★★★	SENIORS ★★★★

What it is Theater-in-the-round stage show. **Scope and scale** Major attraction. **Fright potential** A bit loud, but otherwise not frightening in any respect. **Bottleneck rating** 9. **When to go** Before 11 a.m. or after 4 p.m. **Special comments** Performance times are listed in the handout park map or *Times Guide*. **Author's rating** Upbeat and spectacular, not to be missed; ★★★★. **Duration of presentation** 25 minutes. **Preshow entertainment** None. **Probable waiting time** 20–35 minutes.

Pocahontas and Her Forest Friends

APPEAL BY AGE	PRESCHOOL ★★★½	GRADE SCHOOL ★★★½	TEENS ★★★
YOUNG ADULTS ★★★½		OVER 30 ★★★	SENIORS ★★★

What it is Conservation-theme stage show. **Scope and scale** Major attraction. **Fright potential** Not frightening in any respect. **Bottleneck rating** 7. **When to go** Before 11 a.m. or after 4 p.m. **Special comments** Performance times are listed in the daily entertainment schedule *Times Guide.*. **Author's rating** A little sappy; ★★½. **Duration of presentation** 15 minutes. **Preshow entertainment** None. **Probable waiting time** 20–30 minutes.

▌ AFRICA

AFRICA IS THE LARGEST OF THE ANIMAL Kingdom's lands, and guests enter through Harambe, Disney's idealized and immensely sanitized version of a modern, rural African town. There is a market (with modern cash registers), and counter-service food is available.

Kilimanjaro Safaris (FASTPASS)

APPEAL BY AGE	PRESCHOOL ★★★★	GRADE SCHOOL ★★★★★	TEENS ★★★★½
YOUNG ADULTS ★★★★½		OVER 30 ★★★★½	SENIORS ★★★★★

What it is Truck ride through an African wildlife reservation. **Scope and scale** Super headliner. **Fright potential** A "collapsing" bridge and the proximity of real animals make a few young children anxious. **Bottleneck rating** 10. **When to go** As soon as the park opens, in the 2 hours before closing, or use FASTPASS. **Author's rating** Truly exceptional; ★★★★★. **Duration of ride** About 20 minutes. **Average wait in line per 100 people ahead of you** 4 minutes. **Assumes** Full-capacity operation with 18-second dispatch interval. **Loading speed** Fast.

Pangani Forest Exploration Trail

APPEAL BY AGE	PRESCHOOL ★★½	GRADE SCHOOL ★★★	TEENS ★★½
YOUNG ADULTS ★★★		OVER 30 ★★★	SENIORS ★★★

What it is Walk-through zoological exhibit. **Scope and scale** Major attraction. **Fright potential** Not frightening in any respect. **Bottleneck rating** 9. **When to go** Before 10 a.m. and after 2:30 p.m. **Author's rating** ★★★. **Duration of tour** About 20–25 minutes.

Rafiki's *Planet Watch*

Rafiki's *Planet Watch* showed up on park maps in 2001. It's not a "land" and not really an attraction either. Our best guess is that Disney is using the name as an umbrella for Conservation Station, the petting zoo, and the environmental exhibits accessible from Harambe via the Wildlife Express train. Presumably, Disney hopes that invoking Rafiki (a beloved character from *The Lion King*) will stimulate guests to make the effort to check out things in this far-flung border of the park. As for your kids seeing Rafiki, don't bet on it. The closest likeness we've seen here is a two-dimensional wooden cutout.

Wildlife Express Train

APPEAL BY AGE	PRESCHOOL ★★★	GRADE SCHOOL ★★★	TEENS ★½
YOUNG ADULTS ★★½	OVER 30 ★★½		SENIORS ★★½

What it is Scenic railroad ride to Rafiki's Planet Watch and Conservation Station. **Scope and scale** Minor attraction. **Fright potential** Not frightening in any respect. **Bottleneck rating** 7. **When to go** Anytime. **Special comments** Opens 30 minutes after the rest of the park. **Author's rating** Ho hum; ★★. **Duration of ride** About 5–7 minutes one way. **Average wait in line per 100 people ahead of you** 9 minutes. **Loading speed** Moderate.

Conservation Station and Affection Section

APPEAL BY AGE	PRESCHOOL ★★½	GRADE SCHOOL ★★	TEENS ★½
YOUNG ADULTS ★★½	OVER 30 ★★½		SENIORS ★★½

What it is Behind-the-scenes walk-through educational exhibit and petting zoo. **Scope and scale** Minor attraction. **Fright potential** Not frightening in any respect. **Bottleneck rating** 6. **When to go** Anytime. **Special comments** Opens 30 minutes after the rest of the park. **Author's rating** Evolving; ★★★. **Probable waiting time** None.

▌ ASIA

CROSSING THE ASIA BRIDGE FROM DISCOVERY Island, you enter Asia through the village of Anandapur, a veritable collage of Asian themes inspired by the architecture and ruins of India, Thailand, Indonesia, and Nepal.

Expedition Everest (FASTPASS)
(scheduled opening spring 2006)

What it is High-speed roller coaster through Mount Everest. **Scope and scale** Super headliner. **Fright potential** **When to go** Before 9:30

a.m., after 4 p.m., or use FASTPASS. **Special comments** Contains some of the park's most stunning visual elements. **Author's rating** Not open at press time. **Duration of ride** Not open at press time. **Average wait in line per 100 people ahead of you** About 3 minutes. **Assumes** 2 tracks operating. **Loading speed** Moderate to fast

Flights of Wonder

APPEAL BY AGE	PRESCHOOL ★★★★	GRADE SCHOOL ★★★★	TEENS ★★★½
YOUNG ADULTS ★★★★		OVER 30 ★★★★	SENIORS ★★★★

What it is Stadium show about birds. **Scope and scale** Major attraction. **Fright potential** Swooping birds startle some younger children. **Bottleneck rating** 6. **When to go** Anytime. **Special comments** Performance times are listed in the handout park map or *Times Guide*. **Author's rating** Unique; ★★★★. **Duration of presentation** 30 minutes. **Preshow entertainment** None. **Probable waiting time** 20 minutes.

Kali River Rapids (FASTPASS)

APPEAL BY AGE	PRESCHOOL ★★★★	GRADE SCHOOL ★★★★	TEENS ★★★★
YOUNG ADULTS ★★★½		OVER 30 ★★★½	SENIORS ★★★

What it is Whitewater raft ride. **Scope and scale** Headliner. **Fright potential** Potentially frightening and certainly wet for guests of all ages; height requirement is 42 inches. **Bottleneck rating** 9. **When to go** Before 10:30 a.m., after 4:30 p.m., or use FASTPASS. **Special comments** You are guaranteed to get wet. Opens 30 minutes after the rest of the park. Switching off available. **Author's rating** Short but scenic; ★★★½. **Duration of ride** About 5 minutes. **Average wait in line per 100 people ahead of you** 5 minutes. **Loading speed** Moderate.

Maharaja Jungle Trek

APPEAL BY AGE	PRESCHOOL ★★★	GRADE SCHOOL ★★★½	TEENS ★★★
YOUNG ADULTS ★★★½		OVER 30 ★★★½	SENIORS ★★★★

What it is Walk-through zoological exhibit. **Scope and scale** Headliner. **Fright potential** Some children may balk at the bat exhibit. **Bottleneck rating** 5. **When to go** Anytime. **Special comments** Opens 30 minutes after the rest of the park. **Author's rating** A standard-setter for natural habitat design; ★★★★. **Duration of tour** About 20–30 minutes.

▌ DINOLAND U.S.A.

THIS MOST TYPICALLY DISNEY OF THE Animal Kingdom's lands is a cross between an anthropological dig and a quirky roadside attraction. Accessible via the bridge from

Discovery Island, DinoLand U.S.A. is home to a children's play area, a nature trail, a 1,500-seat amphitheater, and Dinosaur, one of the Animal Kingdom's two thrill rides.

Dinosaur (FASTPASS)

APPEAL BY AGE	PRESCHOOL †	GRADE SCHOOL ★★★★½	TEENS ★★★★½
YOUNG ADULTS ★★★★½		OVER 30 ★★★★½	SENIORS ★★★½

† Sample size too small for an accurate rating.

What it is Motion-simulator dark ride. **Scope and scale** Super headliner. **Fright potential** High-tech thrill ride rattles riders of all ages. **Bottleneck rating** 8. **When to go** Before 10:30 a.m., in the hour before closing, or use FASTPASS. **Special comments** Must be 40 inches tall to ride. Switching-off option provided (see pages 133–135). **Author's rating** Really improved; ★★★★½. Duration of ride 3⅓ minutes. **Average wait in line per 100 people ahead of you** 3 minutes. **Assumes** Full-capacity operation with 18-second dispatch interval. **Loading speed** Fast.

TriceraTop Spin

APPEAL BY AGE	PRESCHOOL ★★★★	GRADE SCHOOL ★★★	TEENS ★★
YOUNG ADULTS ★★		OVER 30 ★★	SENIORS ★★

What it is Hub-and-spoke midway ride. **Scope and scale** Minor attraction. **Fright potential** May frighten preschoolers. **Bottleneck rating** 9. **When to go** First 90 minutes the park is open and in the hour before park closing. **Author's rating** Dumbo's prehistoric forebear; ★★. **Duration of ride** 1½ minutes. **Average wait in line per 100 people ahead of you** 10 minutes. **Loading speed** Slow.

Primeval Whirl (FASTPASS)

APPEAL BY AGE	PRESCHOOL ★★★	GRADE SCHOOL ★★★★½	TEENS ★★★½
YOUNG ADULTS ★★★		OVER 30 ★★★	SENIORS ★★

What it is Small coaster. **Scope and scale** Minor attraction. **Fright potential** Scarier than it looks; 48-inch minimum height. **Bottleneck rating** 9. **When to go** During the first 2 hours the park is open, in the hour before park closing, or use FASTPASS. **Special comments** 48-inch minimum height. Switching-off option provided (see pages 133–135). **Author's rating** Wild Mouse on steroids; ★★★. **Duration of ride** Almost 2½ minutes. **Average wait in line per 100 people ahead of you** 4½ minutes. **Loading speed** Slow.

Theater in the Wild

APPEAL BY AGE	PRESCHOOL ★★★	GRADE SCHOOL ★★★	TEENS ★★★
YOUNG ADULTS ★★★	OVER 30 ★★½		SENIORS ★★½

What it is Open-air venue for live stage shows. **Scope and scale** Major attraction. **Fright potential** Not frightening in any respect. **Bottleneck rating** 6. **When to go** Anytime. **Special comments** Performance times are listed in the handout park map or *Times Guide*. **Author's rating** For *Tarzan Rocks*, ★★½. **Duration of presentation** 25–35 minutes. **Preshow entertainment** None. **Probable waiting time** 20–30 minutes.

The Boneyard

APPEAL BY AGE	PRESCHOOL ★★★★½	GRADE SCHOOL ★★★★½	TEENS —
YOUNG ADULTS —	OVER 30 —		SENIORS ★★★★

What it is Elaborate playground. **Scope and scale** Diversion. **Fright potential** Not frightening in any respect. **Bottleneck rating** 5. **When to go** Anytime. **Special comments** Opens 30 minutes after the rest of the park. **Author's rating** Stimulating fun for children; ★★★½. **Duration of visit** Varies. **Probable waiting time** None.

PARADES

THE ANIMAL KINGDOM NOW HAS A FULL-FLEDGED afternoon parade, Mickey's Jammin' Jungle Parade (the park closes too early for a nighttime parade). The parade features the Disney characters in a safari theme.

PART NINE

THE DISNEY-MGM STUDIOS

ABOUT HALF OF DISNEY-MGM STUDIOS is set up as a theme park. The other half, off-limits except by guided tour, is a working motion picture and television studio. Though modest in size, the Studio's open-access areas are confusingly arranged (a product of the park's hurried expansion in the early 1990s). As at the Magic Kingdom, you enter the park and pass down a main street, only this time it's Hollywood Boulevard of the 1920s and 1930s. Because there are no "lands" as in the other parks, the easiest way to navigate is by landmarks and attractions using the park map.

Guest Relations, on your left as you enter, serves as the park headquarters and information center, similar to City Hall in the Magic Kingdom. Go there for a schedule of live performances, lost persons, package pick-up, lost and found (on the right side of the entrance), general information, or in an emergency. If you haven't received a map of the Studios, get one here. To the right of the entrance are locker, stroller, and wheelchair rentals.

The Twilight Zone **Tower of Terror (FASTPASS)**

APPEAL BY AGE	PRESCHOOL ★★★	GRADE SCHOOL ★★★★★	TEENS ★★★★★
YOUNG ADULTS ★★★★★		OVER 30 ★★★★★	SENIORS ★★★★½

What it is Sci-fi-theme indoor thrill ride. **Scope and scale** Super headliner. **Fright potential** Visually intimidating to young children; contains intense and realistic special effects. The plummeting elevator at the ride's end frightens many adults. Switching-off option is provided. **Bottleneck rating** 10. **When to go** Before 9:30 a.m., after 6 p.m., or use FASTPASS. **Special comments** Must be 40 inches tall to ride. Walt Disney World's best attraction; not to be missed; ★★★★★.

Duration of ride About 4 minutes plus preshow. **Average wait in line per 100 people ahead of you** 4 minutes. **Assumes** All elevators operating. **Loading speed** Moderate.

Rock 'n' Roller Coaster (FASTPASS)

APPEAL BY AGE PRESCHOOL ★★★   GRADE SCHOOL ★★★★ TEENS ★★★★
YOUNG ADULTS ★★★★   OVER 30 ★★★★   SENIORS ★★★

What it is Rock music–themed roller coaster. **Scope and scale** Headliner. **Fright potential** Extremely intense for all ages; the ride is one of Disney's wildest. 40-inch minimum height requirement. **Bottleneck rating** 9. **When to go** Before 10 a.m. or in the hour before closing. **Special comments** Must be 48 inches tall to ride; children younger than age

Motion Sickness

WARNING!

7 must ride with an adult. Switching-off option provided (pages 133–135). **Author's rating** Disney's wildest American coaster; not to be missed; ★★★★. **Duration of ride** Almost 1½ minutes. **Average wait in line per 100 people ahead of you** 2½ minutes. **Assumes** All trains operating. **Loading speed** Moderate to fast.

The Great Movie Ride

APPEAL BY AGE PRESCHOOL ★★½ GRADE SCHOOL ★★★½ TEENS ★★★½
YOUNG ADULTS ★★★★   OVER 30 ★★★★   SENIORS ★★★

What it is Movie-history indoor adventure ride. **Scope and scale** Headliner. **Fright potential** Intense in parts, with very realistic special effects and some visually intimidating sights. **Bottleneck rating** 8. **When to go** Before 11 a.m. or after 4:30 p.m. **Special comments** Elaborate, with several surprises. **Author's rating** Unique; ★★★½ **Duration of ride** About 19 minutes. **Average wait in line per 100 people ahead of you** 2 minutes. **Assumes** All trains operating. **Loading speed** Fast.

Star Tours (FASTPASS)

APPEAL BY AGE PRESCHOOL ★★★★ GRADE SCHOOL ★★★★ TEENS ★★★★
YOUNG ADULTS ★★★★   OVER 30 ★★★★   SENIORS ★★★★

What it is Indoor space flight–simulation ride. **Scope and scale** Headliner. **Fright potential** Extremely intense visually for all ages; the ride is one of Disney's wildest. Likely to cause motion sickness. Switching-off option is provided. 40-inch minimum height requirement. **When to go** First 90 minutes

Motion Sickness

WARNING!

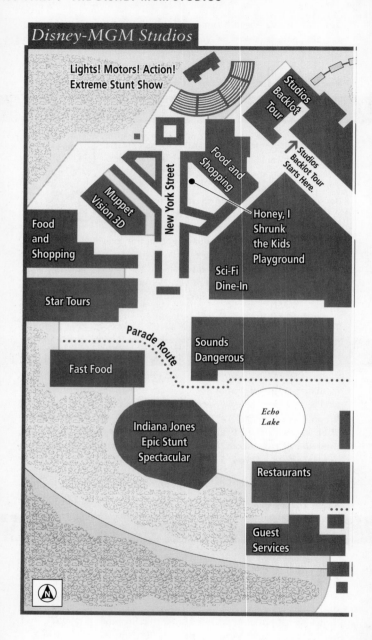

Disney-MGM Studios

Lights! Motors! Action!
Extreme Stunt Show

Studios
Backlot
Tour

Studios
Backlot Tour
Starts Here.

Food and
Shopping

New York Street

Muppet
Vision 3D

Honey, I
Shrunk
the Kids
Playground

Food
and
Shopping

Sci-Fi
Dine-In

Star Tours

Parade Route

Sounds
Dangerous

Fast Food

*Echo
Lake*

Indiana Jones
Epic Stunt
Spectacular

Restaurants

Guest
Services

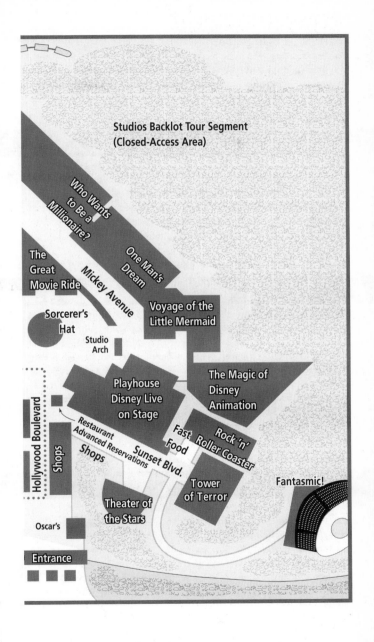

Studios Backlot Tour Segment
(Closed-Access Area)

Who Wants to Be a Millionaire?

One Man's Dream

The Great Movie Ride

Mickey Avenue

Sorcerer's Hat

Voyage of the Little Mermaid

Studio Arch

The Magic of Disney Animation

Playhouse Disney Live on Stage

Hollywood Boulevard

Restaurant Advanced Reservations

Shops

Shops

Fast Food

Rock 'n' Roller Coaster

Sunset Blvd.

Oscar's

Theater of the Stars

Tower of Terror

Fantasmic!

Entrance

after opening. **Special comments** Expectant mothers and anyone prone to motion sickness are advised against riding. Too intense for many children younger than age 8. Must be 40 inches tall to ride. **Author's rating** Not to be missed; ★★★★. Duration of ride About 7 minutes. **Average wait in line per 100 people ahead of you** 5 minutes. **Assumes** All simulators operating. **Loading speed** Moderate to fast.

Sounds Dangerous

APPEAL BY AGE	PRESCHOOL ★★½	GRADE SCHOOL ★★★½	TEENS ★★★
YOUNG ADULTS ★★★	OVER 30 ★★★		SENIORS ★★★★

What it is Show demonstrating sound effects. **Scope and scale** Minor attraction. **Fright potential** Sounds in darkened theater frighten some preschoolers. **Bottleneck rating** 6. **When to go** Before 11 a.m. or after 4 p.m. **Author's rating** Funny and informative; ★★★. **Duration of presentation** 12 minutes. **Preshow entertainment** Video introduction to sound effects. **Probable waiting time** 15–30 minutes.

Indiana Jones Epic Stunt Spectacular (FASTPASS)

APPEAL BY AGE	PRESCHOOL ★★★	GRADE SCHOOL ★★★★	TEENS ★★★★
YOUNG ADULTS ★★★★	OVER 30 ★★★★		SENIORS ★★★★

What it is Movie-stunt demonstration and action show. **Scope and scale** Headliner. **Fright potential** An intense show with powerful special effects, inclluding explosions. Presented in an educational context that young children generally handle well. **Bottleneck rating** 8. **When to go** First 3 morning shows or last evening show. **Special comments** Performance times posted on a sign at the entrance to the theater. **Author's rating** Done on a grand scale; ★★★★. **Duration of presentation** 30 minutes. **Preshow entertainment** Selection of "extras" from audience. **Probable waiting time** None.

Beauty and the Beast—Live on Stage

APPEAL BY AGE	PRESCHOOL ★★★★	GRADE SCHOOL ★★★★	TEENS ★★★
YOUNG ADULTS ★★★	OVER 30 ★★★★		SENIORS ★★★★

What it is Live Hollywood-style musical, usually featuring Disney characters; performed in an open-air theater. **Scope and scale** Major attraction. **Fright potential** Not frightening in any respect. **Bottleneck rating** 5. **When to go** Anytime; evenings are cooler. **Special comments** Performances are listed in the daily *Times Guide.*. **Author's rating** Excellent; ★★★★. **Duration of presentation** 25 minutes. **Preshow entertainment** None. **Probable waiting time** 20–30 minutes.

Fantasmic!

APPEAL BY AGE PRESCHOOL ★★★★ GRADE SCHOOL ★★★★★ TEENS ★★★★½
YOUNG ADULTS ★★★★½   OVER 30 ★★★★½   SENIORS ★★★★½

What it is Mixed-media nighttime spectacular. **Scope and scale** Super headliner. **Fright potential** Loud and intense with fireworks and some scary villains, but most young children like it. **Bottleneck rating** 9. **When to go** Only staged in the evening. **Special comments** Disney's best nighttime event. **Author's rating** Not to be missed; ★★★★★. **Duration of presentation** 25 minutes. **Probable waiting time** 50–90 minutes for a seat; 35–40 minutes for standing room.

Voyage of the Little Mermaid (FASTPASS)

APPEAL BY AGE PRESCHOOL ★★★★ GRADE SCHOOL ★★★★ TEENS ★★★½
YOUNG ADULTS ★★★★   OVER 30 ★★★★   SENIORS ★★★★

What it is Musical stage show featuring characters from the Disney movie *The Little Mermaid*. **Scope and scale** Major attraction. **Fright potential** Not frightening in any respect. **Bottleneck rating** 10. **When to go** Before 9:45 a.m., just before closing, or use FASTPASS. **Author's rating** Romantic, lovable, and humorous in the best Disney tradition; not to be missed; ★★★★. **Duration of presentation** 15 minutes. **Preshow entertainment** Taped ramblings about the decor in the preshow holding area. **Probable waiting time** Before 9:30 a.m., 10–30 minutes; after 9:30 a.m., 35–70 minutes.

Jim Henson's Muppet-Vision 3-D

APPEAL BY AGE PRESCHOOL ★★★★½ GRADE SCHOOL ★★★★★ TEENS ★★★★½
YOUNG ADULTS ★★★★½   OVER 30 ★★★★½   SENIORS ★★★★½

What it is 3-D movie starring the Muppets. **Scope and scale** Major attraction. **Fright potential** Intense and loud, but not frightening. **Bottleneck rating** 8. **When to go** Before 11 a.m. or after 3 p.m. **Author's rating** Uproarious; not to be missed; ★★★★½. **Duration of presentation** 17 minutes. **Preshow entertainment** Muppets on television. **Probable waiting time** 12 minutes.

Honey, I Shrunk the Kids Movie Set Adventure

APPEAL BY AGE PRESCHOOL ★★★★½ GRADE SCHOOL ★★★½ TEENS ★★
YOUNG ADULTS ★★½   OVER 30 ★★★   SENIORS ★★½

What it is Small but elaborate playground. **Scope and scale** Diversion. **Fright potential** Everything is oversized, but nothing is scary. **Bottleneck rating** 7. **When to go** Before 11 a.m. or after dark. **Special comments** Opens an hour later than the rest of the park. **Author's rating** Great for young children, more of a curiosity for adults; ★★½.

Duration of presentation Varies. **Average wait in line per 100 people ahead of you** 20 minutes.

Lights! Motors! Action! Extreme Stunt Show

APPEAL BY AGE	PRESCHOOL ★★	GRADE SCHOOL ★★★★	TEENS ★★★★
YOUNG ADULTS ★★★½		OVER 30 ★★★½	SENIORS ★★★½

What it is Auto stunt show, **Scope and scale** Headliner. **Fright potential** Loud with explosions but not scary. **When to go** First show of the day or after 4 p.m. **Author's rating** Good stunt work, slow pace; ★★★½. **Duration of presentation** 25–30 minutes. **Preshow entertainment** Selection of audience "volunteers."

Streets of America

APPEAL BY AGE	PRESCHOOL ★½	GRADE SCHOOL ★★★	TEENS ★★★
YOUNG ADULTS ★★★		OVER 30 ★★★	SENIORS ★★★

What it is Walk-through backlot movie set. **Scope and scale** Diversion. **Fright potential** Not frightening in any respect. **When to go** Anytime. **Author's rating** Interesting, with great detail; ★★★. **Duration of presentation** Varies. **Average wait in line per 100 people ahead of you** No waiting.

Who Wants to Be a Millionaire

APPEAL BY AGE	PRESCHOOL ★★	GRADE SCHOOL ★★★★	TEENS ★★★★
YOUNG ADULTS ★★★★		OVER 30 ★★★★	SENIORS ★★★★

What it is Look-alike version of the TV game show. **Scope and scale** Major attraction. **Fright potential** Not frightening in any respect. **Bottleneck rating** 6. **When to go** Before noon, or after 4 p.m., or use FASTPASS. **Special comments** Contestants play for points, not dollars. **Author's rating** No Regis, but good fun; ★★★★. **Duration of presentation** 25 minutes. **Preshow entertainment** Video of Regis. **Probable waiting time** 20 minutes.

One Man's Dream

APPEAL BY AGE	PRESCHOOL ★	GRADE SCHOOL ★★½	TEENS ★★★
YOUNG ADULTS ★★★½		OVER 30 ★★★★	SENIORS ★★★★

What it is Tribute to Walt Disney. **Scope and scale** Minor attraction. **Fright potential** Not frightening in any respect. **Bottleneck rating** 2. **When to go** Anytime. **Author's rating** Excellent! . . . and about time; ★★★★. **Duration of presentation** 25 minutes. **Preshow entertainment** Disney memorabilia. **Probable waiting time** For film, 10 minutes.

Playhouse Disney Live on Stage

APPEAL BY AGE   PRESCHOOL ★★★★★   **GRADE SCHOOL** ★★★½   **TEENS** ★★
YOUNG ADULTS ★★★   **OVER 30** ★★   **SENIORS** ★★★

What it is Live show for children. **Scope and scale** Minor attraction.
Fright potential Not frightening in any respect. **Bottleneck rating** 8.
When to go Per the daily entertainment schedule. **Author's rating** A
must for families with preschoolers; ★★★★. **Duration of presentation** 20 minutes. **Special comments** Audience sits on the floor.
Probable waiting time 10 minutes.

The Magic of Disney Animation

APPEAL BY AGE   PRESCHOOL ★★★   **GRADE SCHOOL** ★★★   **TEENS** ★★★
YOUNG ADULTS ★★★★   **OVER 30** ★★★★   **SENIORS** ★★★★

What it is Overview of Disney Animation process with limited hands-
on demonstrations. **Scope and scale** Minor attraction. **Fright
potential** Not frightening in any respect. **Bottleneck rating** 7. **When
to go** Before 11 a.m. or after 5 p.m. **Special comment** Opens an hour
later than the rest of the park. **Author's rating** Not as good as
previous renditions; ★★½. **Duration of presentation** 30 minutes.
Preshow entertainment Gallery of animation art in waiting area.
Average wait in line per 100 people ahead of you 7 minutes.

Disney-MGM Studios Backlot Tour

APPEAL BY AGE   PRESCHOOL ★★★   **GRADE SCHOOL** ★★★★   **TEENS** ★★★★
YOUNG ADULTS ★★★★   **OVER 30** ★★★★   **SENIORS** ★★★★

What it is Combination tram and walking tour of modern film and
video production. **Scope and scale** Headliner. **Fright potential** Sedate
and nonintimidating except for "Catastrophe Canyon," where an
earthquake and flash flood are simulated. Prepare younger children for
this part of the tour. **Bottleneck rating** 6. **When to go** Anytime.
Author's rating Educational and fun; not to be missed; ★★★★.
Duration of presentation About 30 minutes. **Special comments** Use
the restroom before getting in line. **Preshow entertainment** A video
before the special effects segment and another video in the tram
boarding area.

█ LIVE ENTERTAINMENT

IN ADDITION TO *FANTASMIC!* (described above), Disney-
MGM Studios offers an afternoon parade.

THE WATER THEME PARKS

WALT DISNEY WORLD HAS TWO SWIMMING theme parks. Typhoon Lagoon is the most diverse Disney splash pad, while Blizzard Beach takes the prize for the most slides and most bizarre theme (a ski resort in meltdown). Blizzard Beach has the best slides, but Typhoon Lagoon has a surf pool where you can bodysurf. Both parks have excellent and elaborate themed areas for toddlers and preschoolers.

Disney water parks allow one cooler per family or group, but no glass and no alcoholic beverages. Both parks charge the following rental prices: towels $1, lockers $7 or $9 (plus a $2 refundable deposit), life jacket $25 refundable deposit. Admission costs for both parks are $34 per day for adults and $28 per day for children (ages 3–9).

The best way to avoid standing in lines is to visit the water parks when they're less crowded. Because the parks are popular among locals, weekends can be tough. We recommend going on a Monday or Tuesday, when locals will be at work or school and most other tourists will be visiting the Magic Kingdom, Epcot, the Animal Kingdom, or Disney-MGM Studios. Fridays are good because people traveling by car often use this day to start home. Sunday morning also has lighter crowds.

unofficial **TIP**
During summer and holiday periods, Typhoon Lagoon and Blizzard Beach fill to capacity and close their gates before 11 a.m.

If you are going to Blizzard Beach or Typhoon Lagoon, get up early, have breakfast, and arrive at the park 40 minutes before opening. Wear your bathing suit under shorts and a T-shirt so you don't need to use lockers or dressing rooms. Wear shoes. The paths are relatively easy on bare feet, but there's a lot of ground to cover. If you or your children have tender feet, wear your shoes as you move around the park, removing them when you raft, slide, or go into the water. Shops in the parks sell sandals, "Reef Runners," and other protective footwear that can be worn in and out of the water.

*un*official **TIP**
If you have a car, drive instead of taking a Disney bus.

You will need a towel, sunblock, and money. Carry enough money for the day and your Disney resort ID (if you have one) in a plastic bag or Tupperware container. Though nowhere is completely safe, we felt comfortable hiding our plastic money bags in our cooler. Nobody disturbed our stuff, and our cash was easy to reach. However, if you're carrying a wad or worry about money anyway, rent a locker.

*un*official **TIP**
Wallets and purses get in the way, so lock them in your car's trunk or leave them at your hotel.

Personal swim gear (fins, masks, rafts, and so on) is not allowed. Everything you need is either provided or available to rent. If you forget your towel, you can rent one (cheap!). If you forget your swimsuit or lotion, they're available for sale. Personal flotation devices (life jackets) are available free of charge, but you must leave $25, a credit card number, or a driver's license as a deposit.

Establish your base for the day. There are many beautiful sunning and lounging spots scattered throughout both swimming parks. Arrive early, and you can have your pick. The breeze is best along the beaches of the lagoon at Blizzard Beach and the surf pool at Typhoon Lagoon. At Typhoon Lagoon, if there are children younger than age 6 in your party, choose an area to the left of Mount Mayday (the one with a ship on top) near the children's swimming area.

*un*official **TIP**
Lost-children stations at the water parks are so out of the way that neither you nor your lost child will find them without help from a Disney employee. Explain to your children how to recognize a Disney employee (by their distinctive name tags) and how to ask for help.

Though Typhoon Lagoon and Blizzard Beach are huge parks with many slides, armies of guests overwhelm them almost daily. If your main reason for going is the slides and you hate long lines, try to be among the first guests to enter the park. Go directly to the slides and ride as many times as you can before the park fills. When lines for the slides become intolerable, head for the surf or wave pool or the tube-floating streams.

Both water parks are large and require almost as much walking as the major theme parks. Add to this wave surfing, swimming, and climbing to reach the slides, and you'll definitely be pooped by day's end. Consider something low-key for the evening.

It's as easy to lose a child or become separated from your party at one of the water parks as it is at a major theme park. On arrival, pick a very specific place to meet in the event you are separated. If you split up on purpose, establish times for checking in.

■ DOWNTOWN DISNEY

DOWNTOWN DISNEY COMPRISES THE DISNEY Village Marketplace, Pleasure Island, and Disney's West Side. All three are shopping, dining, and entertainment complexes. Admission is charged at Pleasure Island in the evening and at the entertainment venues on Disney's West Side. Otherwise, you can roam, shop, and dine without paying any sort of entrance fee.

PLEASURE ISLAND Pleasure Island offers eight nightclubs with entertainment ranging from comedy to Celtic music to various genres of rock. Once you have paid your admission and passed through the turnstiles, you can hop from club to club without any additional entrance fee or cover charge. You can buy drinks at the various clubs, or if you prefer, just soak up the entertainment without buying a thing. From a family perspective, what's different about Pleasure Island is that kids in the company of their parents are welcome in several of the clubs. For most children, going to a nightclub and dancing to a live band with mom and dad is very cool, an experience they won't soon forget; nor, as this mom from Somerset, Kentucky, reports, will their parents:

> I danced with my 10-year-old at the Beach Club. First thing
> I know he's down on his back, spinning on his head, and
> doing all these amazing break-dancing moves! Who knew?
> I wish we had a video camera.

Under 21s at Pleasure Island are given a wrist band that identifies them as underage for alcohol consumption, so if you turn your teens loose, you won't have to worry about them boozing it up. Pleasure Island really cranks up around 9 or 10 p.m. An admission cost of $21 is charged after 7 p.m.

DISNEYQUEST If your children are 11 and older, Disney-Quest on Disney's West Side is a special treat you might want to consider. DisneyQuest is Disney's pioneering prototype of a theme park in a box, or more literally, in a modest five-story building.

Opened in the summer of 1998, DisneyQuest contains all the elements of the larger Disney theme parks. There is an entrance area that facilitates your transition into the park environment and leads to the gateways of four distinct themed lands, referred to here as zones. As at other Disney parks, everything is included in the price of your admission.

unofficial **TIP**
Weekdays before 4 p.m. are least crowded.

It takes about two to three hours to experience DisneyQuest, once you get in. Disney limits the number of guests admitted to ensure that queues are manageable and that guests have a positive experience.

DisneyQuest is aimed at a youthful audience, say 8 to 35 years of age, though younger and older patrons will enjoy much of what it offers. The feel is dynamic, bustling, and noisy. Those who haunt the electronic games arcades at shopping malls will feel most at home at DisneyQuest.

From the turnstile, you enter the Departure Lobby and a "Cyberlator," a sort of "transitional attraction" (read: elevator) hosted by the genie from *Aladdin,* that delivers you to an entrance plaza called Ventureport. From here you can enter the four zones. Like in the larger parks, each zone is distinctively themed. Some zones cover more than one floor, so, looking around, you can see things going on both above and below you. The four zones, in no particular order, are Explore Zone, Score Zone, Create Zone, and Replay Zone. In addition to the zones, DisneyQuest offers two restaurants and the inevitable gift shop.

Each zone offers several attractions, most based on technologies like simulators that work well in confined spaces. The Explore Zone is representative. You enter through a recreation of the tiger's-head cave from *Aladdin.* The headline attraction in Explore Zone is the Virtual Jungle Cruise, where you paddle a six-person raft. The raft is a motion simulator perched on top of blue air bags that replicate the motion of water. Responding to the film of the river projected before you, you can choose several routes through the rapids. The motion simulator responds to sensors on your paddle. As if navigating the river isn't enough, man-eating dinosaurs and a cataclysmic comet are tossed in for good measure.

Some DisneyQuest attractions tap your imagination. In the Create Zone, for example, you can use a computer to design your own roller coaster, including 360° loops, then take a virtual reality ride on your creation. Sid's Make-a-Toy, also in the Create Zone, lets you design a toy and receive the parts to actually construct it at home. Other creative attractions include virtual beauty salon makeovers and painting on an electronic canvas.

Like all things Disney, admission to DisneyQuest is not cheap. But especially for teens and technology junkies, it's an eye-opening experience and a fun time.

THE BEST *of the* REST

UNLESS YOU'RE A GAMBLER OR A NUDIST, you'll probably find your favorite activity offered at Walt Disney World. You can fish, canoe, hike, bike, boat, play tennis and golf, ride horses, work out, take cooking lessons, even drive a real race car or watch the Atlanta Braves' spring training. It's all there, along with myriad worthy out-of-the-World diversions such as SeaWorld, Busch Gardens, and the Universal parks. You may experience bankruptcy, but probably not boredom. And though we cover all of the above in our *Unofficial Guide* family of books on Walt Disney World and central Florida, it's way too much to cram into this modest guide.

Your kids will go nuts for the Wilderness Lodge Resort, and so will you. While you're there, have a family-style meal at the children-friendly Whispering Canyon restaurant and rent bikes for a ride on the paved paths of adjacent Fort Wilderness campground. The outing will be a great change of pace. The only downside is that your kids might not want to go back to their own hotel.

unofficial **TIP**
We recommend you visit the Wilderness Lodge Resort.

INDEX